RTI in
Middle School
Classrooms

Proven Tools
and Strategies

Kelli J. Esteves, Ed.D.,
and Elizabeth Whitten, Ph.D.

free spirit
PUBLISHING®

Library of Congress Cataloging-in-Publication Data

Esteves, Kelli J.

RTI in middle school classrooms : proven tools and strategies / Kelli J.Esteves, Ed.D. & Elizabeth Whitten, Ph.D.

pages cm

Summary: "Provides practical, research-based Response to Intervention (RTI) instructional strategies for middle school teachers and administrators. Includes examples of RTI strategies in diverse settings; information about implementing co-teaching and RTI; and customizable digital forms"— Provided by publisher.

Includes bibliographical references and index.

ISBN 978-1-57542-481-1 (paperback) — ISBN 1-57542-481-9 () 1. Reading—Remedial teaching. 2. Reading (Middle school) 3. Response to intervention (Learning disabled children) I. Whitten, Elizabeth. II. Title.

LB1050.5.E856 2014

428.4071'2—dc23

2014011993

Edited by Alison Behnke
Cover and interior design by Tasha Kenyon

10 9 8 7 6 5 4 3 2 1
Printed in the United States of America

Free Spirit Publishing Inc.
Minneapolis, MN
(612) 338-2068
help4kids@freespirit.com
www.freespirit.com

Free Spirit offers competitive pricing.

Contact edsales@freespirit.com for pricing information on multiple quantity purchases.

Dedication

For Ava and Alex
—Kelli

For Mackenzie, Mallory, and Matthew
—Liz

Acknowledgments

We would like to thank our families for their unending support and encouragement. Without them, this book would not have been a reality.

To our colleagues at Butler University and WMU, thank you for sharing your wisdom with us. To the schools that opened their doors to us for observations and conversations about RTI, thank you for letting us learn from you and for the difference you make in the world.

Our thanks go to Alison Behnke for her thoughtful questions and her sharp editorial eye. Her insights, along with the work done by the entire editorial team, were invaluable in the production of this book. Finally, our gratitude also goes to the president and founder of Free Spirit Publishing, Judy Galbraith, for seeing how we could be a part of her vision of Free Spirit to help children develop socially, emotionally, and intellectually.

Contents

List of Figures viii

List of Reproducible Forms viii

Digital Content ix

Introduction 1

Why Is RTI Valuable at the Middle School Level? 1

    Developing Young Adolescent Readers 1

    Engaging Learners in Community 2

    Embracing a Diverse Classroom 2

About This Book and Digital Content 2

**Chapter 1: Response to Intervention
in Middle School—An Overview** 5

RTI as a Path to Student Achievement 5

RTI and Social, Emotional, and Academic Development
at the Middle School Level 6

What Does RTI Look Like in Middle School? 7

Implementing and Using RTI's Multi-Tiered System of Support 9

    Tier I 10

    Tier II 12

    Tier III 14

    Managing Middle School Students' Social Awareness
        in Tiers II and III 15

RTI Models and What They Mean for Middle School Teachers 17

    Traditional Model 17

    First-Year Focus 18

    Strategy Instruction Across Subjects 18

Teaming Models 20

    Navigation Team 20

    Instructional Teams 21

    Support Team 21

    Evaluation Team 22

To Sum Up 26

Chapter 2: Creating and Sustaining Positive Learning Environments 31

Making Learning Personal 31
    Getting to Know Your Students (and Helping Them Know Themselves).............32
    Building Community 34

Flexible and Purposeful Grouping in a Multi-Tiered System of Support 34
    Grouping Guidelines 35
    Grouping Students Within the RTI Tiers 40

Academic Conversations and Collaborative Problem Solving 41

Strategies for Building a Positive Learning Environment 42

To Sum Up 58

Chapter 3: Academic Assessment 73

Screening Process 73
    Identify Characteristics of Students at Risk 74
    Use Multiple Measures 74
    Focus on Incoming Students 75
    Implement School-Wide Screening for Students Receiving
        Tier II and III Support 75

Diagnostic Evaluation 76

Progress Monitoring 79
    Curriculum-Based Measurement 79
    Additional Progress Monitoring Tools 81

Outcome Assessment 82

Finding Time to Assess and Manage Data 84

Using Assessment to Determine Level of Support 85
    Movement from Tier I to Tier II Support 86
    Movement from Tier II to Tier III Support 86
    Movement from Tier III to Tier II or I 87

RTI and Special Education Eligibility 88

To Sum Up 90

Chapter 4: Co-Teaching 105

Co-Teaching in RTI Middle Schools and Classrooms 105

Quality Indicators of Successful Co-Teaching 106
    Common Planning and Reflecting Time 106
    Administrative Support 108
    Flexibility and Spontaneity in Teaching 108

Differentiated Instruction and Teaching to Various
   Learning Preferences 109
Balancing Theory and Practice, and Understanding of
   Educational Philosophies 110
Choreographing the Co-Teaching "Dance" 111

Co-Teaching Models 111
   Complementary Teaching 111
   Station Teaching 115
   Parallel Teaching 117
   Alternative Teaching 118
   Shared Teaching 119

The Importance of Using Multiple Co-Teaching Models 124

To Sum Up 124

Chapter 5: Research-Based Teaching **131**

Evidence-Based Instructional Methods and Universal Design for Learning 131
   Set Learning Goals 132
   Provide Strategy Instruction 132
   Incite Curiosity and Activate Prior Knowledge 133
   Design Multiple Opportunities to Learn Content 134
   Promote Higher-Level Thinking 134
   Use the Gradual Release of Responsibility Framework 136
   Integrate Project-Based Learning 137

Research-Based Strategies and Programs 140
   Word Recognition 142
   Reading Fluency 142
   Reading Comprehension 143
   Language and Vocabulary Development 144
   Writing to Communicate 145
   Inquiry and Research 146
   Critical Thinking 147
   Self-Management and Learning Strategies 148

A Final Word **201**

References and Resources 203
Index 209
About the Authors 213

List of Figures

Figure 1.1: RTI Terminology 101 8

Figure 1.2: Characteristics of the Three-Tier Model of Instruction 10

Figure 1.3: Components of Tier I 11

Figure 1.4: Components of Tier II 13

Figure 1.5: Components of Tier III 14

Figure 1.6: Five Principles of RTI 15

Figure 1.7: This We Believe: Keys to Educating Young Adolescents
by the Association for Middle Level Education (AMLE) 23

Figure 2.1: Grouping Methods and Key Benefits 37

Figure 2.2: Example of Clock Grouping 52

Figure 3.1: RTI Assessment 83

Figure 4.1: Co-Teaching Activities 112

Figure 4.2: Complementary Teaching Classroom Picture 114

Figure 4.3: Station Teaching Classroom Picture 116

Figure 4.4: Parallel Teaching Classroom Picture 117

Figure 4.5: Alternative Teaching Classroom Picture 118

Figure 4.6: Shared Teaching Classroom Picture 120

Figure 4.7: Examples of Using Co-Teaching Models at Each RTI Tier 121

Figure 4.8: Key Points of Co-Teaching 122

Figure 5.1: Bloom's Taxonomy 135

List of Reproducible Forms

Download these forms and the additional digital content at
***www.freespirit.com/RTIMSC-forms**. Use the password **4success**.*

Chapter 1
RTI Implementation for Schools and Classrooms: An Overview 27

Chapter 2
Job Application 59

Student Interest Inventory 60–62

Thinking Styles and Learning Preferences Inventory 63–64

Thinking Styles and Learning Preferences Inventory Scoring Guide 65

What Makes a Great Teacher? 66

What Would You Do? 67

Coat of Arms 68

Yellow Pages Expert Form 69

Clock Grouping Template 70

Shuffling the Deck Grouping Template 71

Chapter 3

Learning Profile

Background Information 91–92

Personalized Learner Data 93

Personalized Learner Data (Student Observation Log) 94

Screening Results 95

Academic Assessment Data (Summary of Achievement
 and Ability Test Results) 96

Diagnostic Evaluation Results 97

Intervention Plan Form 98

Progress Monitoring Data 99

Progress Monitoring Data (Graph) 100

Documentation of Interventions 101

Observation of Fidelity of Implementation 102

Parent Contact Log 103

Chapter 4

Tier I Lesson Plan 125

Tier I & II Lesson Plan 126

Using the Problem-Solving Process for Co-Teaching 127

Problem-Solving Process for Co-Teaching 128

Two Plus One Reflection Log 129

Digital Content

Reproducible Pages from the Book

PDF Presentation for Professional Development

PLC/Book Study Guide

Introduction

As every middle school teacher knows, middle school is an extremely exciting and important period in the lives of students. During these years, young adolescents discover and explore their personal identities through their talents, interests, learning preferences, strengths, and areas of need. They form values and make choices that will affect them into adulthood. At the same time, many students are also intensely influenced by their peers while they figure out how they fit into their new, larger school and social group, and as they recognize ways in which they are similar to and different from their classmates. As they navigate this terrain, students in middle school need thoughtful modeling and encouragement to become aware of their roles and responsibilities as members of the diverse school community and beyond. By focusing on personalized, high-quality instruction, *RTI in Middle School Classrooms* can help you guide middle school students through this critical development of their academic and personal selves.

▲ Why Is RTI Valuable at the Middle School Level?

The multi-tiered structure of Response to Intervention (RTI) is designed to provide personalized support for all learners in the diverse classrooms of middle schools today. It emphasizes the importance of high-quality, flexible, and differentiated instruction; productive goal setting; and ongoing monitoring of instruction and intervention. Through the use of the multitude of strategies, programs, and keys to effective teaching provided in this book, schools and educators can harness their own skills, strengths, and resources to best meet the needs of every student. While the use of RTI *can* lead to a diagnosis of a student's specific learning disability, it provides a school with a great deal more. When implemented well, it can be a powerful engine for improving the achievement and engagement of all students. *RTI in Middle School Classrooms* provides you with the practical information and tools you need to put RTI in place, to harness its benefits, and to successfully tackle its challenges.

> RTI can be a powerful engine for improving the achievement and engagement of all students.

Developing Young Adolescent Readers

Middle school students are learning to use abstract reasoning to ask questions, solve problems, understand connections, and make inferences about what they read and learn. Across all grades, RTI emphasizes literacy instruction in addition to its other goals. In order for RTI to be truly successful at the middle school level, *all* teachers need to be involved in teaching and strengthening literacy skills. This book offers strategies for smoothly integrating assessment and instruction.

Engaging Learners in Community

RTI in Middle School Classrooms addresses academic achievement, but also offers a myriad of strategies for engaging and motivating learners by creating a strong community in the classroom. In order for RTI to work properly, *everyone* has to be on board—including students. RTI requires a shift in the way we think about who is responsible for teaching and learning. Students must see themselves as accountable for their own learning, and as meaningful participants in, contributors to, and collaborators in the school community.

This book presents a variety of methods to help you use purposeful grouping as a way to promote this productive collaboration. Most of these methods achieve multiple benefits at once. While teachers focus on students in small groups, other students are responsible for independent study and learning, for monitoring their success, and for helping one another learn. These skills and strengths are all necessary components of RTI. Perhaps more importantly, they are necessary for a successful and meaningful learning community in the 21st century. Tools for promoting academic conversations among peers, building relationships in the classroom, and creating a positive and collaborative culture can be found throughout the book.

Embracing a Diverse Classroom

Educators know that students are not all the same in terms of their academic readiness, their interests, or their learning preferences. By starting with a foundation of high-quality teaching for all learners and then differentiating for specific student needs, RTI's multi-tiered system of support is a natural fit for addressing all students' strengths, needs, and differences. *RTI in Middle School Classrooms* will help you implement the essential components of this system, one chapter at a time. Key concepts the book explores include:

- A focus on making learning personal for all students (Chapter 2)
- Differentiation and flexible, purposeful grouping (Chapter 2)
- Focus on setting and achieving goals (Chapter 3)
- Instruction that is driven by thoughtful assessment (Chapter 3)
- Uses of and approaches to co-teaching as a powerful tool in combination with RTI (Chapter 4)
- Instruction that is founded upon evidence-based strategies (Chapter 5)
- Consistently high-quality instruction for all learners (all chapters)

▲ About This Book and Digital Content

We wrote *RTI in Middle School Classrooms* to give teachers, administrators, and education students a resource as they implement RTI specifically for middle school students. With this goal in mind, we were intentional about including ideas and strategies that could be used across multiple content areas and with all grades of middle school learners. Critical to the success of RTI is the school-wide understanding that RTI is not simply the job of the special education staff, school interventionists, or the designated RTI classroom aides. It takes a coordinated effort from all educators. This can often be a challenge in middle schools, which have structures built on the content area expertise of teachers who may see as many as a hundred or more students every day. Creative thinking and problem solving focused on potential obstacles can lead to a well-coordinated structure with increased collaboration among educators and students.

This book is written for a wide audience of educators, and is designed for both individual and school-wide use. You may find that some sections are especially suited to your needs, and you should feel free to pick and choose the methods that work best for you and your school. *RTI in Middle School Classrooms* is broken down into the following chapters.

Chapter 1: Response to Intervention and Middle School—An Overview offers an overview of RTI and an introduction to different approaches that can be implemented in middle schools. The chapter explains the core beliefs behind RTI; introduces the Assess, Set Goals, Instruct, and Monitor (ASIM) approach; discusses teaming strategies; and emphasizes how RTI fits into a middle school setting. All of this information can serve as a starting point for those who are new to the RTI framework, or as a refresher for those who have used the system before.

Chapter 2: Creating and Sustaining Positive Learning Environments provides ideas and tools for promoting a strong classroom culture. The chapter explores connections between strong student-teacher relationships and academic achievement, and examines how RTI supports these goals. The chapter also features comprehensive information about purposeful grouping in RTI classrooms. It offers a plethora of grouping styles so that a teacher can seamlessly navigate among groups and strategies in order to build student relationships and encourage academic conversations and collaboration.

Chapter 3: Academic Assessment addresses the primary types of assessment needed within RTI and the ASIM system. The chapter also presents the Learning Profile, a valuable tool that allows educators to record and share crucial assessment data in one easy-to-use form. The Learning Profile helps educators throughout a middle school communicate critical information with one another regarding students' needs for individual instruction, purposeful grouping, and more.

Chapter 4: Co-Teaching explores how teachers can work together in RTI classrooms to maximize student learning and strengthen all educators' effectiveness. Descriptions of different co-teaching models are provided, along with key quality indicators for evaluating your approaches and a range of evidence-based strategies for effective co-teaching practices.

Chapter 5: Research-Based Teaching provides guidance on using a wide range of proven instructional methods, and information on how these methods fit the context of RTI at the middle school level. The chapter's What to Try When charts highlight goals to target, and map these goals to the strategies and programs that can help address and achieve those goals. More than fifty evidence-based strategies and programs are provided to meet a variety of needs.

Throughout the book, you'll find helpful charts and tables, as well as Spotlight sidebars that call attention to relevant topics, while RTI in Action vignettes give you snapshots of RTI at work in middle school classrooms. At the back of the book is an extensive list of references and resources for further exploration. In addition, reproducible forms are provided to help you conduct assessment, plan lessons, work with co-teachers, and successfully implement RTI in your school and with your students. The digital content associated with the book includes these reproducible forms, along with a presentation that you can use in professional development. See page viii for details on how to access this material from Free Spirit Publishing's website.

Whether you are brand new to RTI or already use it in your school, *RTI in Middle School Classrooms* offers you practical ideas, helpful tips, and field-tested advice. We wish you all the best as you undertake this process, and we would enjoy learning about your RTI journey—the ups and the downs! To share your thoughts with us, please contact us in care of our publisher:

Kelli J. Esteves, Ed.D., and Elizabeth Whitten, Ph.D.
Free Spirit Publishing
217 Fifth Avenue North, Suite 200
Minneapolis, MN 55401-1299
help4kids@freespirit.com

CHAPTER

▲ 1

Response to Intervention in Middle School— An Overview

For young people, middle school is a critical juncture and often a tumultuous but exciting time. Students come to middle school with established academic and behavioral records, yet most experience significant personal growth and development during this period. Middle school students also deal with evolving social and emotional pressures. At the same time, students—and their parents—are anticipating high school and possibly post-secondary education. In handling all of these factors and addressing the many challenges in today's diverse middle school classrooms, teachers and students at the middle school level will gain significant benefits from RTI's multiple tiers and its customized system of support.

▲ RTI as a Path to Student Achievement

RTI is about personalizing instruction in order to meet students' needs and to maximize students' potential. For this reason, it is just as useful in challenging and motivating high-achieving students as it is in preventing and reversing academic deficits in those students who need more support. The structure can be especially advantageous for those middle school students who have a history of academic or behavioral struggles but who have not qualified for special education. In all cases, the aim of RTI is to intervene while academic deficits are small, thus preventing larger gaps down the road. RTI also helps teachers target and strengthen essential skills—such as critical thinking, content area vocabulary, text comprehension, and problem solving—that will give students the tools to tackle challenges and make progress in all content areas, in middle school and beyond.

RTI helps students achieve their personal best through the following key elements, which will be explored in greater depth over the course of this book:

- high-quality instruction for all students
- differentiation of instruction
- purposeful grouping
- instruction and intervention at varying levels of intensity for students in need of extra support

- teaming and collaboration among educators, administrators, and other stakeholders
- assessment to identify students' needs, strengths, learning preferences, and interests
- ongoing progress monitoring of all students

Many effective educators already practice some or all of these approaches in their daily teaching, and the core elements comprise a related method we will refer to as ASIM—Assess, Set Goals, Instruct, and Monitor. The ideas and methodology of ASIM are supported in the Individuals with Disabilities Education Act (IDEA). IDEA recognizes RTI as an alternative to the discrepancy formula, which used the presence of a severe discrepancy between IQ and academic achievement to identify students with specific learning disabilities. Other educational reforms such as No Child Left Behind (NCLB) influenced IDEA policymakers to design a more responsive way to address the diverse needs of students in today's classrooms. RTI did originally emerge from special education legislation. However, the focus on screening, evidence-based teaching, and classroom-based interventions truly make it a general education initiative. RTI is designed to ensure meaningful instruction and targeted progress monitoring for *all* students—not only those who are at risk of learning difficulties. By closely monitoring students at each tier, educators can determine the need for additional instruction, whether that instruction is administered to a whole class, small groups, or individuals.

▲ RTI and Social, Emotional, and Academic Development at the Middle School Level

RTI's focus on individual strengths, needs, and interests, combined with its active engagement of students as participants in their own progress, will help you fully support middle school learners. This period is a time of great individual growth and identity development for students—not only academically, but also socially, emotionally, and even physically. Students at this level are rapidly building a more complete awareness and understanding of their own identities. They are eager for—and increasingly ready for—more significant autonomy and independence in their learning and beyond.

> Middle school students are rapidly building a more complete awareness and understanding of their own identities. They are eager for—and increasingly ready for—more significant autonomy and independence in their learning and beyond.

Even as middle school students are working to define themselves as individuals, they are also trying to figure out how they fit into their larger peer group. Peer relationships become more important than ever. Meanwhile, middle school students attempt to develop meaningful connections with adults, including teachers, coaches, and advisors. During this pivotal period in students' lives, they need encouragement to become aware of their roles and responsibilities as members of a learning community.

In addition, with the onset of adolescence, young people begin developing a more complex awareness of and curiosity about the world. As part of this development, middle school students are ready to use abstract reasoning to ask questions, solve problems, understand connections, and make inferences. They are also eager to investigate and engage with the world in meaningful ways. Schools implementing RTI are well prepared to build on this evolving academic readiness through personalized learning instruction.

▲ What Does RTI Look Like in Middle School?

There is no single correct approach to implementing RTI in middle schools. Most approaches, however, include the use of tiered support, with increasing intensity of instruction from Tier I to Tier III. Tier I includes all students in the general education setting. At Tier II, students are instructed using small-group settings based on academic need. Tier III provides intense targeted instruction to students who are still struggling academically after Tier II services have not produced the anticipated or desired results. (For more detailed information on the tiers, see pages 9–15.)

All RTI models encompass the following basic principles:

Implementation of the ASIM Approach

- Students are assessed to determine baseline performance and to set desired outcomes.

- Students are taught using the ASIM method. This approach is implemented using research-based instruction and strategies.

- For more information, see "RTI Implementation for Schools and Classrooms: An Overview" on page 27. This graphic provides a snapshot of how the ASIM approach dovetails with the process of putting RTI in place.

Data-Based Decision Making and Personalized Learner Assessment

- Educators make data-driven decisions using a multifaceted approach to assessment, including personalized learner assessment. Every teacher knows each student's learning preferences and interests. Getting to know your students not only helps you make informed decisions regarding their instruction, but also promotes a positive climate in the classroom.

Evidence-Based Strategies

- All teachers use evidence-based instructional strategies. Ideally, many of these strategies have been adopted school-wide, and all teachers—as well as students—are well prepared to use them. This broad implementation and understanding of the system is especially important in middle school, as it results in a more seamless broadening of the strategies from subject to subject and classroom to classroom. The school-wide strategies are carefully selected by teachers and administrators to support students during class-wide instruction, giving learners the tools they need for content comprehension across all subjects.

Effective Instructional Methods

- Teachers have in-depth knowledge of effective instructional methods. This includes the use of multiple materials that are developed or chosen by teachers, multiple forms of assessment to inform and guide instruction, and a range of devices and services. For example, teachers use books written at students' reading levels to teach basic reading skills, conduct frequent assessment to analyze those reading skills, and help students use available and appropriate technology such as audiobooks, tablets, or voice recognition software to best achieve lesson and curricular objectives.

Purposeful Grouping

- Teachers design instruction to include a range of grouping techniques. While whole-group instruction is often appropriate and effective, RTI also calls for purposefully placing students in small groups to meet their needs and learning preferences.

Integration of Literacy Instruction

- Teachers respond to the need to integrate literacy instruction across diverse content areas. Because some students advance from the elementary grades without reading at grade level, it is essential for teachers to instruct students using evidence-based reading strategies that help them understand content area vocabulary, comprehend texts, and maintain or increase their motivation to learn. This is not only a good practice in general, but also a key component of the Common Core State Standards.

- Educators provide students with access to texts at their reading level. Reading levels can vary widely in middle school, and it is essential that students are provided with reading material from which they can learn.

▲ **Figure 1.1: RTI Terminology 101**

General Education Teacher	A teacher responsible for general education classroom instruction, typically focused on subject area instruction and working with general education students as well as those receiving special education.
Special Education Teacher	A teacher responsible for students with Individualized Education Programs (IEPs), which include annually set goals chosen to facilitate student attainment of grade-level academic standards. The special education teacher may also work with students who are not on his or her caseload of students officially receiving special education. Special education teachers collaborate with general education teachers and often support Tier I and II instruction through collaborative teaching.
Specialized Personnel or Specialist	A teacher who specializes in a given area such as literacy, instructional coaching across content areas, study skills, English language learners, behavior intervention, and so on.
Interventionist	An expert teacher who is in charge of implementing interventions. This may be the general education teacher, a special education teacher, or a specialist.
Paraeducator	A person responsible for assisting teachers with various instructional and non-instructional tasks. This person might also be called a paraprofessional, classroom aide, or instructional assistant.

Collaboration and Teaming

- School personnel participate in school-wide collaboration, strong communication, and problem solving. Teaming is essential. Educators need to be intentional about building relationships with colleagues and students, and educators and students need to work as a team with a shared primary goal—student success.

SPOTLIGHT
WHAT RTI IS *NOT*

Many states, provinces, and school districts have made progress toward full implementation of RTI, and some have mandated K–12 adoption of the initiative. However, some schools encounter the pitfall of implementing RTI in name only. Calling study hour "Intervention Hour" does not equate to implementation of the model. RTI does not consist of a single endorsed model, and each school's faculty and staff will want to consider what best fits their specific setting. Nevertheless, staying true to the major tenets of RTI is critical to your students' success. Ask and consider the following questions to facilitate a conversation with your colleagues about whether your school's implementation of RTI is in line with best practices:

- Are academic and behavior screening processes in place to accurately and meaningfully identify students who may be at risk?

- If a student is not making progress, is a team of educators analyzing the student's strengths and specific areas of need?

- Do students have specific written goals targeting the areas of greatest concern?

- Do students receive instruction purposefully focused on meeting their individual goals?

- Is progress toward meeting these goals monitored and documented?

- Is your school implementing evidence-based strategies and research-based curriculum and interventions?

▲ Implementing and Using RTI's Multi-Tiered System of Support

The most commonly used RTI model consists of three tiers, with each tier characterized by an increased intensity of intervention. Tier I is considered the universal level available to all students, while Tier II targets students at risk or those in need of specialized support. Tier III is the most intensive level, designed to support students with the highest degree of academic or behavior needs. (Some schools consider special education programming to be Tier IV, but in this book we will focus on the three-tier model.) What follows is an overview of the three tiers and the characteristics they commonly feature. Remember, however, that your school's students may have unique needs that require tailoring the RTI model to fit your circumstances.

▲ **Figure 1.2: Characteristics of the Three-Tier Model of Instruction**

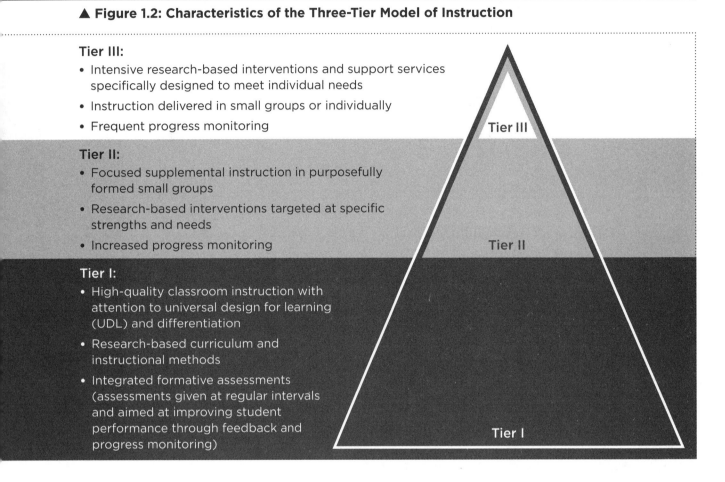

Tier III:
- Intensive research-based interventions and support services specifically designed to meet individual needs
- Instruction delivered in small groups or individually
- Frequent progress monitoring

Tier II:
- Focused supplemental instruction in purposefully formed small groups
- Research-based interventions targeted at specific strengths and needs
- Increased progress monitoring

Tier I:
- High-quality classroom instruction with attention to universal design for learning (UDL) and differentiation
- Research-based curriculum and instructional methods
- Integrated formative assessments (assessments given at regular intervals and aimed at improving student performance through feedback and progress monitoring)

Tier III

Tier II

Tier I

Tier I

Tier I is considered the universal level of RTI because it emphasizes high-quality instruction designed to meet the needs of all learners. At Tier I, you factor in what is known about both universal design for learning (UDL) and differentiation.

The term *universal design for learning* is defined as "a framework for guiding educational practice that (a) provides flexibility in the ways information is presented, in the ways students respond or demonstrate knowledge and skills, and in the ways students are engaged; and (b) reduces barriers in instruction, provides appropriate accommodations, supports, and challenges, and maintains instructional accommodations."[*]

UDL allows for accommodations in materials or procedures to help students learn. At the same time, UDL recognizes that these accommodations do not alter the standards that all students need to achieve. Rather, UDL's accommodations allow students to learn *within* a standards framework, giving all learners an equal opportunity to meet the required goals. For example, one student might be a strong auditory learner who benefits from clearly articulated verbal explanations. Another student in the same class might learn best through visual depictions. A third student might need hands-on practice and movement incorporated into the lesson. Designing a lesson that encompasses all three of these instructional inputs will support the

[*]Thompson, Morse, Sharpe, and Hall, 2005.

understanding and achievement of all students in the class, regardless of their primary learning preferences. Acknowledging similarities and differences among learners as you design your lessons and instruct your students will prevent some students from needing a Tier II level of support.

Even with the most carefully crafted curriculum and instructional methods suited to a variety of learners, there will be a need to differentiate further. Students who have significant learning difficulties, English language learners, and highly advanced students will still need specialized support beyond the basic principles of UDL. At Tier I, general education teachers are responsible for implementing differentiation and supporting students who have different levels of academic readiness, learning preferences, and interests. Flexible small groups are an effective way to accomplish this. Then, if some students are still not making progress with this high-quality instruction, further differentiation may be needed at a Tier II level of support.

> Designing a lesson that encompasses multiple instructional inputs will support the understanding and achievement of all students in the class, regardless of their primary learning preferences.

Tier I involves:

- highly qualified teachers delivering universally designed instruction and a research-based curriculum

- differentiated instruction

- a variety of research-based instructional methods

- comprehensive and authentic assessment of students' strengths, learning preferences, interests, and academic needs

- thoughtful approaches to academic and behavioral screening

- flexible and purposeful grouping

- ongoing professional development for educators

▲ **Figure 1.3: Components of Tier I**

Target Audience	All students
Instructional Focus	Universal design for learning; research-based programs, strategies, and instructional methods
Grouping	Purposeful and flexible grouping formats within the general education classroom
Assessment	Record review of all incoming students, including additional screening if needed; formative assessment of learning
Interventionist	General education classroom teacher
Setting	General education classroom

RTI in Action

Miss Sanchez, a sixth-grade social studies teacher, uses RTI in combination with an integrated model of instruction. Miss Sanchez's integrated model views behavior and academic progress—particularly in reading level—as components of the same support system, and sees these components as influencing each other. Unless discipline issues in the classroom are at a minimum, Miss Sanchez's instruction will be interrupted and she will lose teaching time. Additionally, poor academic performance may lead to her students engaging in problem behavior, which in turn can result in students avoiding or escaping academic tasks.

In carrying out the integrated model with RTI, Miss Sanchez consistently uses four evidence-based strategies in her daily teaching: Interactive Word Wall (page 163), Clock Grouping (page 51), Think Pair Share (page 56), and Jigsaw Teaching (page 54). These four strategies promote student achievement and successful inclusion in all classes. All teachers at Miss Sanchez's school are prepared to implement the same or similar strategies within their content areas. At the beginning of the school year, teachers show students how to use each strategy across the content areas, making learning accessible for all students. Miss Sanchez's sixth-grade team meets weekly to discuss vocabulary terms they can use across the curriculum in their Interactive Word Walls. This activity reinforces students' use and generalization of the content vocabulary. Miss Sanchez utilizes Clock Grouping to seamlessly move her students from one activity or group to another. For example, she pairs students for her 3:00 grouping when she uses the Think Pair Share strategy. She has found that using Think Pair Share frequently throughout a lesson helps students reuse the information she just taught and move it into long-term memory. Next she uses a Jigsaw as an independent practice time and closure activity. Students are moved to their 9:00 clock groups to complete the Jigsaw. She finds her students enjoy working in their expert groups and then moving back to home groups to teach the information in which they are now the experts. Miss Sanchez has found this grouping activity supports all levels of learners in her classes.

Tier II

At Tier II, increased intervention helps students who need more support, enabling them to reach their goals and meet academic benchmarks. This tier is characterized by small-group instruction targeting students' specific areas of need. Tier II may also include supplemental classes specifically geared toward learning goals, ideally with a reduced class size. Progress is monitored throughout the intervention period.

The Tier II interventionist can be the general classroom teacher, a specialist, or a special education teacher. The person implementing the intervention should have a level of expertise matched with the intervention itself. That is, if the interventionist is teaching reading comprehension skills, he or she should be highly qualified to teach reading. While paraeducators play a valuable role at Tier II, RTI teams will want to be cautious about using these personnel to deliver scripted lessons or programs as a means of Tier II or III intervention. Students who have academic needs have the right to a skilled teacher who understands the nuances of academic development.

In some cases, interventionists may need or want additional training, depending on schedules and availability of personnel. At the same time, as intervention is stepped up at this tier, it is vital that teachers and specialists implement these interventions correctly and in keeping with the goals and vision of the RTI team. Therefore, a measure called *fidelity of implementation* is put in place at Tier II to ensure proper and consistent implementation. Fidelity can be assessed in a number of ways, ranging from teacher observation to self-reporting of lesson effectiveness. At a minimum, lesson plans will document the frequency and duration of the intervention, and student work samples will be saved and filed. This is the responsibility of the interventionist and the support team.

Students who are identified as needing Tier II instruction receive interventions that are centered on their unique needs. Tier II involves:

- thorough analysis of students' academic strengths and needs
- collaborative problem solving by the RTI team
- involvement of families in the problem-solving process
- research-based interventions that target identified goals
- small-group instruction
- monitoring fidelity of implementation
- a minimum of biweekly progress monitoring

If Tier II support proves effective, gains are made and goals are met. Some students may no longer need extra support and could move to a Tier I level of support. If, on the other hand, significant improvement is not made during the intervention period, the intensity of the support would be increased again and the student would move on to receive Tier III support.

▲ **Figure 1.4: Components of Tier II**

Target Audience	Students who have been identified as needing additional differentiation and support to reach learning goals
Instructional Focus	Research-based interventions consisting of programs and/or strategies designed and employed to supplement, enhance, and support core instruction
Grouping and Frequency	• Small-group instruction based on academic readiness and/or similar learning goals • Minimum of 30 minutes per day, three or four times per week in small groups
Assessment	Progress monitoring of target skills weekly or biweekly to ensure adequate progress and learning
Interventionist	Usually a general education teacher or specialist, as assigned by the school and the RTI team
Setting	General education classroom or pull-out sessions outside of class

Tier III

Students at Tier III receive an increased level of support compared to Tier II. Tier III's increased intensity can be accomplished in two ways that may overlap. One way is to increase the amount of time spent working on the targeted goals. The other primary way to increase intensity is to decrease the student-to-interventionist ratio. The team should also consider whether a change in the type of intervention is needed. For example, if a student has not progressed after focused Tier II attention on developing organizational strategies, educators will reevaluate both the students' needs and the intervention approach. As in Tier II, progress will be closely monitored throughout the intervention period. Typically, the Tier III interventionist is either the special education teacher or a specialist, not the general education teacher.

Tier III involves:

- more intensive interventions
- increased one-on-one instruction and/or small-group learning
- evidence-based strategies specifically designed to meet students' individual academic needs, interests, and learning strengths
- monitoring fidelity of implementation
- progress monitoring a minimum of once a week

Keep in mind that while most students will move to Tier III only after spending some time at Tier II, this will not always be the case. When students enter the middle school (whether as first-year students or as transfers), it is important for school personnel to review the records of these incoming students to gain a sense of their intervention history, current academic levels, and individual needs. For example, students who are reading more than two grade levels below their peers may need Tier III from the beginning, bypassing Tier II support.

▲ **Figure 1.5: Components of Tier III**

Target Audience	Students who have been identified as having marked difficulties, and who have not fully responded to Tier II efforts; students whose reading level is two or more grade levels behind
Instructional Focus	Research-based interventions consisting of programs and/or strategies that supplement, enhance, and support core instruction
Grouping and Frequency	• Small group instruction or individual instruction • Minimum of 60 minutes per day, three to five times per week
Assessment	Progress monitoring weekly on target skills
Interventionist	Usually a specialist or special education teacher, as assigned by the school
Setting	Appropriate setting designated by the school

Managing Middle School Students' Social Awareness in Tiers II and III

Most young adolescents have a strong desire to avoid being singled out as needing extra help or perceived as being academically behind (or even ahead of) their peers. When RTI is used in middle school, it is more essential than ever to keep the emphasis of intervention on helping students reach their academic and behavioral goals, not on punishing them for deficits or drawing attention to their needs. The RTI structure works for all students, including high achievers whose needs might not be met with standard Tier I supports. However, Tier III is typically seen as intense intervention only for struggling students who are at risk and who have significant needs.

> Students' involvement in personal goal setting and progress monitoring can help them see growth and personal progress, which in turn will increase their motivation.

It is also important to remember that students might react negatively to Tier II and Tier III support if they lack confidence that the intervention will succeed. Therefore, it is imperative that instruction be targeted toward specific, individualized, and measurable goals for each student. Students' involvement in personal goal setting and progress monitoring can help them see growth and personal progress, which in turn will increase their motivation. This is true at all tiers, but can be especially powerful for students who are struggling.

▲ **Figure 1.6: Five Principles of RTI**

The National Association of State Directors of Special Education (NASDSE) identified eight principles of RTI in a publication titled *Response to Intervention: Policy Considerations and Implementation*. Building on these principles, we have identified five core beliefs embraced by schools that have implemented RTI effectively. These core beliefs can be useful when examining how your school's mission and vision align with your implementation of RTI.

1. All students can learn.	RTI is founded on the belief that *all* students—whether they are struggling, have advanced academic readiness, or are having a difficult time adjusting to the rigor of middle school—can learn, make progress, and achieve their personal best. Toward this end, the RTI process involves a thoughtful approach to screening, and demands prompt and intentional intervention targeted toward specific learning goals. As educators evaluate students' strengths and needs, they can determine if and how additional support and differentiation are needed. And when schools have the necessary structures in place to respond to these needs, that support can be smoothly and efficiently supplied through RTI.
2. Quality assessment informs instructional practices.	Educators must thoughtfully observe their students and make data-driven decisions to ensure the best outcomes for all students. While progress monitoring is essential to the RTI process, it is not the only type of assessment needed. Personalized learner assessment promotes understanding of students' learning strengths and interests. Diagnostic evaluation targets specific academic strengths and needs. Outcome assessment reveals whether or not instruction was effective, and whether or not goals were met. When teachers use a multifaceted approach to assessing learners, they can best use the information they gather to guide instruction.

3. Quality teaching makes a difference.	A critical element of RTI is high-quality Tier I instruction with attention to universal design for learning. The focus is on proactively creating an instructional environment that sets up all students for success and fosters student engagement. This means that the core curriculum, interventions, and instructional methods are grounded in evidence and have a high probability of success. Built on a foundation of research-validated programs and strategies, quality teaching also recognizes the many connections among RTI, differentiated instruction, and the need for teachers to understand their students' learning strengths, interests, and academic readiness. These factors are essential to strong instruction in a multi-tiered system of support.
	Quality teaching cannot be an isolated act. Educators need to support one another in both assessment and instruction. As a result, teachers need to collaborate to ensure that strategies and programs are put into action properly. One way to address this fidelity of implementation is to observe one another during the teaching of an intervention. The goal of the observation is not to judge the teacher, but to evaluate the degree to which the intervention is being implemented as designed. Fidelity also involves documenting the frequency and duration of intervention.
4. Positive relationships within the classroom maximize learning.	Students are more likely to engage in learning if they sense that their teachers truly care about them and are invested in helping them succeed. Studies validate the importance of positive, supportive student-teacher relationships, revealing that when students feel safe and accepted by their teachers, they demonstrate greater academic growth. Additionally, flexible grouping and peer-assisted learning can build positive relationships within the classroom. Both allow the students to strengthen skills in teamwork, effective communication, and problem solving.
	Teachers who are invested in fostering positive relationships are continually asking themselves: • Do I know each one of my students on a personal level? • Do I encourage a sense of community in my classroom? Do my students know and respect one other? • Do I understand developmental characteristics of the population of students with whom I am working? • Do my students trust me? Respecting students' learning strengths and interests not only promotes learning, but creates an environment in which students can thrive.
5. Educators must work as a team.	RTI is both a general education and a special education initiative. However, the full weight of RTI is not meant to be carried *only* by the general education and special education teachers. Given that RTI takes school-wide coordination, administrators must also offer thoughtful guidance and strong leadership. When RTI is at its most effective, all educators participate in various forms of teamwork ranging from problem solving through teaming to differentiating instruction through co-teaching and partnering with families. For the strongest teaming, all participants must also be knowledgeable about and competent in the skills of collaboration and effective communication.

▲ RTI Models and What They Mean for Middle School Teachers

RTI can be implemented in middle school using multiple models. This section explores three of the most common models. As you know, resources, structures, and methods can differ widely among middle schools. While reading through the model descriptions that follow, you may notice that some elements are in place already in your school. As you develop and implement your RTI program, your team (see pages 20–23 for more on forming and using teams) will need to determine what works best for your school and your students. A carefully constructed "mixed" approach—blending or overlapping elements of the various models—based on the unique needs of your school is likely to be the most effective. Understanding the big picture and keeping the key principles of RTI in mind is of utmost importance as you design and refine your model.

Traditional Model

In a traditional RTI model, students in need of Tier II or Tier III interventions are provided with support in what is typically thought of as a specialized class. Maximizing learner growth is the primary intention of RTI. As a result, each student receiving Tier II or III support will have an intervention plan. The time in supported instruction should be spent working toward clear, documented goals. The interventionist (whether this is a classroom teacher, specialist, or other educator) may use a combination of individual and small-group instruction, while implementing a variety of research-based programs and strategies depending on students' needs.

A successful traditional model is designed so that intervention classes have a low student-to-teacher ratio. At minimum, the interventionist has the opportunity to provide instruction in a 3:1 group for at least 30 minutes three times per week. So, for example, if your school has adopted block scheduling, the support may be provided every other day for approximately 90 minutes. And to keep the ratio appropriate, if the class meets for an hour and a half every Monday, Wednesday, and Friday, the class would have no more than fifteen students per highly qualified teacher. While the interventionist is teaching a small group, other students can be reading and responding to text written at their reading level, taking part in progress monitoring with a paraeducator, engaging in collaborative or self-guided projects, or learning through computer-aided instruction. Alternatively, the class could meet for 45 minutes to an hour every day of the week. These exact logistics are less important than the student-to-teacher ratio and the interventions implemented during this scheduled time.

The small-group instruction arrangement is by no means a rigid system. There may be times when the interventionist delivers whole-group instruction on critical strategies to improve note-taking, organizational skills, or reading comprehension. However, the focus remains on the intense work required to provide students with the academic boost they need to meet goals and reach desired levels of achievement.

Because the intervention is mainly provided in isolation from other classes, it is important for interventionists to communicate with each student's general education teachers. A potential challenge of the traditional model is that students and teachers could come to view RTI as something that is achieved in the "RTI class," when it is truly a school-wide initiative and everyone's responsibility. Coordination of instructional intervention is ideally evident throughout the school day, not just in the intervention class. General classroom teachers are kept informed of students' progress toward goals. They are also up-to-date on the effectiveness of specific strategies that have resulted in students' success. These strategies can then be implemented in other classes as appropriate.

First-Year Focus

Schools implementing a first-year focus approach concentrate on students entering the middle school. These schools focus on making the transition from elementary to middle school a success by providing useful learning strategies for all new students and implementing academic interventions when necessary. Educators select evidence-based learning strategies to use school-wide. Each classroom teacher agrees to teach his or her subject utilizing the selected strategies.

In the first week of the school year, all teachers focus on introducing and explaining the chosen learning strategies to students. Additionally, educators assess students entering middle school to determine if they have academic delays in core areas such as reading and math. From this data, a school-wide academic student baseline is determined. Students who are identified as struggling are then further assessed to determine specific areas of need and to prioritize the appropriate strategies for addressing those needs. Goals are written for each student so individual progress can be monitored.

It's important to realize that initial screenings can sometimes produce false positives. That is, students who were initially thought to be at risk may not actually be behind, and may not need extra support after all. For this reason, initial assessment must be paired with a systematic look at each student's academic history. By examining all the data, the school can direct its efforts toward the students who will benefit most from developing and strengthening specific learning strategies.

A key benefit of the first-year focus is that *all* first-year students work toward developing strategies that increase their awareness of how they best learn. Differentiation comes with the level of intensity of intervention. While some students will be ready to move right to the application phase of a given strategy, others will need Tier II support to develop understanding before moving to higher levels of learning. At Tier III, students with greater needs receive more intense instruction individually or in small groups for a longer period of the school day. At both Tiers II and III, focused instruction is provided to bring struggling students up to grade level and increase their metacognition. Meanwhile, the team provides ongoing progress monitoring to ensure the interventions are effective and students are progressing. The team will also ensure that students move fluidly among the tiers according to their progress and need.

Strategy Instruction Across Subjects

In an RTI model focused on strategy instruction across subjects, all students (Tier I) are taught learning strategies selected by faculty and implemented across all disciplines and content areas. The chosen learning strategies are embedded in the instruction of the core content courses, as well as instruction at Tiers II and III.

Through school-wide assessments and student record reviews, educators will determine which strategies best address their students' specific needs. Students will benefit most when schools choose three or four learning strategies to teach consistently across all content areas.*

At Tiers II and III, research-based interventions will be implemented to address the specified problem area of each student, while educators also continue to use the learning strategies chosen for Tier I instruction. Typically, content-area literacy skills are a focus for students at Tiers II and III, especially given the importance in middle school of informational texts in many content areas.

In this model, using consistent learning strategies across disciplines helps students understand the content in their core courses. It also gives students the tools to problem solve when they encounter challenges. When the chosen learning strategies are carefully selected based on students' needs, the strategies will give students the resources to be active learners who engage in the content and solve problems using the information they have gathered.

*Torgesen, Houston, and Rissman, 2007.

SPOTLIGHT
THE COMMON CORE STATE STANDARDS, ADOLESCENT LITERACY, AND RTI

The goal of the Common Core State Standards (CCSS) is to "provide a consistent, clear understanding of what students are expected to learn, so teachers and parents know what they need to do to help them."* Throughout the CCSS are standards in reading, writing, speaking, listening, and language that apply across content areas. RTI is a good match for helping students achieve these standards by using strategy instruction across the content areas. No matter what the discipline, a strong, standards-based curriculum must be made accessible to all students. Similarly, regardless of a student's reading level, access to the content is the responsibility of all teachers.

To achieve these goals, educators need to reach a new level of collaboration through grade-level teams and interdisciplinary teams. Conversations within these teams will ideally support differentiation of instruction across the content areas, while drawing on teachers' subject-specific expertise to promote the mastery of content standards. For example, teachers may adjust their mindset to "I am teaching not only social studies or science, but the CCSS." This collaboration and cross-content planning can take many forms. For example, the members of a grade-level team could choose to provide explicit vocabulary instruction by dedicating a portion of their lessons each week to agreed-upon vocabulary that supports standards and applies to multiple content areas. Daily, repeated exposure to the new vocabulary words in different contexts, supported by practice sessions in vocabulary use, will increase students' achievement within the common core framework.** This level of collaboration and teamwork will set in motion successful student outcomes. Chapter 5 includes strategies for content area literacy that further connect to the CCSS for middle school learners.

*www.corestandards.org.

**Nelson and Stage, 2007.

As in all models of RTI, the key purpose of strategy instruction across subjects is to help students reach clearly defined goals. In support of core content instruction, emphasis on school-wide learning strategies will continue in Tiers II and III. At the same time, students in Tiers II and III will be provided with intervention plans consisting of thoughtfully chosen research-based programs and learning strategies to meet their individual needs above and beyond Tier I instruction in each subject area.

> As in all models of RTI, the key purpose of strategy instruction across subjects is to help students reach clearly defined goals.

This approach is similar to the traditional model, but it differs given the focus on strategy instruction with special attention to content-area literacy skills. In this model, Tier II and III interventions are often designed to address literacy skills that can then be generalized to all content areas. Additionally, targeted strategy instruction is delivered by an interventionist who specializes in literacy, while the same strategies are simultaneously supported by general education teachers in content area classes. This approach can also apply to strategy instruction focused on organizational skills, information processing, problem solving, and other academic tools that will serve students well across all subjects.

▲ Teaming Models

RTI is a comprehensive, school-wide approach to education. As part of successful implementation, various types of teams are formed that then work together to support the model. This section provides an introduction to the key types of teams, their members, and their responsibilities.

Navigation Team

When a school adopts RTI, an important first step is to assemble a Navigation Team. This team represents a variety of stakeholders, including teachers, specialists, administrators, and families. As a school-wide team, the Navigation Team oversees the implementation of RTI. In doing this, it's important for the team to start with the question "How does RTI support the mission and vision of the school, and how will our method of implementation reflect these values?"

In asking and answering this core question, the Navigation Team will:

- draft RTI procedures for the middle school
- consider the level of need for professional development for the school and for specific groups of educators, and work to provide it
- determine methods to measure fidelity of implementation
- define and implement the use of progress monitoring tools
- conduct a systematic inventory of school resources that support RTI, such as necessary personnel, classroom space, research-based curriculum, and intervention materials

These issues, along with other big-picture matters, are the responsibility of the Navigation Team.

Instructional Teams

Most middle schools implementing RTI will have several Instructional Teams. Each of these teams is composed of general education teachers implementing RTI in their specific subject areas. Teachers can form teams based either on grade level or content area, and will meet on a regular basis.

At the beginning of the school year, Instructional Teams work on completing student learning profiles so they may begin to effectively group students for instruction. Once they establish instructional groups, they can move on to discussing the research-based curriculum, ongoing student-centered assessment, and procedures for progress monitoring of students. Members of the Instructional Teams chart student results and identify students who need Tier II instruction. They also collaborate with appropriate specialists regarding students who need Tier III instruction, or they may work with the Support Team to refer a student for further evaluation.

Support Team

The Support Team includes special education teachers, specialists (such as literacy specialists, behavior specialists, and speech and language pathologists), and at least one general education representative. The Support Team collaborates with Instructional Teams to evaluate the needs of students who are not meeting benchmarks in content areas.

The Support Team's key role is in Tier II, where the team serves two purposes. Members of the Support Team may provide small-group instruction in the general education classroom or pull-out sessions to students needing intervention. In addition, the Support Team may collect assessment data to determine if students are responding to effective instruction or are learning significantly below the level of their peers. In most cases, members of the Support Team are also part of the Evaluation

Team (see the following section). This helps provide for a smooth flow of information to determine if a student is in need of further assessment or a comprehensive evaluation.

It's important for the Support Team and Instructional Teams to work together on setting a clear focus for each intervention. A disjointed, piecemeal approach is very unlikely to be successful over the long term. These teams also need to compile and draw upon a varied portfolio of effective intervention strategies and programs. Chapter 5 is a good place to start investigating these strategies.

Evaluation Team

If a student does not respond to instruction at Tiers I and II, the Evaluation Team may be called upon. This team may include members from Instructional Teams and

SPOTLIGHT
RTI AND GROWTH MINDSET

RTI works best when teachers and students share a growth mindset. This concept, studied in depth by Carol Dweck and her colleagues, is in contrast to a fixed mindset. When students have the mindset that intelligence is fixed or permanent, they see themselves as good or bad, smart or dumb, and so forth. On the other hand, those who hold a growth mindset believe that their intelligence increases with learning. They tend to think that while a task may be difficult at first, it will get easier with meaningful instruction.

Often, by the time students reach middle school, they do have a fixed outlook, having drawn conclusions in the elementary grades about what they are "good" and "bad" at, and viewing these characteristics as unchanging. If some of your students view their capabilities as permanent, they need you to provide them with evidence to the contrary. Setting realistic goals, providing focused instruction, and offering regular feedback on progress all give evidence that hard work pays off. This is true for students who tend to be high achievers just as much as it is for those who struggle. Helping your students move from a fixed view to a growth mindset will not only help them learn and succeed, but will also dovetail with your use of RTI.

When implementing RTI and the Assess, Set Goals, Instruct, and Monitor approach, using growth-mindset language can help your students embrace their potential and take ownership of their learning. The quoted text that follows offers an example of framing and explaining each stage of ASIM to your students through a growth-mindset lens.

Assess: "The initial assessments give us a starting point for how you are doing right now. This will help us determine what you already know and what you're ready to take on as the next step."

Set Goals: "Let's set goals based on what you are ready for now and where you'd like to be in about eight weeks."

Instruct: "I've picked out several teaching ideas aimed at helping you learn. Are you comfortable with the strategy we have for meeting your goal?"

Monitor: "You're getting closer and closer to reaching your goal. Look at how far you've come based on your hard work." *or* "We aren't seeing much progress toward the goal yet. Why do you think that is? Maybe we need to come up with a different approach."

the Support Team. Whether there is overlap in these teams or not, the Evaluation Team works closely with both the Support and Instructional Teams to gather information about students. Members of the Evaluation Team also often include a school psychologist, the principal or another administrator, special education teachers, general education teachers, English language learner specialists, literacy specialists, and other appropriate personnel.

The Evaluation Team provides ongoing support to the Instructional and Support Teams by overseeing the implementation of intensive interventions. When a student is not responding as expected at any tier, the Evaluation Team may be asked to examine a student's history and consider whether a different type of intervention is needed. If the severity of a student's learning difficulties is not successfully addressed at Tiers II or III, the Evaluation Team may administer a comprehensive evaluation to determine whether the student has a specific learning disability.

▲ **Figure 1.7: This We Believe: Keys to Educating Young Adolescents by the Association for Middle Level Education (AMLE)***

The Association for Middle Level Education's 2010 position paper, *This We Believe: Keys to Educating Young Adolescents*, defines 16 research-based characteristics of effective middle level education. The paper organizes these characteristics into three main areas: Curriculum, Instruction, and Assessment; Leadership and Organization; and Culture and Community. *This We Believe* articulates a foundational philosophy for middle level education that fits with this book's goal of helping teachers and administrators implement the RTI model in middle school. Each of the book's chapters was written with attention to the research-based characteristics outlined in AMLE's position statement. As you use *RTI in Middle School Classrooms*, consider the following characteristics and how you can combine them with RTI's principles to support and enhance your students' learning.

CURRICULUM, INSTRUCTION, AND ASSESSMENT

Educators value young adolescents and are prepared to teach them.
(Value Young Adolescents)

Effective middle grades educators make a conscious choice to work with young adolescents and advocate for them. They understand the developmental uniqueness of this age group, the appropriate curriculum, effective learning and assessment strategies, and their importance as models.

Students and teachers are engaged in active, purposeful learning.
(Active Learning)

Instructional practices place students at the center of the learning process. As they develop the ability to hypothesize, to organize information into useful and meaningful constructs, and to grasp long-term cause and effect relationships, students are ready and able to play a major role in their own learning and education.

*Reprinted with permission from the Association for Middle Level Education, formerly NMSA (National Middle School Association). *This We Believe: Keys to Educating Young Adolescents*. Westerville, OH: 2010.

Curriculum is challenging, exploratory, integrative, and relevant.
(Challenging Curriculum)
Curriculum embraces every planned aspect of a school's educational program. An effective middle level curriculum is distinguished by learning activities that appeal to young adolescents, is exploratory and challenging, and incorporates student-generated questions and concerns.

Educators use multiple learning and teaching approaches.
(Multiple Learning Approaches)

Teaching and learning approaches should accommodate the diverse skills, abilities, and prior knowledge of young adolescents, cultivate multiple intelligences, draw upon students' individual learning preferences, and utilize digital tools. When learning experiences capitalize on students' cultural, experiential, and personal backgrounds, new concepts are built on knowledge students already possess.

Varied and ongoing assessments advance learning as well as measure it.
(Varied Assessments)

Continuous, authentic, and appropriate assessment measures, including both formative and summative ones, provide evidence about every student's learning progress. Such information helps students, teachers, and family members select immediate learning goals and plan further education.

LEADERSHIP AND ORGANIZATION

A shared vision developed by all stakeholders guides every decision.
(Shared Vision)

When a shared vision and mission statement become operational, middle level educators pursue appropriate practices in developing a challenging academic program; they develop criteria to guide decisions and a process to make needed changes.

Leaders are committed to and knowledgeable about this age group, educational research, and best practices.
(Committed Leaders)

Courageous, collaborative middle level leaders understand young adolescents, the society in which they live, and the theory of middle level education. Such leaders understand the nuances of teaming, student advocacy, exploration, and assessment as components of a larger middle level program.

Leaders demonstrate courage and collaboration.
(Courageous Collaborative Leaders)

Leaders understand that successful schools committed to the long-term implementation of the middle school concept must be collaborative enterprises. The principal, working collaboratively with a leadership team, focuses on building a learning community that involves all teachers and places top priority on the education and healthy development of every student, teacher, and staff member.

Ongoing professional development reflects best educational practices.
(Professional Development)

Professional development is a continuing activity in middle level schools where teachers take advantage of every opportunity to work with colleagues to improve the learning experiences for their students.

Organizational structures foster purposeful learning and meaningful relationships. (Organizational Structures)

The ways schools organize teachers and group and schedule students have a significant impact on the learning environment. Interdisciplinary teams' common planning time, block scheduling, and elimination of tracking are related conditions that contribute to improved achievement.

CULTURE AND COMMUNITY

The school environment is inviting, safe, inclusive, and supportive of all. (School Environment)

A successful school for young adolescents is an inviting, supportive, and safe place, a joyful community that promotes in-depth learning and enhances students' physical and emotional well-being.

Every student's academic and personal development is guided by an adult advocate. (Adult Advocate)

Academic success and personal growth increase markedly when young adolescents' affective needs are met. Each student must have one adult to support that student's academic and personal development.

Comprehensive guidance and support services meet the needs of young adolescents. (Guidance Services)

Both teachers and specialized professionals are readily available to offer the assistance many students need in negotiating their lives in and out of school.

Health and wellness are supported in curricula, school-wide programs, and related policies. (Health Wellness)

Abundant opportunities are available for students to develop and maintain healthy minds and bodies and to understand their personal growth through health-related programs, policies, and curricula.

The school actively involves families in the education of their children. (Family Involvement)

Schools and families must work together to provide the best possible learning for every young adolescent. Schools take the initiative in involving and educating families.

The school includes community and business partners. (Community Business)

Genuine community involvement is a fundamental component of successful schools for young adolescents. Such schools seek appropriate partnerships with businesses, social service agencies, and other organizations whose purposes are consistent with the school's mission.

▲ To Sum Up

When RTI is explained to education students, a common response is: "Well, that's just good teaching!" or "You mean that's not what is already being done in schools?" These questions see RTI for what it should be—a team approach to meeting the needs of all students through strong, personalized instruction based on each learner's individual progress toward academic and behavior goals.

Those of us who have been in the field of education for a while tend to be skeptical of new initiatives, because we've seen them come and we've seen them go. It's true that RTI is relatively new as a means of determining eligibility under IDEA. But as a framework designed to meet the needs of all students, it might not seem new at all to a middle school that has long been focused on universal design for learning, differentiation, formative assessment, and a thoughtful pre-referral process. This foundation is why RTI, in some form or another, is here to stay—because at its core, it is based on principles that are well worth our time and effort. *RTI in Middle School Classrooms* will help you implement and sustain a model that benefits you, your students, and your school community.

RTI Implementation for Schools and Classrooms: An Overview

The Assess, Set Goals, Implement, and Monitor (ASIM) process is helpful not only for crafting student intervention plans, but also for the implementation of RTI at the school-wide and classroom levels. The graphic below will guide your thinking as you and your team assess your readiness for RTI, set implementation goals, carry out plans to reach those goals, and monitor your progress. At the end of your goal cycle (typically one school year), evaluate your progress and your school's responsiveness to the implementation. Begin the process again by reassessing and setting new goals for the next year.

School-Wide Implementation	Classroom Implementation	Notes
Assess the school's current structures, resources, and overall climate. **Essential Questions:** • Does my school understand the purpose and value of school-wide implementation? If not, how can we work toward that understanding? • Is there a team of professionals that can help with decision-making and initial navigation? • To what extent does my school's culture need to change to be more student-centered, personal, inclusive of all students, and so on? • What multi-tiered support structures are already in place? Whom are they serving? What support services are still needed? • Does my school have a method for screening all students to identify the need for support services? If not, what steps need to be taken to put such a method in place? • Does my school have a method for documenting intervention plans? If not, how will we establish this method?	**Assess** your instructional design, assessment methods, and overall classroom culture. **Essential Questions:** • To what extent is my classroom a positive learning environment? Would all students describe it as such? • In what ways is my instruction in line with UDL principles? How do I differentiate to meet the needs of all learners? • To what extent do I purposefully group students to either build community or meet academic needs? • What formative evaluation methods are already in place? • How effective am I as a co-teacher? Do I have a strong grasp of co-teaching models? If not, how will I build my understanding of those models? • To what extent is my teaching grounded in research?	Write down your assessment of your school's readiness for implementation, as well as your personal readiness for classroom implementation. Use the "Essential Questions" at left to guide your response.

Assess

➡

Implementation for Schools and Classrooms (*cont.*)

	School-Wide Implementation	Classroom Implementation	Notes
Set Goals	***Set goals* for school-wide implementation.** • Based on the information gathered through the Assess phase, the Navigation Team articulates the school's strengths and needs when it comes to RTI implementation. • The Navigation Team sets two or three goals for the first year of implementation. At the end of the year, the team will re-evaluate these goals and establish new ones and/or refine existing ones as needed to support and strengthen school-wide implementation of RTI.	***Set goals* for classroom implementation.** • Based on the information gathered through the Assess phase, each teacher articulates his or her strengths and readiness for RTI. • Each teacher sets two or three goals based on the assessment of his or her classroom readiness for RTI's implementation. • The Navigation Team is informed of and knowledgeable about these goals, and helps the teacher work toward achieving them.	Identify and record two or three goals for your school, plus two or three goals that pertain specifically to your class.
	Note: There may be a need for professional development prior to implementation at the school and/or classroom level. After analyzing the responses to the questions in the Assess phase, customize your approach to professional development to meet school and individual needs. Options include book studies, consultation from experts, in-service training, webinars, and/or facilitated work sessions.		
Implement	***Implement* RTI in your school and classroom.** • The implementation of RTI requires a coordinated effort among many school professionals. Ensure that a member of the Navigation Team takes on the role of RTI coordinator to oversee this implementation. The level of responsibility placed upon the RTI coordinator will vary based on your school's needs. For instance, the coordinator might be called on to offer big-picture analysis, or to manage more day-to-day details of implementation. • Identify a method for monitoring fidelity of implementation. How will the school assess whether goals are being met? • Face obstacles head-on and address them with the Navigation Team as they arise. • Offer professional development throughout the first years of implementation so that educators may continually learn how to support students using the RTI framework.		Write down your role and responsibilities in the implementation of RTI. Identify potential challenges and how you might overcome them.

	School-Wide Implementation	Classroom Implementation	Notes
Monitor	*Monitor* progress toward achieving your goals and reassess those goals to improve implementation. • Keep track of your progress through data collection. This can involve work samples, journaling, and/or other means of documenting progress. • Reevaluate your goals and your progress after each semester or at the end of the school year to establish new goals and/or revise the existing goals as needed.		Propose ideas for how your school and team can monitor implementation at the school-wide level, as well as how you will monitor progress toward your classroom goals.

Practice and Patience: Rolling Out RTI in Your School and Classroom

Remember that it may take up to five years before RTI is fully implemented in all classrooms. Identifying the existing structures your school already has in place is a good start. In addition, it's likely that your school will need to make gradual adjustments to the roles played by some personnel, the way colleagues work together, the way lessons are presented and classes are structured, and the support services available to students and to educators. Meanwhile, teachers and other school staff can benefit from professional development focused on the identified goals of the school and of individual classrooms. With time, commitment, and collaboration, you'll find the approach to RTI that works for you, your middle school, and your students.

Creating and Sustaining Positive Learning Environments

A teacher's core belief that every student can learn is key to establishing a positive learning environment. However, this belief alone will not ensure such an environment unless you take the time to deliberately plan activities for students to get to know one another. It's also essential for teachers to emphasize, model, and practice the idea that "different" doesn't mean "wrong" and that our unique qualities can be our strengths. Establishing this philosophy helps build a community that benefits students' development as well as school climate. In addition, teaching students how to meaningfully engage in discussions will open the door for them to be truly active in their learning groups and accepted in their classrooms.

Building this supportive and inviting environment in an RTI classroom requires, among other things:

- using thoughtful, ongoing dynamic assessment of learning
- making instructional decisions based on the unique needs of each learner
- building teacher-student relationships
- building relationships among peers
- purposefully grouping students
- guiding students as they engage in academic conversations and problem solving

This chapter explores the many ways educators can foster an inclusive mindset and establish a positive learning environment for all middle school students.

▲ Making Learning Personal

One of a middle school teacher's most important tasks is keeping young adolescent students focused on and engaged in learning. Assessments and activities aimed at making learning personal help teachers accomplish this task by exploring students' motivations, interests, hobbies, strengths and weaknesses, and academic readiness, and then using these characteristics in lesson planning. At the same time, these activities and assessments can help create a positive culture and climate in your classroom.

You can start the process by getting to know each of your students at a personal level. Gather information about their backgrounds, interests, communication skills, and learning preferences. The knowledge you acquire through the personalized learning assessments and strategies in this chapter will also give you insight that you can use to make meaningful connections between the curriculum and the information students already know or understand—in other words, insight into how you can connect classroom content to students' prior knowledge or skills.

All of this information can then be incorporated into daily lesson planning and instruction to meet each student's unique learning needs. It will give you the data you need to individualize instruction and purposefully group students; employ examples and strategies focused on how your students learn best; and provide whole-group instruction that engages all students through multiple approaches and methods.

> By teaching students at their levels of academic readiness, you show them that they can be successful. And by incorporating students' areas of interest, you demonstrate respect for their uniqueness as individuals.

By teaching students at their levels of academic readiness, you show them that they can be successful. And by incorporating students' areas of interest, you demonstrate respect for their uniqueness as individuals. The Assess, Set Goals, Instruct, and Monitor (ASIM) model provides a structure for working toward personalized learning goals within the framework of RTI.

Through this entire process, you will also be modeling acceptance of learning differences and setting the tone for a positive classroom environment. By spending time at the beginning of the school year or semester to get to know your students' personalities and learning needs, you will be more likely to meet those needs in an engaging and meaningful way. Sharing this information with other members of your school's RTI teams will help your fellow teachers do the same throughout the school year.

Getting to Know Your Students (and Helping Them Know Themselves)

Successful middle school students tend to share two qualities: self-efficacy and self-regulation. Students who have developed self-efficacy believe they have the skills to complete learning objectives, and those with self-regulation skills believe that they control the steps necessary to successfully perform tasks. To build self-efficacy, students need opportunities to learn what their strengths are, and then need to be given opportunities to use those strengths to reach academic goals and sustain achievement in the middle grades and beyond. The assessment strategies covered in this chapter move students toward self-efficacy by helping you get to know your students, and by helping students get to know themselves better.

The time you spend on assessments will pay off when making instructional decisions for individuals, small learning groups, or a class as a whole. You will be better prepared to develop and deliver lessons that address the learning needs of your students by understanding their backgrounds, experiences, and interests. By making learning meaningful for your students, you will also reduce classroom management issues. Knowing and considering what students need to be successful learners ensures that you do not leave classroom success to chance.

Two examples of such assessments are the Student Interest Inventory (page 60) and the Thinking Styles and Learning Preferences Inventory (page 63). The Student Interest Inventory will provide you with information helpful in setting academic goals, planning instruction, engaging students, and grouping students. Using the information in your daily teaching will let students know that you value them as individuals, and they will appreciate your consideration of their interests. This will help build strong relationships between you and your students. Furthermore, through the self-reflective activity of completing the inventory, students will gain self-awareness about how they prefer to learn and how they prefer to spend their time.

The Thinking Styles and Learning Preferences Inventory identifies how students best process information and how they feel most confident communicating what they know. With this knowledge, you can plan instruction based on students' learning strengths, which in turn will keep students motivated and engaged. As students are grouped for tiered instruction across content areas, the information you've gathered becomes valuable data to ensure that teachers throughout the middle school account for students' thinking styles and learning preferences.

RTI in Action

MAKING LEARNING PERSONAL

At the beginning of the school year, Mr. Ferguson, a seventh-grade science teacher, administers assessments to gather information about his students' learning and thinking preferences and needs. Of the twenty-eight students in his third-period biology class, ten prefer to learn through visual means, six prefer to hear the information, and twelve prefer to learn using a hands-on approach. Mr. Ferguson decides that the best way to meet the needs of all of his learners is to address each lesson through multiple means of representation. First, however, he wants to make sure students are cognizant of their own learning preferences so they can make good choices for themselves.

To help students understand these ideas, Mr. Ferguson presents students with examples of how each type of learner might prefer to learn and complete work after a typical lecture providing new information. On Day 1, he provides graphic organizers for students to complete. On Day 2, he uses a free online survey to gather student responses. On Day 3, he posts questions on a screen and has students respond using clickers. On Day 4, he lectures from a PowerPoint presentation projected on the screen.

After each lesson, Mr. Ferguson asks students to respond to the following statement:

The way this lesson was taught helped me learn.

☐ Strongly Disagree
☐ Disagree
☐ Agree
☐ Strongly Agree

On Day 5, after collecting and assessing all the data, Mr. Ferguson shares the results with his class. He describes the different learning preferences and explains how important it is for students to know what style of learning works best for them.

Building Community

Among the many benefits of getting to know students at a personal level is the cultivation of positive peer relationships and strong community—both in your classes and in the middle school as a whole. As you identify the strengths of each student and incorporate that information in your daily lesson planning, students will observe the recognition and admiration you show each student. Some students will naturally follow your lead. Others might need more time and practice. Overall, the outcome will be a positive learning environment that encourages students to capitalize on their personal strengths, appreciate others' differences, and stay focused on learning. As the semester and school year progress, continue to lead classes in community-building activities to strengthen the bonds that you established early on and to deepen your understanding of each individual student.

> Among the many benefits of getting to know students at a personal level is the cultivation of positive peer relationships and strong community—both in your classes and in the middle school as a whole.

Your efforts to build community and respect among students are critical in middle school, since intervention can often be especially stigmatizing and isolating for adolescents. To keep all students feeling connected as a group, you can implement community-building activities with the whole class. Giving students the opportunity to learn in smaller groups will also help build relationships. In addition, providing all students with evidence that you have a growth mindset for them as individuals will help lower the level of competition in the classroom by emphasizing personal development.

Of course, no matter how well you know your students and no matter how much you plan and prepare, the unexpected will happen. A student may come to school upset because her mother is in the hospital, an unplanned fire drill may disrupt a class schedule, or two students might bring an outside disagreement into the classroom. Yet having established a positive environment and a supportive community will help you cope with each difficult situation.

▲ Flexible and Purposeful Grouping in a Multi-Tiered System of Support

Students in middle school tend to be curious and eager to learn—as long as their teachers make lessons interesting, challenging, and engaging. During the middle school years, students also tend to be quite social, which can sometimes make it difficult to keep them focused on learning. However, you can harness this sociability for good, since meaningful learning often occurs through interaction, collaborative activities, and academic conversations. Creating and sustaining a strong class community and a collaborative atmosphere is another way you can support individuals' learning.

Grouping is a proven teaching method to realize all of these goals. This chapter will give you the knowledge necessary to purposely group your students while addressing academic and social challenges.

Effective grouping also shifts the control of learning from the teacher to the student, an important goal to reach with middle school students. Giving your students practice in skills such as problem solving, decision-making, and trying out different paths toward achieving their learning objectives will support student-centered learning.

As you plan for learning, think about grouping your students with these aims:

- enhancing instruction by using a variety of methods

- shifting control of learning to the students

- helping students with moving information into long-term memory

- engaging students in critical thinking and problem solving

In considering these aims, also ask yourself the following questions:

- How thoughtful am I in deciding how to group students? Am I using student data to make these decisions?

- What type of grouping will best meet my goals and my students' learning objectives?

- How mindful am I of keeping groups flexible? Is it easy for students to join, leave, and change groups as their needs change?

- How well do students understand the purpose of groups?

Asking these questions will help you plan effective lessons and use your class time wisely. Additionally, using the data you've already gathered about your students will help you choose the best grouping strategies for each of your classes.

Naturally, not every student works well independently and not every student works best in a group. But when you use flexible, purposeful, and data-driven grouping techniques across RTI's tiers, you give all students a better chance of achieving academic success. Grouping also helps learners construct social knowledge and skills through collaborative work. This section will explore a range of ways you can group students, and the benefits of each.

> When you use flexible, purposeful, and data-driven grouping techniques across RTI's tiers, you give all students a better chance of achieving academic success. Grouping also helps learners construct social knowledge and skills through collaborative work.

Grouping Guidelines

Grouping students effectively can help them extend, expand, enrich, enhance, and accelerate their learning, and gives you a valuable tool to specifically address the needs of each student and to engage students in productive partnerships with their peers.

There are a variety of ways to group students, along with a variety of purposes for grouping. Group composition can be determined by social skills, background knowledge of the content area, skill level, reading levels, interest areas, thinking and learning preferences, leadership skills, and other factors. The overarching goal is to group students in the way that most effectively addresses their learning needs, while being mindful of keeping groups flexible as these needs and circumstances change.

The best purposeful grouping uses a range of techniques based on what you know about your students and what their target learning outcomes are. Grouping is based on the data acquired from the assessments and activities in this chapter, the results of class-wide assessment, or other sources and observations. Taking into consideration the various learning needs of each student, think about how you might deliver a lesson so that every student will successfully master the content. As you plan your instruction, ask yourself, "How do I best address the needs of my students?" At this point in your planning, decide if and when grouping your students will enhance their learning. Lessons that are well planned to meet the needs of your students will likely use more than one grouping technique. The key is to use a variety of grouping techniques to ensure that all students are engaged and contributing as valued members of your classroom community. Try to avoid overusing any single type of grouping.

As you consider if and how to group your students, use these six key questions to start and guide your thought process:

1. Will grouping support the classroom community?

2. Will grouping increase student achievement?

3. Will grouping promote academic conversation among peers?

4. Can specific content or skills be best reinforced through group work?

5. What grouping configuration best fits the activities required or best supports the lesson goals?

6. How can I group to increase student engagement?

GROUPING METHODS: FROM THE TOP DOWN

In the broadest sense, there are three high-level ways to group your students: as a whole class, in small groups that are subsets of the class, or individually for focused, independent study. Each of these groupings has unique benefits and characteristics.

Whole-class instruction is just what its name suggests—a situation in which students are taught as one large group. Often, teachers will begin a lesson with whole-group instruction and then break into another form of grouping for guided study or independent practice. Whole-class instruction can be especially useful when you are:

- modeling what students will do independently
- introducing new material
- explaining assignments
- conducting closure activities

Small groups break your classes into subsets for focused work. You may use various methods to determine the composition of those groups. For example, skill area grouping is a type of homogeneous grouping in which students with similar needs work together. In this scenario, students:

- work with peers toward similar learning goals
- experience reteaching, review, or extension of specific skills or content
- are pre-taught a lesson for which they'll need extra support to understand particular concepts, or for which they need to practice relevant skills

Another type of small grouping is heterogeneous grouping, which places students with different characteristics into the same group. This grouping technique can be used for:

- project-based work
- group collaboration that requires students to fulfill different roles and combine their various strengths
- group discussion

Keep in mind that, for many grouping strategies, the groups do not all need to be equal in size. Groups can range from two to eight students. Like other grouping decisions, use what you know about your students to choose group sizes. For more details on ways to form and use small groups, see pages 38–39.

Individual instruction gives students the chance to work on their own. Its common uses include:

- preparation for group work
- journaling, essay writing, or other composition
- reading or other independent study

The following table shows an overview of these major grouping types and some of their most significant benefits to students.

▲ **Figure 2.1: Grouping Methods and Key Benefits**

Type of Group	Whole-Class Instruction	Small Groups	Individual Instruction
Key Benefits	• Ensures that all students are receiving the same information • Ideal structure for short lectures • Efficient means of introducing information or content before students break into groups • Good way to conclude a lesson after group work	• Students come to understand and appreciate the value of teamwork and collaboration • Students model skills for one another, including self-efficacy and self-regulation • Students in **heterogeneous groups** appreciate and benefit from the differences they bring to the group, and learn to value people who think and learn differently than they do • Students in **homogeneous groups** can receive tailored instruction based on student need	• Students have time to individually acquire new skills in their preferred style of learning and to practice those skills • Students are able to work at their own personal pace • Students can think through ideas on their own without social pressures

USING SMALL GROUPS IN YOUR CLASSROOM

When you're implementing purposeful grouping, small groups are likely to be your most frequently used tool to accomplish specific learning objectives. As mentioned earlier, there are many ways you can go about forming small groups, depending on the needs of your students and the goals of your lesson. In this section, we'll explore several options for creating and using small groups.

Heterogeneous grouping provides opportunities for using peer role models within each group. With grouping according to mixed levels of academic readiness and guidance that supports group interdependence, each group member is encouraged by the teacher and peers to fully participate in the learning objective. Students are evaluated based on group and individual performance.

Skill area grouping places students in homogenous groups with students who have similar needs. In these groups, students cooperate with peers who are working toward similar learning objectives. These groups are frequently monitored and adjusted as goals are met and needs change.

Learning preference grouping allows students to work with peers who have the same or different types of learning preferences and perspectives. By using the information gathered through assessments, you can easily group students in either way. Grouping students with *the same* learning styles allows peers to share how they use their strengths in various situations and also how they deal with challenges. Students grouped by *different* learning preferences can give each other insight on how to expand and strengthen additional learning preferences and build different study skills and methods.

Peer pairing allows you to pair students who will benefit from working together for quick and efficient review of information, as well as more in-depth studying of content to move it into long-term memory. Peer pairing and similar methods such as cross-age tutoring have been shown to improve on-task behavior, promote stronger student-to-student relationships, and increase academic growth for both the tutor and the tutee.

In determining the peers for pairing, create a list of your students based on your assessment of their content knowledge. Once you've compiled this list, pair the most confident student with the student listed first on the bottom half of the list, pair the student listed second from the top with the second student in the bottom half of the list, and so on.

Mastery grouping brings together students who need additional time to explore content in a variety of ways to fully grasp the taught concept. For example, students who are having difficulty acquiring new vocabulary introduced in a lesson might work together to master the vocabulary by using content area literacy strategies. This grouping will change with each lesson based on your evaluation of students' mastery of the content, and based on your assessment of their need for further reteaching and reviewing.

Interest grouping brings together students who have similar interests. This is especially relevant for project work. Grouping students by interest areas allows them to share their knowledge of, enthusiasm for, and skills related to the content. This type of grouping can also lead to new friendships and strengthen the community in your classroom.

Opportunity grouping is a strategy in which groups are determined based on the opportunities students have to work together. Groups match up students who have had little if any opportunity to work together. This grouping will build community in your classroom and give students a chance to expand their relationships with peers.

Random grouping places students together through randomization. For example, using your class list, choose every fifth student and make a group until you are down to the last group of students. The purpose of random grouping is to continually mix up your grouping throughout the week, month, and semester.

Student choice grouping gives students the opportunity to work with their friends. Instruct students to privately list the top three choices of peers with whom they would like to do group work. Collect the lists and use them to form groups. You may want to gather this information every ten weeks or so, since friendships can change frequently in middle school.

Remember never to let your groups stagnate. In addition, use random grouping rarely. Instead, mix and match your grouping approaches to meet the needs of your different classes and to complement your lesson objectives.

SPOTLIGHT
ABILITY GROUPING VS. ACADEMIC READINESS GROUPING

Research has consistently shown that grouping by ability level should be done sparingly.* Students with low academic achievement perform more poorly when they are grouped by ability with similarly performing peers. In addition, ability grouping has been identified as a source of lowered self-esteem and motivation among struggling students.

Grouping students while implementing RTI often means putting together students who are ready for similar levels of academic challenge in specific content areas. This is *not* equivalent to ability grouping, in which you group and teach students through a more fixed-mindset view of their aptitude: above average, average, or below average. Rather, in academic readiness grouping, students are grouped more purposefully by learning goals or needs with the intention of improving their performance in a specific area and within a specific time frame. Purposeful groups should never become stationary, but be ever-changing in response to students' varying needs over time and across content areas, in response to students' movement between RTI tiers, and in harmony with students' learning preferences and interests.

*Marzano, Marzano, and Pickering, 2003

Grouping Students Within the RTI Tiers

When you consider how to combine purposeful grouping with RTI, revisit these six guiding questions introduced earlier in the chapter:

1. Will grouping support the classroom community?

2. Will grouping increase student achievement?

3. Will grouping promote academic conversation among peers?

4. Can specific content or skills be best reinforced through group work?

5. What grouping configuration best fits the activities required or best supports the lesson goals?

6. How can I group to increase student engagement?

Use your answers to these questions to help you make decisions about how best to apply grouping at each tier. In this section, we'll explore the relationships between tiers and grouping.

TIER I

When you are providing Tier I instruction, your classes will most likely be composed of students with different levels of academic readiness who respond differently to the curriculum you teach and instructional methods you use. Along with other strategies, grouping is one way to address these differences.

Tier I teaching is typically a combination of whole-class and small-group instruction. Your choice of grouping at this tier will be determined by the learning goals and by your observation of student achievement before, during, and after the lesson. In Tier I, purposeful grouping helps you reduce the student-teacher ratio while still allowing students with different levels of academic readiness to work together. It also allows you to carry out individual assessment, goal setting, targeted instruction, and progress monitoring.

As the class works in purposeful groups, you can monitor to ensure students are achieving benchmarks and chosen goals. Close monitoring of progress can help you recalibrate groups as necessary, and will also give you information to use in making ongoing decisions regarding the need for Tier II intervention.

TIER II

Though fewer students receive Tier II support, it still isn't practical (or in many cases even possible) to provide individualized instruction for each student. Instead, you can continue to carefully form student groups to ensure that individual learning needs are met for students who need support beyond Tier I instruction.

Students at Tier II are best grouped by similar levels of academic readiness (rather than general ability), similar learning goals, or both. This will give you the opportunity to work with each group as needed to introduce new information, reteach certain concepts, or give learners additional practice in key skills or knowledge areas. At the same time, when students are grouped according to their specific learning strengths, they can engage with and teach one another. This helps resolve a classroom challenge at Tier II—ensuring that all students are involved even as teachers work specifically with small groups of students.

Groups at Tier II remain fluid and flexible, with students moving in and out of their small groups within eight to sixteen weeks, as determined by frequent progress monitoring.

TIER III

Tier III instruction typically comprises small-group or individual instruction to meet specific areas of concern. Tier III focuses on students who are not successfully responding to Tier II interventions and who show a need for more intense instruction. Tier III instruction will most likely take place outside of the general classroom and be implemented by a specialist trained to provide more intensive instruction in the identified deficit area. Close collaboration between the specialist and the classroom teacher is essential so the student can move to Tier I or II level of support as soon as possible and appropriate.

Tier III instruction can be offered at the same time as Tier II instruction. As students move to groups for Tier II instruction, Tier III students can go to the specialist trained to provide more intensive instruction in their areas of need.

Remember to view tiers as differing levels of support rather than a placement or location. As students' needs change, movement among the tiers will be fluid. This will require ongoing progress monitoring and collaboration from the RTI teams.

▲ Academic Conversations and Collaborative Problem Solving

Students in middle school are more prepared than ever before in their lives to engage in meaningful academic dialogue with one another. With the development of greater abstract reasoning and more complex thought processes, adolescents are ready and eager to dig deeper into ideas, lessons, and questions. Conversation with their peers is a powerful tool for this exploration.

In their book *Academic Conversations: Classroom Talk that Fosters Critical Thinking and Content Understandings*, Jeff Zwiers and Marie Crawford identify five core communication skills:

- elaborating and clarifying
- supporting ideas with evidence
- building on and/or challenging ideas
- paraphrasing
- synthesizing

Many middle school students will need to be taught these conversation dynamics, and will need support and guidance as they learn to employ these skills in group settings. Putting students together in purposeful groups is not enough. For those groups to be truly productive, students need to be guided in a structured way as they develop these conversational tools. Providing such structure, with clearly defined roles and expectations, will prepare your students for success.

At the same time that middle school students are improving their facility for academic conversation, they are also developing the skills to work collaboratively and to

> With the development of greater abstract reasoning and more complex thought processes, adolescents are ready and eager to dig deeper into ideas, lessons, and questions. Conversation with their peers is a powerful tool for this exploration.

solve problems as partners and teammates with their peers. True classroom community is built and strengthened when students work collaboratively on projects. Guiding students in this social and emotional element of learning and problem solving is essential. To solve problems in a group setting, students have to be able to clearly articulate their points of view. The strategies presented in this book provide you with a starting point for promoting academic conversations and collaborative problem solving. From this foundation, you can create and customize your own strategies based on your knowledge of your students.

▲ Strategies for Building a Positive Learning Environment

The work you do to promote a positive learning environment and to build a strong sense of community in your classrooms and schools will pay off as the semester and year continue. This process opens the doors for all students to be truly active in their learning and to feel accepted in their classrooms. The strategies and assessments that follow in the rest of this chapter will give you the tools to do this work. They will help you get to know your students, create a strong school and class community, purposefully group students, and implement strategies for promoting academic conversations.

Each of the following strategies focuses on one of these key goals:

- Making Learning Personal
- Creating Community
- Purposeful Grouping
- Encouraging Academic Conversations and Collaborative Problem Solving

In the following section you'll find a summary of each strategy. Many of these strategies also include tips that you can use for implementation and customization.

Job Application

Area Addressed: *Making Learning Personal*

Strategy Summary

This activity provides students with multiple opportunities to fill out job applications, as well as exposure to a variety of work experiences. This is not only a skill-building opportunity for students, but also provides teachers with valuable support in maintaining an organized classroom.

Each student completes a typical job application form (page 59) every two weeks, identifying the job for which he or she would like to be "hired." Align the job application and descriptions with your classroom needs. By switching every two weeks, students get the opportunity to experience a variety of jobs. You will most likely have more students than jobs, so it's a good idea to create and maintain a master schedule to ensure students have the opportunity to experience their first-choice jobs at some point in the semester. Another option is to assign teams of two or three students to each job so that it can be accomplished more efficiently using teamwork. Additionally, if a student is absent, the other team members will carry out the job responsibilities.

In addition to this activity's other benefits, it exposes students to a variety of skills and tasks that may help them determine types of part-time jobs they want to pursue. It can even give them ideas for the careers they might want as adults. It also underscores the fact that everyone has a role to play in a community and that everyone is important and valuable.

Teacher Tips

- Write a short description of each job to help students choose which tasks they may prefer.

- You may choose to provide students with performance evaluations, as well as the opportunity for them to provide self-evaluations. Your feedback on their job performance will help them determine their areas of strength, while self-evaluation will encourage them to reflect on how they see their strengths.

Student Interest Inventory

Area Addressed: *Making Learning Personal*

Strategy Summary

Stimulating students' interests and motivating them to learn requires teachers to gather information to address the learning needs of all students. The Student Interest Inventory (page 60) collects information that will help you plan effective classroom instruction, engage learners, set academic goals, differentiate content for unique student needs, and effectively group students.

Introduce the inventory to students by telling them you want to know as much as possible about what interests them and how they like to learn. Be sure to tell them there are no wrong answers to the inventory's questions and that you will use the information they share to better plan your lessons.

You may vary the way you administer the inventory depending on the time you have available, the attention spans of your students, and the ages and levels of students you teach.

Teacher Tips

Consider these variations in administering the Student Interest Inventory:

- Spread the process over multiple days (for example, students could fill out one page per day).

- Allow students to complete the inventory on computers rather than in hard copy (using the form in this book's digital content).

- Make the inventory into a private online survey using a site such as SurveyMonkey and have students complete it by a given date.

- Customize the inventory by selecting questions appropriate for an individual or group of students, adding additional comments you deem important, and/or omitting any that don't apply to your students or the content area you teach.

Understanding Thinking Styles and Learning Preferences

Area Addressed: *Making Learning Personal*

Strategy Summary

Teachers and students can benefit from analyzing thinking styles and learning preferences. Explain the following thinking styles and learning preferences to students to help them understand themselves. As a group, talk about each style and preference, and the way these factors affect how we learn, work, and communicate. Ask students to describe to one another how they best think and learn depending on different contexts, such as when they read, study, practice skills, review information, engage in project work, or learn something new.

Thinking Styles

- **Global thinkers** are typically in need of less structure in how they learn and process information. They work best if introduced to the big picture first, as problem solving and concepts make more sense to them when they are able to understand the greater context. When introduced to new information, they need a strong lesson introduction that connects to prior knowledge. They are comfortable working on multiple projects simultaneously. They are generally "idea" people who prefer open-ended tasks.

- **Analytic thinkers** prefer structure in the learning process. Their approach to learning and processing information is linear. They generally prefer order and are purposeful in carrying out tasks. Students who are analytic thinkers are usually detail-oriented in completing work. They typically prefer to work on projects in a step-by-step process with minimal interruption.

Learning Preferences

- **Visual learners** generally learn best through pictures, charts, infographics, and other visual representations of information. These students are skilled in remembering and processing information that comes in the form of images.

- **Auditory learners** learn best by listening. For these learners, lectures and other spoken information can be most easily remembered and synthesized.

- **Kinesthetic learners** generally process information best when they are able to incorporate touch or movement into learning.

Teacher Tips

Learning preferences go beyond visual, auditory, and kinesthetic. Some students prefer to learn in solitude. Others prefer social learning in collaborative groups. The list of ways in which to learn is a long one, and most students benefit from a variety of learning modalities. Whatever your students' preferences are, understanding them will help you build relationships with learners, vary your instructional methods, and help students do their best work.

Thinking Styles and Learning Preferences Inventory

Area Addressed: *Making Learning Personal*

Strategy Summary

Sometimes teachers get into the habit of delivering instruction only one way—usually the way in which *they* learn best. In this situation, all students may be expected to complete the same task as proof that they have acquired key skills or content knowledge. However, the way in which you teach your students and how they demonstrate their understanding of lesson objectives will have a great impact on their academic achievement. That is why "one-size-fits-all" teaching often doesn't produce the most positive outcome for students or teacher.

The Thinking Styles and Learning Preferences Inventory (page 63) will help you determine how your students take in and process information. Understanding students' thinking and learning preferences will give you powerful information when designing your lessons. It will also build stronger relationships with your students, who will appreciate the fact that you're considering what works best for them in the learning process. Giving your students multiple means of meeting goals sends them the message that you realize they all learn differently and that you want to give them all the opportunity to show their best work. The inventory will also help students know and understand their own strengths and learning preferences so they can make informed choices about their learning and their academic goals.

Once the inventory is complete and has been scored, explain to students what the results mean for them as learners. Share descriptions of the thinking styles and learning preferences, and take the time to provide examples of how they might use this information to their advantage when choosing how to best process and show their work. For instance, students might choose their study strategies based on what they learn from the inventory.

Once you know the thinking styles and learning preferences of your students and how these styles and preferences are distributed in each of your classes, you can use this information to plan lessons and to group students. In your instruction, to ensure you are addressing both global and analytic thinkers, always provide students with the lesson objective—the "big picture"—as well as the sequential steps needed to meet the objective. To meet varied learning needs, give students options to present their work in ways involving visual, auditory, and kinesthetic styles.

Teacher Tips

You may find that administering this inventory as a whole-class activity provides the most accurate results, because it gives you an opportunity to explain concepts and offer examples and context as necessary. You might choose to project the inventory on a large screen visible to all students. This way, you can read and discuss each question with the class before individuals respond. For example, question number one reads, "I decorate my written work with pictures and doodles." You may want to elaborate on this statement by saying, "This means that while you're taking notes or thinking about content, it helps you to draw pictures of what you're thinking or to doodle designs as you process the information." You can also explain to students that answering a question with "This often describes me" doesn't mean that they don't pay attention. It's important for students to understand that their answers will help them make better choices on how they best think and learn, and that you will not use the information to isolate or penalize them in any way.

What Makes a Great Teacher?

Area Addressed: *Making Learning Personal*

Strategy Summary

Knowing and understanding what your students value in a teacher gives you worthwhile information for establishing a positive learning environment. It will also give you important knowledge regarding the most effective ways to communicate with your students and the best ways to plan instruction that meets their social and academic needs.

The What Makes a Great Teacher? questionnaire (page 66) is most useful at the beginning of the school year as you establish relationships with your students. It will be most effective if each student individually responds to the questions, but a small-group approach can also be effective.

Teacher Tips

You can have students complete this questionnaire in a variety of ways, including:

- filling out a hard-copy version
- filling out the form on a computer
- answering it in the form of a private online survey
- answering questions aloud in a personal interview

What Would You Do?

Area Addressed: *Making Learning Personal*

Strategy Summary

This activity presents students with a set of thought-provoking vignettes (page 67). Through students' responses to these scenarios, you can determine individuals' interests and comfort levels with various leadership roles. As a result, you can make more informed decisions about student leadership as well as decisions about how to structure small-group instruction.

Instruct students to read each vignette, think carefully about the scenario, and consider how they would respond in that situation. Students can respond through reflective writing, small-group conversation, or class discussion.

Assure students that you want their honest descriptions of how they would respond in these or similar situations. Clarify that you're not looking for specific answers, and that you don't expect everyone's answers to be the same, since each of us reacts differently to the same situations. Your goal is to get to know them better through their responses to these hypothetical scenarios.

Teacher Tips

- You may choose to add to or replace any of the five vignettes based on specific situations relevant to your particular class, school, or community.
- This activity can be administered by giving your students one vignette per day or per week, or you could consider all or several vignettes in one or two class periods. Many teachers find that using just one or two vignettes a day gives students the chance to provide more thoughtful responses and not hurry through the activity.

- The information collected from the vignettes will give you insight on whether peer pressure outweighs rational decision-making for a student. It can also help you determine if a student is more likely to be a leader or follower in a group of peers.

SPOTLIGHT

DETERMINING LEVELS OF PEER LEADERSHIP

Mrs. Sheahan, an eighth-grade language arts teacher, used one vignette every week for the first two months of the semester. She started by using the vignettes on page 67 and soon developed and added her own. Mrs. Sheahan found the vignettes provided her with strong discussion points for students, and through 15-minute whole-class discussions she was able to get many students to open up about difficult experiences and decisions about how to handle them. She also felt she was able to help students think of alternative ways to handle tough situations.

Just as Mrs. Sheahan did, you may choose to develop additional vignettes and use one per week as a teaching tool. You may also want to add to the discussion, having students consider and talk about the scenario in small groups before coming back to the large group and sharing their ideas for further discussion.

Coat of Arms

Areas Addressed: *Making Learning Personal/Creating Community*

Strategy Summary

Coat of Arms is an activity that allows students to share important events from their lives. The purpose is to give your students an opportunity to reflect on those significant events and share them with their peers. This exercise can reveal student interests and values and build community.

You can do this activity at the beginning of the school year or semester, when many of your students are still getting to know each other, or you can wait until later in the semester when they may feel more comfortable sharing information. The timing you choose will depend on whether your primary goal is to learn basic information about your students up front, or to build trust before asking for more personal information that may also be more illuminating.

Have each student create a coat of arms by using pictures to answer the first five questions that follow, and composing a motto in response to the sixth. A template for a traditional coat of arms is provided on page 68. Encourage students to be creative. They can use photos, hand-drawn pictures, magazine pictures, or clipart, or you may have them create their coats of arms as electronic graphics.

The following questions are recommended as starting points for guiding students as they assemble their coats of arms. However, feel free to modify these questions according to your needs and your goals for the activity.

1. What is an important event in your life—something that has made you the person you are today?

2. What is your favorite sport, hobby, or activity?

3. What is the best part of your school day?

4. Who is your favorite person in the world?

5. What are you proudest of or happiest about?

Number 6 is to be answered in words.

6. What is the motto you try to live your life by every day?

After students have completed the activity, set aside a little time each week or each day of class for students to share their creations. They can do this through formal presentations or in a more casual setting. As you observe, facilitate discussion highlighting each student's unique qualities. Ask questions of each presenter, modeling for your students, and then encourage peers to ask questions of their own to promote interest and acceptance. Make notes of the key qualities and experiences explored by each student and add them to students' personal learner profiles.

Teacher Tips

- Ask for students' permission to post their coats of arms in the classroom so all students—including those from other classes—can look at them and get a sense of their peers' unique experiences.

- For another example of this activity, see the following Spotlight, "What's in My Bag."

SPOTLIGHT
WHAT'S IN MY BAG

Mrs. Edison, a seventh-grade Spanish teacher, told her students they could choose between making a coat of arms or describing "What's in My Bag" to share with their classmates. To help them choose, she modeled both activities. For the Coat of Arms, she followed the directions listed in the Coat of Arms activity and created a graphic on her computer using pictures of significant events in her life. For "What's in My Bag," she put personal mementos in a bag. She pulled out one item at a time and explained its significance and importance in her life. She had a trophy that she won showing Black Angus cattle while growing up. She pulled out a T-shirt from Trinity College in Dublin, Ireland, where she had attended a semester of college. The T-shirt was also a reminder of the trip she took through Ireland to meet her relatives. She had three small knit hats—two pink and one blue—from the births of her children. The last item in the bag was an apple. She told her students she included it to represent her teaching, her lifelong passion. She encouraged her students to ask questions throughout the presentation to get to know her better as a person and as their teacher.

Digital Storytelling

Areas Addressed: Making Learning Personal/Creating Community

Strategy Summary

Digital storytelling invites students to produce short, first-person narratives on meaningful subjects, using a variety of digital media. Offering a range of digital options enables students to learn new technologies while stretching their creativity. Students might choose to create videos, assemble slideshows, design websites, or use a combination of these and other formats, depending on the technologies available at your school.

After students create their digital stories, they will share them with classmates. These personal stories can lead to deeper student-to-student understanding, resulting in a more positive, supportive atmosphere in your classroom.

In addition, while all students have interesting and important stories to tell, they don't always have the appropriate tools or opportunities to share those stories. For example, some students will struggle with written expression, but will excel at telling their stories aloud. You may find that students who have been somewhat nonproductive or unengaged in written work nevertheless have colorful, intense, and rich stories just waiting to be told. In turn, these stories can provide you with valuable information on how to better meet the learning needs of your students. For all of these reasons, digital storytelling can have a powerful impact on the climate of your classroom and the compassion of your students.

There are no strict rules for storytelling, so tailor this activity according to the interests, needs, and strengths of your students. You may want to start the creative process by providing a prompt. For example, you could ask students to tell stories about important adults in their lives, whether those people are relatives, celebrities, individuals within the community, or figures connected to the curriculum you are teaching. The important thing is that the stories come from students' personal experiences, perceptions, and beliefs.

Digital storytelling gives students an opportunity to reflect on the things they admire most in others, what they may aspire to be or do with their lives, what they find most interesting, or what their opinions are on specific subjects. At the same time, it will give you insight on how you might capture their interest or how best to motivate them in your teaching.

Teacher Tips

- Visit the website of the Center for Digital Storytelling at www.storycenter.org for more information and resources.

- If your school has access to electronic tablets, storytelling applications can be very helpful with this strategy.

Where I Come From

Areas Addressed: Making Learning Personal/Creating Community

Strategy Summary

Experts predict that by the year 2020, nearly half of the public school population in the United States will be made up of students whose first language is not English. Therefore, teachers have a responsibility to embrace and appreciate the cultural differences in their students. As a teacher, you already gather a range of student information and use it to enhance your teaching and meet student needs. This activity goes a step further by encouraging students to get to know more about their peers and their backgrounds, building community and compassion in your classroom.

In this activity, you will assign each student to interview a classmate with whom they are not very familiar or with whom they do not typically socialize outside of class. Explain to students that they are going to be reporters. Inform them that they will choose three highlights from the interview—three key facts about the other person that stand out as especially thought-provoking. Encourage students to ask follow-up questions that build on the responses they get from the required questions. Provide class time for students to conduct and transcribe the interviews. Review students' first transcriptions and, if appropriate, make suggestions for the top three facts they might choose to focus on. Then assign students the homework of turning their transcriptions into narrative reports in which they'll share the three facts or insights from the interviews that they found most interesting or illuminating.

This activity can be a path to building positive and respectful connections among students who may not be drawn to each other naturally, while helping those students better understand the cultural differences that exist among them. This activity also creates a safe, supportive, and welcoming forum for sharing culturally different views and experiences, and focuses on understanding and accepting the differences among students' backgrounds, cultures, and interests. Additionally, it provides students with opportunities for interviewing, summarizing, writing, and presenting.

Teacher Tips

- If possible, provide students an example of an interview you have conducted with a colleague, focusing on three key facts you took away from the interview. Try to choose a colleague with cultural differences so you can model respect for and acceptance of differences.

- If desired—and if it's acceptable to all members of the class—students could share the three key facts of their narratives in presentations. Interview subjects could then answer follow-up questions from the class.

Chat

Area Addressed: *Creating Community*

Strategy Summary

This activity is an opportunity for students in small groups to get to know more about each other and to build empathy and understanding for their peers. As the semester or school year progresses, students find enjoyment, interest, comfort, and reassurance in sharing news with their groups. This activity requires a small amount of class time in exchange for a very positive and beneficial outcome.

Using information you've gathered on students' leadership abilities, learning preferences, cultural differences, and academic readiness, purposefully place students in heterogeneous small groups. On the first day of class each week, students share within groups their highs and lows from the weekend. The teacher monitors the group discussion and often sits in on various groups modeling appropriate responses and questions.

This valuable activity builds community in your classroom, gives students a supportive space in which to talk about their lives, and provides you with insight regarding the challenges individual students may face and how those challenges might affect their learning and your classroom.

Teacher Tips

- Make sure to use Chat consistently, offering it every Monday (or on whatever weekday your class first meets) so students build trust within their groups.

- Encourage students to ask follow-up questions in the week or weeks after a big issue has been raised. For example, in Mrs. Enicks's sixth-grade math class, one of her students shared during Chat how scared she was because her mother was very sick and had to go to the hospital. Each week until her mother recovered, the student's group asked her for an update.

Yellow Pages

Area Addressed: *Creating Community*

Strategy Summary

The Yellow Pages activity highlights and promotes students' unique abilities, talents, and interests. This activity also has the potential to bring together students who haven't previously made a connection or who haven't had a reason to work together.

In this activity, students identify themselves as skilled or knowledgeable in specific areas in which they can provide peers with expertise or demonstration when needed. For instance, students could identify special computer skills, a flair for graphic design, or a talent for proofreading papers. Students can then describe these areas of expertise on the Yellow Pages Expert Form on page 69. Once students have completed the form, gather all the information and create a single document that lists students' names and contact information under the appropriate categories. Encourage students to refer to these Yellow Pages when they feel like they need expert assistance.

Teacher Tips

- To get students thinking about their skills and areas of expertise, you could have them peruse the local Yellow Pages to get an idea of the various categories. You could also compile and distribute your own list of categories for students to consider.

- The Yellow Pages activity can be implemented school-wide, at individual grade levels, or within a single classroom. It can also include parents and other members of the community. The final list of people and their areas of expertise can be printed or distributed in electronic format.

Clock Grouping

Area Addressed: *Purposeful Grouping*

Strategy Summary

Clock grouping is a method that is easy to implement and appropriate for all subjects. This method is most helpful when you want to group students several different ways and transition among these groupings within the same class period. It allows you to easily manage the grouping of students in up to twelve different ways, and to smoothly transition students from group to group by listing the clock time of each activity. (These groupings are not related to actual time; they are just a way to identify transitions.)

Steps

1. For each of your classes, group students according to your lesson objectives and your knowledge of student interests and attributes, as well as any specific learning needs that might be present.

2. Customize the clock reproducible on page 70 by adding student groupings to the clock. You can make additions to or rearrange groups as necessary throughout the semester or school year as student needs, points of instructional emphasis, and other factors change. Either display the clock in an area where it will be visible to all students (on a projector or interactive whiteboard, for instance), or make a copy of the clock for each student.

3. During transition times, identify new groupings by referring to the appropriate clock group. For example, you may start your lesson by addressing your class as a whole group (12:00 group), then direct students to move to their 3:00 groups for an activity (3:00 groups are based on heterogeneous grouping of learning preferences), and for closure have them move to their 9:00 groups (peer pairs) for a quick review of the content learned.

Teacher Tips

• This strategy is especially helpful for middle school teachers managing multiple classes, because it organizes multiple grouping structures for a class on a single page. Each class would have a clock grouping structure purposefully planned ahead of time by the teacher.

▲ **Figure 2.2: Example of Clock Grouping**

12:00 Group (whole class)

9:00 Groups (peer pairs)

Li	Chandra
Blake	Raymond
Tammy	Stephanie
Maria	Hector
Asma	Anthony
Thomas	Sasha
Naima	Jesse
Alejandro	Asad
A.J.	Amy
Desiree	Ben

3:00 Groups (heterogeneous groups based on learning preferences)

Hector	Ben
Desiree	Maria
Jesse	Alejandro
Sasha	Blake
Naima	Asad
Thomas	Chandra
Li	Amy
Tammy	Stephanie
Anthony	A.J.
	Raymond
	Asma

6:00 Groups (homogeneous groups based on skill area)

Jesse	Tammy	Asma	Li	Asad
Stephanie	Desiree	Chandra	Anthony	Sasha
Hector	Ben	Maria	Alejandro	Thomas
Naima	Amy	Raymond	Blake	A.J.

Shuffling the Deck Grouping

Area Addressed: *Purposeful Grouping*

Strategy Summary

This grouping method allows you to create groups of varying size for different lessons. Each student is featured on a card along with identifying categories used to form groups. Before a session of small-group work, take out the deck of cards and based on the number of students you'd like in groups and the objective of the lesson, choose which category you'll use to determine groups. Following are directions for using this grouping method.

Steps

1. Using 3" × 5" index cards or the template on page 71, create a card for each student in each of your classes. Color-code the cards for each class or distinguish them in some other way. Place the student's name in the middle of his or her card. Various grouping criteria will appear in the card's four corners.

2. Determine how you want to group students, and how many members you want per group. This grouping method gives you the option of creating four different groups. For example, the first group can be your largest grouping, based on learning preferences. If you have twenty-four students and want three groups of eight, then you will use numbers 1, 2, or 3 in the top right corner of each student's card. This is your first grouping.

3. In the top left corner of each card, write one of six colors. In a classroom of twenty-four students, each color group will be composed of four students. This grouping could be based, for instance, on leadership skills for collaborative grouping.

4. In the bottom right corner of each card, write SC for "Student Choice." When using this grouping, let students work with others of their choosing during unstructured activities or free periods. Also offer the option of working alone for students who prefer independent time.

5. In the bottom left corner of each card, write PP for "Peer Paired." Use this grouping for quick reviews of information, as well as for more in-depth studying of content to move to long-term memory. Refer to the description of peer pairing on page 38 to match students for learning.

Teacher Tips

- Keep a tally of how often you use each of the four grouping methods so that you can determine whether you're over-relying on any one option.

Peer Tutoring

Area Addressed: *Purposeful Grouping*

Strategy Summary

Peer tutoring is another successful way to group students to enhance their learning and provide needed practice in Tier I. Pairing a student with more advanced academic readiness with a student who needs additional practice in an identified content or skill area provides the tutee with that practice while giving the tutor an opportunity to practice and solidify the skills being taught. The common saying "The best way to learn something is to teach it" is put into action with this strategy. As part of this method, you will determine content material to be used for tutoring, set a specific time for tutoring groups, prepare tutors and tutees for their roles, explain the behaviors required for successful tutoring, and monitor student performance.

Teacher Tips

- Use this strategy only when it benefits both learners and can be carried out in a positive and productive way. Not all students work well with partners, so being sensitive to the pairing dynamic is important.

Jigsaw Teaching

Area Addressed: *Encouraging Academic Conversations and Collaborative Problem Solving*

Strategy Summary

Jigsaw teaching is a strategy that builds comprehension, encourages effective communication, and gives students practice in problem solving. It is best used with class sizes of twenty to thirty students. This strategy allows all students to be experts in specific, assigned areas. When you have critical elements or areas of research you want students to know and you need to be sure of actively engaging all students, this is the strategy to use.

Jigsaw uses two types of grouping. First, students gather in collaborative groups. Within these groups, members count off, up to the number of critical elements being studied. Once students have their numbers, they report to their expert groups, the members of which all have the same number (all the ones together, all the twos, and so on).

Give each expert group a critical element or area of research to discuss and master. For example, for a unit on graphing, expert groups could be assigned to study the pros and cons of using a line graph, bar graph, or pie chart to communicate different kinds of information. Within the expert group, students take notes as they become experts in whichever area they are studying. After a specified amount of time, experts return to their collaborative groups. In turn, the experts teach their collaborative group members about their areas of expertise.

Teacher Tips

- To build on the jigsaw analogy and take it a step further, you could create a paper jigsaw puzzle for each group, with pieces large enough for making notes. Each member receives a piece and records his or her findings on it. Then, upon returning to the collaborative group, experts place their puzzle pieces together as they share their expert knowledge with the group.

Reciprocal Teaching

Area Addressed: Encouraging Academic Conversations and Collaborative Problem Solving

Strategy Summary

Reciprocal teaching in its most general definition is an instructional activity that asks students to teach one another. Palincsar and Brown developed a specific method for reciprocal teaching that uses four strategies to promote comprehension across the curriculum. The four strategies used are summarizing, questioning, clarifying, and predicting. Before using reciprocal teaching, teach students the required strategies and give them time to practice each one. You may want to share the following chart with students as a reference tool to remind them of each role, especially when your class is just getting familiar with reciprocal teaching.

Summarizing	Questioning	Clarifying	Predicting
Students identify key ideas, critical points, and new and vital vocabulary. Students analyze what information is central and what details are relatively unimportant.	Students ask clarifying questions on confusing points, unclear information, the roles of characters or key players, and whether there are connections to prior concepts taught. They create and ask "why" and "how" questions in order to understand a specific text or idea.	Students provide responses to the questions posed by the questioner and ask other team members for their points of view. Students recognize and question any words, phrases, or ideas that are unclear, unfamiliar, confusing, or easily misinterpreted.	Students make predictions about the next reading requirement, task, or lesson goal. These predictions are usually made using prior knowledge learned during previous steps. This step helps all group members with the retention of content.

It is not necessary to use all four strategies every time you use reciprocal teaching. Based on your students' learning preferences and the lesson, skill, or subject matter you're teaching, determine what strategy or strategies work best for the situation. Then group students according to the number of strategies you choose to use. For example, if using all four strategies, you would place your students into groups of four and assign each group member a role: summarizer, questioner, clarifier, or predictor. Instruct students to read a few paragraphs of the selected text and to use highlighting, underlining, or sticky notes to support their roles in the group discussion. Each student then performs his or her assigned role to increase the entire group's comprehension of the content.

Teacher Tips

- When using this strategy, switch students' roles frequently to build student competency in each area.

Palincsar, A.S., and A.L. Brown. "The Reciprocal Teaching of Comprehension-Fostering and Comprehension-Monitoring Activities." *Cognition and Instruction,* 1, 117–175 (1984).

Think Pair Share

Areas Addressed: *Encouraging Academic Conversations and Collaborative Problem Solving/Reading Comprehension*

Strategy Summary

Think Pair Share is a collaborative strategy that gives students the opportunity to think about what they've just read, individually summarize the information, and share their summaries with assigned peers. This quick summarization strategy ensures students have a chance to confirm their understanding of what was read, and engages all students in active participation.

Steps

After reading, students use the Think Pair Share mnemonic to build comprehension through summarization and verbal rehearsal. Use the following steps to implement Think Pair Share.

1. **Think:** Students read a passage and reflect on what they read.

2. **Pair:** Students form pairs as assigned by the teacher.

3. **Share:** Students share their summaries with their partners. If differences of opinion arise, students refer back to the passage to confirm the information or to amend their summaries to make them more accurate.

Teacher Tips

- When you are first introducing this strategy to students, consider modeling its steps with a colleague.

- Pair students using a purposeful grouping technique so you can quickly transition to Think Pair Share.

- Use this strategy often to help students move information from short-term memory to long-term memory.

- Consider always pairing students with the same peers when using Think Pair Share. Having an established partner helps make this strategy a quick yet meaningful way to engage learners in a focused, purposeful way.

Santa, C.M. "A Vision for Adolescent Literacy: Ours or Theirs?" *Journal of Adolescent & Adult Literacy,* 49:6, 466–476 (2006).

Silent Conversation

Area Addressed: *Encouraging Academic Conversations and Collaborative Problem Solving*

Strategy Summary

Silent conversation is a nonverbal way for students to reflect, generate ideas, demonstrate and reinforce learning, think through projects, or solve problems. It can also be a way to involve all students in a problem-solving activity, even those students who tend to be quiet or reserved.

Steps

1. Before using this strategy for the first time, explain briefly that this is a silent activity. No one may talk out loud, but everyone is expected and encouraged to add comments

to the "conversation." Students can respond to other people's ideas, underline or put various expressive marks (such as exclamation points, question marks, hearts, or smiley faces) next to comments, and write questions in response to others' points.

2. Start the idea-sharing process by writing a thought-provoking question in the center of the board or on a piece of chart paper.

   Sample questions:

   - What was the clearest point made in the lesson?
   - What questions do you have about _____?
   - What do you think about _____?
   - What do you know about _____?
   - How is _____ connected to _____?

3. Hand a marker or other writing utensil to each student, or place many writing utensils at the board.

4. Students join in and write notes on the board as they feel moved. At times, there may be long periods of quiet waiting as students read comments, reflect on their thoughts, and decide how to comment.

5. You may want to stand back and let the conversation unfold without input, but if needed you can also spark interaction and expand thinking by:

   - circling interesting ideas
   - writing questions about a participant comment
   - adding comments of your own
   - connecting two comments with a line and adding a question mark or a remark

Teacher Tips

- This strategy can be an excellent way to get quiet or shy students involved in classroom discussion.
- Because this activity takes place in silence, it gives students a change of pace and encourages thoughtful reflection.

Wentworth, M. (based on work by H. Smith, Foxfire Fund), National School Reform Faculty, "Chalk Talk," www.nsrfharmony.org/protocol/doc/chalk_talk.pdf (accessed April 22, 2014).

Conversation Norms

Area Addressed: Encouraging Academic Conversations and Collaborative Problem Solving

Strategy Summary

Establishing class norms as a group is a powerful way to be clear and open about the expectations students have of one another and the expectations you have for the class. Establish these norms early and revisit them often to make sure they are followed consistently. The following steps will guide you through the process of developing a set of norms with your class.

Steps

1. Ask all students to write a list of things they need in order to work productively in the class.

2. Have each student name one thing from his or her written list. Go around the whole class, with no repeats, and take as many cycles as necessary to list all points.

3. Ask for any clarification needed. For instance, one student may not understand what another student has listed, or may interpret the language differently.

4. If the list has more than ten items, ask students if some of them can be combined, and how.

5. Ask if everyone can abide by the listed norms. If anyone dislikes or doesn't want to comply with one of the items, discuss that point and work to guide the class toward the decision to keep the norm on the list.

6. Once you've established the norms for a class, refer to them whenever they would help the group make progress. For example, if a student is continually interrupting or not sharing "air" time, make an extra effort to reinforce the students who are implementing the class norms to encourage the student who is interrupting to follow the norms.

Teacher Tips

- Some common norms include: We listen to each other; we share our ideas and explain them; when we disagree, we do so respectfully and try to see the other view.

- Revisit this strategy as often as needed. The class might need to revise or reword the conversation norms on occasion as their understanding of what makes a group productive in their work deepens throughout the semester or year.

- You can use conversation norms to address behavioral issues as well as academic practices. For instance, your class can set up specific expectations and established norms applying to collaborative projects or study groups, and you can reinforce and support students in meeting those expectations.

Adapted from *Academic Conversations: Classroom Talk That Fosters Critical Thinking and Content Understandings* by Jeff Zwiers and Marie Crawford. Portland, ME: Stenhouse, 2011.

▲ To Sum Up

Central to RTI is a classroom that embraces universal design for learning, and one of UDL's key considerations is the removal of barriers to learning. Creating and sustaining a positive learning environment helps remove barriers that social pressures and stigma could bring in association with differing levels of academic and behavioral support. These steps can take time, and they usually demand a measure of trial and error. But the outcome is invaluable: students who are deeply engaged, feel safe, and find joy in learning. This chapter's many techniques for making learning personal, building community, using purposeful grouping, and teaching students how to have academic conversations are designed to help you meet this goal.

Job Application

Name:	Date:

Student ID #:	Birthday:	Phone number:

Address:

Please place a check mark next to the classroom job for which you are applying. Each job will last for a two-week period, at which time new employees will be hired.

☐ Student Substitute	☐ DJ	☐ Operator
☐ Attendance Clerk	☐ Paper Pusher & Sorter (2)	☐ Technology Specialist
☐ Lunch Counter	☐ Door Holder (2)	☐ Environmentalist
☐ Planner Assistant (2)	☐ Host & Hostess (1 each)	☐ Board Technician
☐ Library Clerk (2)	☐ Gamer	
☐ Courier	☐ Greeter	

Why would you like to have this job? *(Please write in complete sentences.)*

What knowledge and/or experience do you have that will help you do this job well? *(Please write in complete sentences.)*

What strengths do you possess that will help you do this job well? *(Please write in complete sentences.)*

Please copy the following statement on the line(s) below:
I promise that if given ANY classroom job, I will perform it to the best of my abilities.

If you are not hired for the job of your choice for this two-week period, what are two other jobs that you would like to be considered for?

1.

2.

By signing below, the student agrees to the above statements.

(student signature)

Student Interest Inventory

Name: Date:

Answer each of the following questions as clearly and completely as you can. Remember, there are no wrong answers. This activity is for learning more about *you* as an individual.

1. What is something you especially liked about school last year? Why?

2. What is something you didn't like about school last year? Why?

3. What hobbies or special interests do you have outside of school?

4. Do you think you will be different in 20 years? How so?

5. Who is one of your best friends? Why are you so close?

6. Who is one of the luckiest people you know? Why is he or she so lucky?

7. What is the best compliment someone could ever give you?

8. Do you ever feel shy? If yes, when?

9. Do you want to go to college? Why or why not?

10. What would you like to do for a job when you finish school?

11. Circle your favorite way to work in class.

a) by myself   b) with a partner   c) in a small group   d) as a whole class

12. Circle the way you learn best.

a) by listening   b) by doing   c) by watching   d) by reading

13. What TV shows do you like to watch? What do you like about them?

14. Who do you think is the smartest person in the world? Why?

15. Does being at school motivate or drain you? Why do you think that is?

16. If you were a teacher, what subject would you like to teach?

17. Whose advice do you listen to? Why can you trust this person?

18. What can teachers do to make learning more interesting for you?

➡

19. What is something you want to learn more about this year?

20. What do you most fear about becoming an adult?

Complete the following statements:

21. I can't understand why

22. I need extra help with

23. Activities I like to do with friends include

24. Activities I like to do by myself include

25. The accomplishments I have achieved that I am most proud of are

a)

b)

c)

Rate how much you like the subjects listed below:

Subject	Love it	It's okay	Not very much	Not at all
	☐	☐	☐	☐
	☐	☐	☐	☐
	☐	☐	☐	☐
	☐	☐	☐	☐

Thinking Styles and Learning Preferences Inventory

Name: _____   Date: _____

Please read each statement and think about how well it describes you. Use this scoring system:

1 — This never describes me.
2 — This sometimes describes me.
3 — This often describes me.

1. .... I decorate my written work with pictures and doodles.

2. .... When making a decision, I like to talk it over with someone.

3. .... It is easier for me to find a new place by looking at a map than by having someone tell me directions.

4. .... I can build things without directions.

5. .... I need to know the "gist" of a story before reading about it or watching it on TV.

6. .... I appreciate it when a teacher gives me detailed directions, because I follow them step by step.

7. .... I don't need to take notes in class. I just listen.

8. .... I can picture information in my head from my papers or book when taking a test.

9. .... It's easier for me to find a new place if someone tells me how to get there than if I look at a map.

10. .... I learn best when I can do something hands-on.

11. .... When I retell a story, I easily explain the main idea or the lessons learned by the main character. I have a hard time remembering the facts and details.

12. .... When I take a math test, I start with the problem I want to do first, not necessarily the first problem on the page.

13. .... When I retell a story, I can easily list the events from beginning to end.

14. .... I move around when studying or taking a test.

15. .... I learn best when a teacher uses lots of overheads, PowerPoint presentations, onscreen displays, and pictures.

16. .... I can read with music on but not in front of the television.

17. .... If given a choice, I'd rather do a class presentation than a written paper.

18. .... When I take a math test, I always start at the beginning.

19. .... I need to hear examples of how a rule can be followed or broken in order to really understand it.

➡

20. .... When trying to decide on the spelling of a word, I write all the possible spellings.

21. .... I can hear the words in my head while I read.

22. .... I can understand a rule without examples.

23. .... When I take notes, they are usually quite messy and difficult for other people to follow.

24. .... I study better when I can take frequent movement breaks.

25. .... I learn best when classes have a lot of discussions and guest speakers.

26. .... I can solve a math problem in my head when I can see the problem written on paper.

27. .... I like to squeeze a tennis ball or play with my pencil while sitting in class.

28. .... I can easily do more than one thing at once.

29. .... I like to follow step-by-step directions.

30. .... I need to see "the big picture" in order to really concentrate on what I am supposed to be learning.

31. .... I understand spelling rules and can apply them.

32. .... When learning a new computer game, I like it when someone tells me how to use it, rather than shows me how to use it.

33. .... I prefer to study by myself.

34. .... I like to solve riddles and logic puzzles.

35. .... It's difficult for me to listen if I can't see the person's face.

36. .... I move my hands a lot while talking.

37. .... I can solve a math problem in my head if I can talk it out.

38. .... I need to hear all of the facts before I believe something is true.

39. .... I make decisions based on what feels right in my gut, not necessarily based on facts.

40. .... If I want to remember something, I have to write it down, but I don't necessarily have to look at it again.

Thinking Styles and Learning Preferences Inventory Scoring Guide

Student name: _____   Date: _____

Transfer student scores to the grid below. For example, if a student scored the first item with a 3 (This often describes me), enter a 3 in the blank. When you have entered every question's score, total each of the five columns.

Item Score	Item Score	Item Score	Item Score	Item Score
1.	2.	4.	5.	6.
3.	7.	10.	11.	13.
8.	9.	14.	12.	18.
15.	17.	20.	19.	22.
16.	21.	24.	23.	29.
26.	25.	27.	28.	31.
33.	32.	36.	30.	34.
35.	37.	40.	39.	38.
Total	Total	Total	Total	Total
Visual	**Auditory**	**Kinesthetic**	**Global**	**Analytic**

Within the first three columns, the highest total indicates a student's favored learning preference (visual, auditory, or kinesthetic). The highest score within the last two columns suggests a student's preferred thinking style (global or analytic).

The lowest score possible for a learning preference or thinking style is 8. This score suggests that students do not feel a particular style describes them. A score of 24, on the other hand, suggests that students strongly prefer a given mode of learning or thinking. A high score of 18 or more is a strong indicator of a student's preferred learning preference or thinking style. A score of 10 or less is a strong indicator that students are not inclined to a particular style of learning or thinking.

What Makes a Great Teacher?

Name: _____   Date: _____

1. What are the five most important qualities in a great teacher? Number these qualities 1–5, with 1 being the most important. Place an X by any other qualities that are important to you but aren't in your top five.

.... Caring	.... Teaches in a variety of ways
.... Fair	.... Enjoys teaching
.... Creative	.... Answers all questions
.... Makes me want to do my best	.... Good listener
.... Respects me	.... Positive role model
.... Praises students	.... Understanding
.... Values me	.... Calm
.... Enthusiastic	.... Disciplinarian
.... Smart	.... Tries new things
.... Acknowledges me	.... Gives me extra help
.... Exhibits "realness"	.... Grades papers right away
.... Enjoys humor	.... Other: ....
.... Likes to have fun	.... Other: ....

2. Look back at what you marked as the most important quality. Why do you believe a great teacher must have this quality?

_____

_____

_____

_____

3. What strategies have teachers taught you that have helped you become a better student?

_____

_____

_____

_____

4. Who is the best teacher you have ever had? Why?

_____

_____

_____

_____

What Would You Do?

Name: _____   Date: _____

Think about what you would do in each of the following situations. Is the decision a difficult one, or not? What other ways might you handle these scenarios?

1. You see a classmate struggling with a question on schoolwork. *What would you do?*

   a. Keep focusing on your own schoolwork.

   b. Tell the teacher that the student doesn't understand.

   c. Make fun of the student for not knowing the answer.

   d. Offer to help the student by working through it together.

   e. Other: _____

2. While playing a sport, you notice a classmate on the sidelines watching. *What would you do?*

   a. Ignore him or her and keep playing the game.

   b. Invite him or her to join in and play.

   c. Wait until the game is over to invite him or her to play next week.

   d. Tell one of your team members or coach that the classmate is watching.

   e. Other: _____

3. You see a classmate taking an illegal drug. *What would you do?*

   a. Look away and mind your own business.

   b. Go tell an adult.

   c. Join your peer.

   d. Talk to him or her about not using drugs.

   e. Join your peer just to save face, and then go tell an adult what happened.

   f. Talk to your friends about what you saw.

   g. Other: _____

4. You see a peer being bullied by a group of other students. *What would you do?*

   a. Join the other students in bullying the peer.

   b. Go tell an adult.

   c. Try to stop the bullying by talking to the students who are doing the bullying.

   d. Try to stop the bullying by helping your peer physically fight the other students.

   e. Wait until the other students leave and then make sure your peer is okay.

   f. Other: _____

5. A classmate posts something mean about you online. *What would you do?*

   a. Ignore the post.

   b. Write something mean back.

   c. Tell an adult.

   d. Talk to the classmate in person the next day and ask about the post.

   e. Other: _____

Coat of Arms

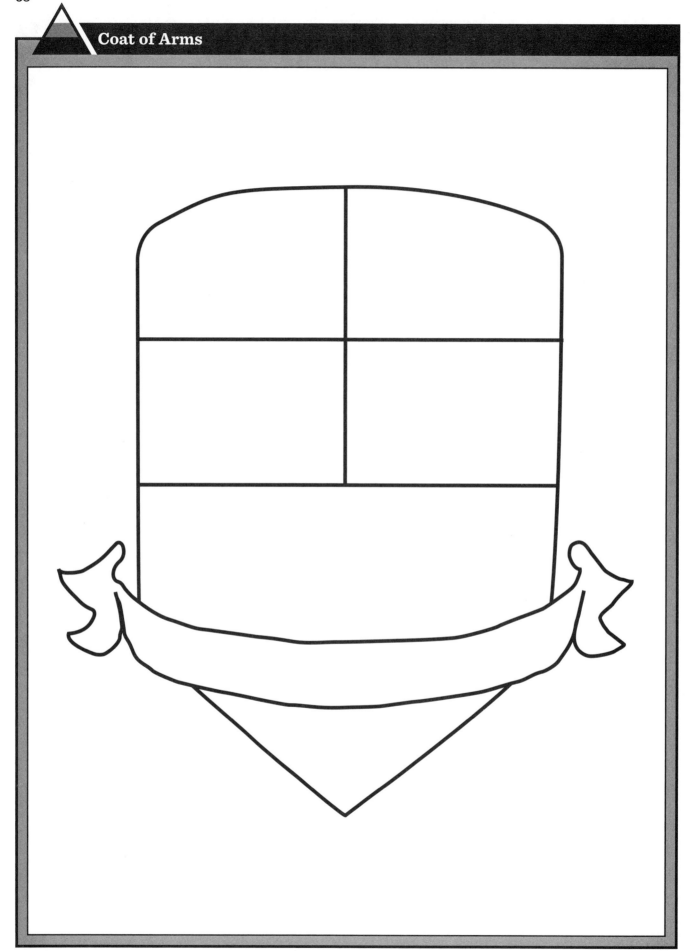

Yellow Pages Expert Form

Name:	
Grade:	Age:
Teacher's name:	Subject area:
Room number:	

Expert Area 1: ....

I spend .... hours a week at this activity.

I consider myself to be .... at this activity (check one)

☐ excellent   ☐ good   ☐ fair

Comments:

....

....

Expert Area 2: ....

I spend .... hours a week at this activity.

I consider myself to be .... at this activity (check one)

☐ excellent   ☐ good   ☐ fair

Comments:

....

....

Expert Area 3: ....

I spend .... hours a week at this activity.

I consider myself to be .... at this activity (check one)

☐ excellent   ☐ good   ☐ fair

Comments:

....

....

Clock Grouping Template

Shuffling the Deck Grouping Template

Academic Assessment

Central to using an RTI framework successfully in middle school is a thoughtful approach to assessment for students at all tiers. This chapter views time-tested assessment practices through an RTI lens. The goal is to help you see how the comprehensive assessment program that you already have in place can fit into an RTI framework. It also may help you strengthen your approach by offering a variety of strategies organized under four primary types of academic assessment:

- screening process
- diagnostic evaluation
- progress monitoring
- outcome assessment

The chapter also addresses how to determine the need for a change in the level of support a student receives, as well as eligibility for special education.

▲ Screening Process

Screening assessments are designed to gauge learners' critical abilities. An optimal screening process yields results that identify students who are at risk for academic problems and accurately predicts the need for increased academic support.

In elementary schools, screening assessments are typically given to all students three times per year. Screening at the middle school level differs for multiple reasons. For one thing, middle school students typically have a well-established academic and behavioral history. The starting point of your assessment cycle will be a review of existing records in an attempt to familiarize yourself with student histories, identify red flags, or determine whether any data is missing.

> You can think of screening at the middle school level not as a single act, but as a process for recognizing students whose strengths and needs require closer examination.

In addition, no single middle school screening tool has, to date, been developed that is uniformly quick, reliable, and able to provide all the data teachers need to make actionable decisions. Yet identification of academic need is central to RTI's success and academic screening cannot simply be abandoned because of the unavailability of such a universal tool. Instead, you can think of screening at the middle school level not as a single act, but as a process for recognizing students whose strengths and needs require closer examination. The first step in this process is to look at what screening methods your school already has in place and compare those to the recommendations that follow.

Identify Characteristics of Students at Risk

Screening for students begins with an understanding of the general characteristics of students who struggle. Put simply, we have to know what we are looking for. Experts point to several factors closely associated with dropping out of school.* Students are defined as being at risk if they have one or more of the following characteristics:

- repetition of a grade or grades
- poor attendance
- behavioral problems
- low socioeconomic status or poverty
- a home life characterized by violence
- a history of low achievement
- substance abuse
- teenage pregnancy

When a student drops out of school it is usually the result of a complex set of circumstances that may or may not have been preventable by academic or behavioral intervention. That said, teachers have a responsibility to identify and respond to risk factors that *are* within their control. For example, strong research points to reading proficiency level in the third grade as an indicator of later success at school. Nevertheless, that doesn't mean that some students might not develop reading problems when the content load becomes more challenging and vocabulary more sophisticated. Formal and informal reading inventories can help you identify late-emerging reading difficulties. In particular, some students may struggle with comprehension as academic language becomes more prevalent in text and instruction. Problems may also arise when students are required to demonstrate a higher level of independence regarding organization and study skills.

The figure on page 78 highlights common areas of difficulty for at-risk students. The What to Try When charts and corresponding strategies found in Chapter 5 also explore these areas and how to address them.

Use Multiple Measures

Using multiple sources of data will give you the most complete and accurate information with which you can make further screening decisions. Major concerns about a few of the areas in the list that follows may warrant the need for additional evaluation. Minor concerns about several areas may also serve as a call for action. There is no specific formula for how to make these professional decisions. When in doubt, err on the side of caution. It's better for a screening process to yield false positives—students identified as potentially at risk when they actually are not—than to overlook students who are struggling but hide it well. Further diagnostic evaluation will help clear up any such false positives.

Ideally, Instructional Teams comprising grade-level educators will review a range of information for each student at least once per semester—preferably before the semester begins. The Instructional Team can also seek the support and input of specialists including special educators, school psychologists, speech and language pathologists, and school social workers. The reviewed information will include:

---

*Slavin and Madden, 2004.

- attendance records
- writing sample(s)
- informal reading inventory results
- standardized test scores from the previous three years
- previous grades across all subject areas
- student self-inventory (if available)
- parent/guardian survey or comments (if available)
- teacher survey or narrative comments (if available)
- English proficiency level (if applicable)

For most students, one screening per year is sufficient, as long as a team of trained educators such as the Support Team is involved in the screening process, and as long as multiple data sources are used. You may find, however, that it's beneficial to screen some students more often, such as incoming students. (See more in the next section about focusing on incoming students.) Students receiving Tier II and Tier III support may also benefit from more frequent screening. Of course, throughout the year, teachers should continue to be careful observers of all students.

Focus on Incoming Students

Students who are entering the school, either as members of the incoming class of the middle school or as new transfer students, should go through the screening process three times per year. Because these incoming students are new to the school's faculty and staff, it will take longer to get to know each learner's level of academic readiness. You can continue to use the multiple measures and sources of data listed in the previous section to repeat your screening of new students midway through the school year, and again at the end of the year.

Implement School-Wide Screening
for Students Receiving Tier II and III Support

Additional screening for students receiving Tier II and III support may seem like an unusual suggestion, given that these students are routinely engaged in progress monitoring and assessment as part of the more intense support and interventions at these tiers. As you'll read in the section on progress monitoring (pages 79–82), at Tiers II and III, teachers and students together monitor a student's progress toward two or three specific academic goals. The purpose of this screening assessment, on the other hand, is to take a step back from this intense day-to-day work to reevaluate the bigger picture. Questions to ask at this point include:

- Are any academic or behavioral barriers getting in the way of meeting the student's goals?
- Is attendance an issue?
- How strong are the student's study skills?
- How are the student and his or her parents or guardians feeling about the level of academic progress being made?

Adding this school-wide approach to Tier II and III screening is less about identifying those who might be at risk and more about ensuring fidelity of implementation, as well as maintaining a team approach to meeting the needs of learners. It also creates the opportunity for someone other than an interventionist to review a student's records and offer additional insight on the intervention plan, progress report, and Learning Profile (pages 91–103).

▲ Diagnostic Evaluation

The initial screening process will help you identify students who might not be reaching their highest levels of learning and will give you an indication of issues that may need to be addressed. Diagnostic evaluation, on the other hand, is designed to offer further insight into the particular challenges a student faces, while also factoring in the physical, social-emotional, and cognitive development of young adolescents. It's a way of shifting the level of analysis into a higher gear for those students who were "red-flagged" in the initial screening, and of going into greater depth to answer the question of how to address the student's specific strengths and needs.

Many assessment tools for diagnostic evaluation—such as formal achievement tests, informal reading or math inventories, writing samples, classroom observations, and student work samples—can shed light on a given student's learning needs, and many of them already are used on a regular basis. The goal of this evaluation, regardless of the specific methods used, is to determine students' capabilities and deficit areas.

In addition, background information on student health, attendance, and family life can all provide insight into why a student may be struggling in a particular area. The Learning Profile on pages 91–103 is a helpful tool for compiling this information for diagnostic evaluation. You can then use all of the information you've gathered to guide instruction across the three tiers to remediate specific skill deficits.

> Students and parents are important allies in making determinations about student learning needs, and they are a valuable part of the decision-making process.

Most importantly, diagnostic evaluation helps educators pinpoint specific skills to target for intervention. The Intervention Plan Form on page 98 will guide you and your team through this process. Aim to write no more than three measurable goals for each student. If a student has more than three areas to work on, document all of them but choose only the three highest-priority goals to focus on during a single eight- to sixteen-week period. Reference the What to Try When charts on pages 142–149 to look for common areas of difficulty and to find corresponding research-based strategies and programs designed to address those areas. In the evaluation process, you may determine that you don't need to write an Intervention Plan, in which case you will want to document this determination. (For instance, an Intervention Plan would not be needed if, after diagnostic evaluation, a student turns out to be making sufficient progress with Tier I level of support.)

Students and parents are important allies in making determinations about student learning needs, and they are a valuable part of the decision-making process. Students are at the center of learning, and teachers must actively involve them in the conversation to be sure that they are invested. When students have a sense of personal agency—a belief that they have control over what happens to them—they understand that hard work can produce favorable results. If instruction is overly teacher-directed, however, students may not have the opportunity to develop that sense of agency.

In addition, parental input can provide deeper insight into the diagnostic process, as well as providing learner support beyond the school day. Guardian consent may not technically be required to carry out diagnostic evaluation as described here, because it consists of general education assessments and is not intended to determine if a disability exists. Nevertheless, adults at home possess a unique depth and breadth of information about students, and they deserve the opportunity to share that knowledge with school staff. You can use the Parent Contact Log on page 103 to document your communication with parents or guardians.

SPOTLIGHT
DOCUMENTING YOUR OBSERVATIONS

In addition to more formal diagnostic evaluation measures, you can use anecdotal information collected as you observe your students. Over time, these observations can illuminate trends and serve as clues for meeting students' needs. Keep notes about what you notice, and record the date, time, place, and full description of significant and relevant events. Here are some techniques you can use to document and keep track of your student observations:

- Write observations on sticky notes. After class, stick the notes on pages specially designed for each student. Keep all the student pages in binders, with one binder for each of your classes.

- Write your observations on index cards and file them in a recipe box. Use tabbed dividers to create separate sections for each of your classes. Add index cards to the section after each observation.

- Use a computer or tablet to record your observations. Create a digital folder for each class and a document within that folder for each student. Applications such as Evernote can be useful, time-saving organizational tools.

- Fill out an academic and/or behavior log and add it to the student's section in a binder.

- Layer overlapping index cards of notes, taped across the top, along the length of a clipboard. Keep the top card blank for confidentiality, and label all other cards with students' names. Use one clipboard for each class of students you see throughout the week.

- Keep these notes confidential. While you might choose to share them with select team members and/or a co-teacher, these should, for the most part, be for your eyes only.

Read through your notes periodically. Have you documented observations for every student? Are there notes written even about the quiet students, the ones who tend to fly under the radar? What is the nature of your observations? Would it be helpful to focus on one or two guiding questions for a set time period? For example, you could spend one week observing specifically on the topic of learning environment, and use this question as your guide: What would it take for [student name] to thrive in our class and do the highest levels of meaningful work?

Not only can these notes contribute to students' diagnostic evaluation, but they can also help you make accommodations, modify instruction, and adjust the learning environment to better serve specific students.

DIAGNOSTIC EVALUATION OF ACADEMIC SKILLS AND COMMON AREAS OF DIFFICULTY

The following information describes common areas of difficulty for middle school students. Use it to help identify students' areas of need and to guide goal setting. Feel free to add to this list as you notice any other areas of difficulty for particular students.

Word Recognition

Student:

- does not recognize affixes or syllabication patterns in words
- over-relies on phonics to read words

Reading Fluency

Student:

- reads at an improper rate (either too fast or too slow)
- reads with little prosody (struggles with expression and proper phrasing)

Reading Comprehension

Student:

- struggles to make inferences
- needs help understanding text structure
- has limited comprehension of historical, technical, or scientific texts
- does not grasp the main ideas or draw conclusions from the text
- has difficulty seeing the author's point of view

Language and Vocabulary Development

Student:

- has difficulty identifying patterns in language
- does not use context to determine the meaning of words and phrases
- needs to strengthen knowledge of roots and affixes

Writing to Communicate

Student:

- needs to improve his or her understanding of the writing process
- has difficulty writing opinion pieces on topics or texts
- struggles to convey ideas and information clearly
- needs help writing narrative pieces
- demonstrates lack of structure in his or her writing

Inquiry and Research

Student:

- seems to lack intellectual curiosity
- needs to develop research skills (generating questions; gathering relevant information by using and citing multiple sources; presenting findings; emphasizing salient points)

Critical Thinking

Student:

- needs help evaluating information from differing perspectives
- does not evaluate the soundness of reasoning
- needs to develop stronger metacognitive and self-reflective thinking

Self-Management and Learning Strategies

Student:

- needs help setting goals
- has difficulty with time management
- needs help initiating a task and following work plans
- lacks test-taking strategies
- needs to improve note-taking skills
- lacks effective study skills
- needs to increase academic motivation

▲ Progress Monitoring

A diagnostic evaluation of a student's strengths and needs will help you and your team determine a specific intervention plan comprising two or three instructional goals. The next logical step is to decide how to monitor progress toward those goals. Progress monitoring evaluates the effectiveness of the interventions. This form of assessment is important because it alerts educators when changes to the educational program are needed, making the assessment formative in nature. Monitoring progress can also be motivating for students, especially if the intervention is working and progress is being made. Progress monitoring emphasizes the need to assess student performance on a routine and frequent basis to determine whether learners are advancing.

When monitoring progress, follow a consistent set of administration and scoring procedures every time so that you and your team can measure growth reliably. You can then graph these results—again, in a consistent way—to be reviewed on a monthly basis by the interventionist and the student. This form of assessment answers the question "Is learning taking place?"

> When students are active participants in their own growth, articulating their learning goals and the progress they've made will come naturally.

By the time students reach middle school, most are fully capable of understanding cause and effect, which can make progress monitoring very powerful. Another benefit is the use of documentation in student-led conferences. When students are active participants in their own growth, articulating their learning goals and the progress they've made will come naturally and will maintain their investment in the process.

Curriculum-Based Measurement

Curriculum-based measurement (CBM) is one type of progress monitoring that reflects what students are learning on a daily basis and what you want students to practice. CBM allows teachers to assess skills by tracking how students perform on probes (quick tests of student knowledge) directly related to intervention goals. It has been widely researched, with more than one hundred studies proving its reliability and validity as an assessment.* This form of assessment is popular because it not only indicates whether learning is taking place, but also the rate at which students are building academic skills. In essence, CBM serves as a barometer of the effectiveness of an intervention or a form of instruction.

CBM is also effective for monitoring academic progress because it is highly standardized. It uses a standard set of directions, consistent standards for evaluating performance, and a standard amount of time for administration.

As more schools adopt and use RTI, some education publishers have started producing prepackaged CBM programs. A variety of websites also offer CBM packages and tools (see the References and Resources section on pages 203–208 for information and examples). Or you can create your own CBMs. See the following pages for more information on how to do this.

---

*Hosp, Hosp, and Howell, 2007.

SPOTLIGHT
CREATING CURRICULUM-BASED MEASUREMENTS

The following six steps outline how you can create and administer your own CBMs.

Step 1: Choose the intervention goal you will measure, and determine how you will collect data on that goal.

This step serves as a good test to see if you wrote a strong measureable goal. If not, you may have to reword the goal so that it can be accurately and meaningfully measured.

Step 2: Locate or create assessment probes.

Assessment probes are the basis for measuring student skill in the CBM process. These probes are composed of multiple forms that measure performance based on the goal. Many probes are available online at teacher sites. Type in your subject area and the words *assessment probe* into any search engine, or see this book's References and Resources for specific sites. You may also want to create your own probes based on your curriculum. To do so, identify the essential information and skills you want students to know and acquire. Create multiple versions of assessments and administer them on a routine basis. The frequency of administration can vary from weekly to monthly depending on the assessment.

Step 3: Establish a baseline of performance.

The next step is to determine the student's baseline in the relevant skill or content area and record it in a graph to which you will add as you proceed with the CBM.

Step 4: Establish learning goals and a timeline for reaching those goals.

When a baseline has been determined, the teacher, in collaboration with the Support or Instructional Team, works to determine goal scores and the length of the assessment period. In determining the CBM timeline—or any progress-monitoring timeline, for that matter—keep in mind that students at Tier II should be monitored at least monthly. Students receiving Tier III support will be monitored more frequently due to the significance of their academic needs. A minimum of biweekly is recommended at the top tier.

Following are two primary standards to use in establishing learning goals.[*] Well-designed learning goals are achievable, yet challenging.

- **Exemplary Sampling:** Choose a sample group of students whom you know to be proficient with the specific skills you're using CBM to measure. Test these students using a standard set of probes, and use their scores to establish criteria on which other performance objectives will be based. This is not used to compare students, but rather to aid in setting goals.

- **Growth Rate Chart:** Researchers have investigated how much progress we can expect a typical student to make given standard instruction. If growth rate charts have been researched for the skills you are measuring, you can take your student's baseline score and add the expected rate of growth to develop the goal line. The References and Resources section features books and websites helpful for identifying norms and growth rate charts for middle school students and classrooms.

Step 5: Plot the baseline and goal line on a graph.

Once the goals and timeline have been established, plot the goal line on a graph, starting from the baseline. Visual representation of academic progress can make it easier to share assessment results with colleagues. Additionally, involving students in graphing scores can be powerful motivation, since documenting their scores and showing them their progress gives them concrete feedback

---

[*]Hosp, Hosp, and Howell, 2007.

on their rate of learning. RTI goals should not feel like they are being done *to* the student, but rather done *with* the student.

Step 6: Assess the student's progress against the goal line.

As checkpoint scores are recorded, evaluate whether the student is on track to meet the established learning goals. If scores fall short of the goal line for three checkpoints in a row, talk with other members of your RTI team about whether the goals or timelines were unreasonable, and whether a new research-based intervention needs to be implemented.

Additional Progress Monitoring Tools

CBM is a valuable form of progress monitoring, but it is by no means the only method you can use. For example, informal reading inventories (IRIs) are an efficient way to measure progress in reading, and are a stronger indication of literacy development than the common reading rates measurement of how many words a student can read in a minute. Another way to monitor progress is to collect students' classroom work samples in a portfolio and evaluate them to determine if progress is being made according to a hierarchy of skills. Maybe you've created an authentic means of assessing learning through digital storytelling that works wonderfully for your classes. Perhaps students document their learning with an electronic portfolio. You might also document your observations or use a rubric to evaluate academic performance. The possibilities are many! Simply ask the following questions to determine if a given assessment can be used for progress monitoring:

- Does it provide information regarding students' academic performance?
- Does it evaluate the effectiveness of instruction and depth of knowledge?
- Are there enough alternate versions or forms so that it can be used on a frequent and regular basis (weekly or monthly)?
- Can it be administered in a standardized fashion?
- Is the tool reliable and valid?

If the answer is "yes" to all of these questions, the assessment may be used as a progress monitoring tool. If not, that certainly doesn't mean that you should abandon your carefully crafted assessment. It just means that it is not a good fit for *this* category of progress monitoring.

Note: Whether or not assessments you generate yourself can be used as a part of special-education eligibility decisions is up to your school's Evaluation Team. In any case, these assessments can be valid progress monitoring tools for formative educational decision-making and purposes other than eligibility decisions. When creating and using your own progress monitoring tools, just be certain that they are thoughtfully developed and implemented to reflect a student's grasp of skills and academic growth. Such informal progress monitoring tools can be used in combination with CBM or other more structured assessments. In fact, a comprehensive assessment program—one that incorporates a full battery of diverse assessments—generally results in the best instructional decision-making and, ultimately, greatest student progress.

▲ Outcome Assessment

For the purpose of RTI, outcome assessment can be broadly defined as summary evaluations of student learning that document the overall effectiveness of instruction. Whereas progress monitoring is related to formative measures, outcome assessment is summative in nature. This form of evaluation looks back on instruction and intervention and helps answer the question "To what extent did the student meet the goal or desired outcome?" Feedback from quality outcome assessments helps students more fully understand what they know and can do as a result of their efforts to learn something new.

Outcome assessment can be given to individual students or to an entire class. Projects, papers, and quizzes administered near the end of a unit of study all constitute outcome assessment. These types of evaluation are many and diverse, and are often already staples of the regular curriculum. Another way to help teachers assess overall growth and know if students have met a desired outcome is to examine pretest and posttest CBM data.

While outcome assessments may have limited value in making day-to-day decisions regarding instruction or intervention, they can prove helpful when making big-picture RTI decisions regarding movement among the tiers. RTI teams can examine both summative and formative data in deciding which tier of instruction is most appropriate for each student.

▲ **Figure 3.1: RTI Assessment**

This chart provides a quick reference to the major forms of assessment used in the RTI framework.

Assessment Type	What is it?	What RTI decisions does it help educators make?	At what point in the RTI process is it used?	What are some examples and resources?
Screening	A formative process of assessment designed to gauge the critical abilities of learners and identify students who might be at risk	It informs educators which students may need additional evaluation and it helps ensure a team approach to fidelity of implementation	At least once a year for all students and at least three times a year (fall, winter, and spring) for incoming students and those receiving upper-tier support	Informal reading inventories such as the Basic Reading Inventory by Jerry Johns; STAR Math; STAR Reading; existing state and district-wide tests
Diagnostic Evaluation	Assessment process designed to determine specific information regarding a student's strengths and needs	It helps teachers target instruction toward specific goals by building on strengths and remediating needs; the process helps educators determine a starting point for instruction	It is used for each student who is "red-flagged" during the initial screening process or for any student a teacher is concerned about; it may or may not result in an intervention plan, depending on the findings of the team	KeyMath-3: A Diagnostic Inventory of Essential Mathematics; Woodcock-Johnson III Normative Update (NU) Tests of Achievement; teacher-created assessments; teacher observations
Progress Monitoring	Formative assessment of student progress on a routine and frequent basis using a standard set of procedures so that growth can be measured consistently and accurately	It tells educators if what they are doing is working or if changes need to be made	Progress monitoring is used primarily in Tiers II and III on a weekly or biweekly basis, depending on the intensity of the intervention and the level of need	Reading A–Z Assessments; aimsweb; easyCBM; Khan Academy; teacher-created assessments

Assessment Type	What is it?	What RTI decisions does it help educators make?	At what point in the RTI process is it used?	What are some examples and resources?
Outcome Assessment	Summative assessments that take place near the end of units of study or other academic transition times; outcome assessment also describes the evaluation period when a collection of work samples and progress monitoring results are pulled together and analyzed	It documents the overall effectiveness of instruction and tells the teacher whether or not the student has met a desired goal or outcome	Outcome assessments are analyzed before major decisions are made regarding a student's instruction and/ or movement among tiers	Teacher-generated assessments such as projects, papers, and presentations; student outcomes can be documented in a variety of ways, such as rubrics, electronic portfolios, and/ or work sample binders

▲ Finding Time to Assess and Manage Data

Given the need for varied assessment and data collection within the RTI model, some educators have wondered how they will find time to actually teach. At first, assessment can feel overwhelming, especially in a middle school setting where you are managing multiple classes and multiple groups of students. Many teachers have worried that these practices will affect their ability to teach the curriculum thoroughly and well. This concern is valid. Education isn't about constant measurement, after all. But it's not really about *teaching,* either. It's about *learning*. An emphasis on teaching places the focus on what the teacher is doing, while an emphasis on learning puts the student at the center. This responsiveness to learners is a hallmark of RTI.

Ultimately, the instructional interventions, not the assessments, will make the difference for the learner. Yet a thoughtful approach to assessments will lead to the right interventions for the right students at the right time. Therefore, high-quality assessments that lead to strong educational decisions are a worthwhile investment of time and resources.

Nonetheless, assessment might still feel like a burden at times. It can help to remember that it is instrumental to effective instruction. Rather than being viewed as an add-on, assessment will ideally be integrated so tightly into the curriculum that students may not even know when they are being assessed. In *This We Believe: Keys to Educating Young Adolescents,* the Association for Middle Level Education explains the role of varied and ongoing assessments in not only measuring learning, but also advancing it. The paper states:

*Continuous, authentic, and appropriate assessment measures, including both formative and summative ones, provide evidence about every student's learning progress. Such information helps students, teachers, and family members select immediate learning goals and plan further education.** *

Still, the question remains: How can educators conduct this assessment and manage the resulting data within the context of an already busy school day? The full responsibility of assessment and data management should not fall solely on the shoulders of classroom teachers. Teaming is key. Given that all students are involved in the screening process, training all educators to participate sends the message that RTI is a school-wide priority. It also gives teachers the opportunity to get to know their students on a deeper level, and makes the task of screening large numbers of students more manageable.

> Education isn't really about *teaching*. It's about *learning*. An emphasis on learning puts the student at the center. This responsiveness to learners is a hallmark of RTI.

Other personnel, such as classroom aides, special educators, and school psychologists, will also be involved with assessment and data collection. These professionals can be helpful in administering assessments and reporting results to Instructional Teams and other RTI groups. Using electronic portfolios and/or customizing the Learning Profile on pages 91–103 can also help you manage data efficiently, especially when this task is systematically coordinated using a team-based approach. In assessment and data management, as in the problem-solving process, all members of the team are collaborative partners in the education of young adolescents. Viewed from the perspective of its long-term benefit, a comprehensive assessment program emerges as an important aspect of effective schools, and therefore is truly a school-wide endeavor.

▲ Using Assessment to Determine Level of Support

A comprehensive assessment program begins with the personalized learner assessment of all students (Tier I). This form of evaluation, which identifies student interests and learning preferences, helps you get to know students personally and gives you information useful for differentiated instruction. Teachers, regardless of their content areas, can use surveys, interviews, and class activities, including those in Chapter 2, to gather this information about students at different points throughout the year.

Academic achievement data at Tier I is also collected from the screening process at the beginning of the year. In many schools, this first line of screening consists of state- and district-required testing. After the initial screening and learner assessment, assessment programs will vary from student to student and depend on the subject area being taught. The frequency of progress monitoring for students will also differ depending on their respective skill levels, and outcome assessments will vary depending on course standards and pedagogical approaches. In essence, all assessment methods are informed by one basic question: What information do I need to guide my instruction and maximize learning for each student?

*Association for Middle Level Education, formerly NMSA (National Middle School Association). *This We Believe: Keys to Educating Young Adolescents.* Westerville, OH: 2010.

Assessment data is critical in the selection of interventions that have the best chance of helping students succeed, but how is it used in determining the level of support needed? The information that follows will help you and your RTI team answer that question.

Movement from Tier I to Tier II Support

A careful screening process can help identify struggling students. However, it is not generally an exclusive determining factor for Tier II intervention. Instead, a collective team of educators (including members from Instructional and Support Teams) will conduct diagnostic evaluation before students are given more intensive interventions. This evaluation may involve administering additional assessments if more are needed, but in many cases, sufficient diagnostic data will already be available in a student's school records. The team will then analyze this data to establish an individual student's respective strengths and areas of need. The team documents all of this activity as part of the diagnostic and evaluative process.

After considering available assessment data, RTI team members also closely examine classroom performance and teacher observations. If they determine from this analysis that a student's needs cannot be met in Tier I, the diagnostic evaluation will result in RTI team members highlighting specific skills that need to be worked on with the learner at Tier II. This identification of skills will include a starting point for instruction during the Tier II intervention. The team will establish a method for monitoring progress, along with baseline information that can be used to help determine whether a given intervention is successful. You can use the Intervention Plan Form (page 98) to record this information.

School schedules can, as appropriate, influence when interventions begin. These logistics are a part of middle school life, and teachers and RTI teams can, within reason, base some educational decisions on schedules if it's in the best interests of students to be minimally disruptive to their routine. There will, of course, be cases in which teachers have to make adjustments to schedules at inopportune times.

As you make decisions about moving a student from Tier I to Tier II and about implementing specific interventions, ask yourself and your team the following guiding questions:

- What are the student's strengths and specific areas of need?
- Can these areas of need be addressed in Tier I? Why or why not?
- Are external factors influencing the student's pace of academic growth? If so, how will these factors be addressed?
- Was Tier I instruction differentiated based on the student's academic readiness, learning strengths, and interests?
- Has the student's Tier I instruction been based on research-based teaching practices?
- How far away is the next natural transition period in the school calendar?

Movement from Tier II to Tier III Support

Determining whether or not to increase a student's level of support to Tier III involves multiple variables. One key factor for RTI team members to consider is the academic growth the student has shown since the introduction of Tier II interventions. If the rate of progress is insufficient and the goals have not been met, the intensity or type of intervention must be changed. If increased concentration on a goal is in the best interest of the student, support will be increased. Every situation is different, but there are typically drawbacks that need to be considered when making the decision. For instance, more intensive support is usually more invasive and involves more time away from peers, which could be stigmatizing. Use your knowledge and that of your team members to determine what will be most beneficial for each student.

Again, as you work through this assessment and decision-making process, help clarify and organize your thinking with key questions including the following:

- Is the student consistently scoring below the predetermined goal line (six to eight data points) according to the data from the progress monitoring tool?
- Did the student receive Tier II level intervention long enough (eight to sixteen weeks) to demonstrate progress?
- Was the intervention implemented correctly?
- Would the student benefit from another round of Tier II level support?
- Is there an approaching natural transition period in the school calendar?

Movement from Tier III to Tier II or I

Support at both the Tier II and the Tier III level is designed to help students reach their goals and eventually experience success without extra support. A sense of independence is crucial to the effectiveness of this process, especially when working with young adolescents. When middle school students meet their individual goals, this acknowledgment and experience of success can be instrumental in fostering agency, motivation, and self-determination.

To move from Tier III to Tier II or I, it is essential that students demonstrate progress over a substantial period of time—preferably a quarter or semester. In addition, students' generalization of the strategies and skills addressed in Tier II or III will be observed and documented prior to moving students from the additional tier of support. Through collaborative review, the grade-level team will review student progress to ensure students are not moved too quickly to a lower level of support. On the other hand, keeping students at higher tiers for too long can also impact growth academically and behaviorally by keeping them from an inclusive education with their grade-level peers. It is crucial to continually monitor student scores and performance after transitions between tiers so that learners do not lose gains they made, especially when moving from a higher tier to a lower one.

When considering a move to a lower tier, answer the following questions:

- Is the student consistently meeting or exceeding the goal line (based on progress monitoring data)?
- Has enough gain been made so that the student will eventually catch up with peers and experience success without the extra support?
- Is the student's academic progress stable enough to remove the extra support provided in Tier II or Tier III?
- Is there an approaching natural transition period in the school calendar?

RTI in Action

Mr. Shapinsky uses the Assess, Set Goals, Instruct, and Monitor (ASIM) approach in his eighth-grade language arts classroom. His school's screening team supports and builds upon his initial assessment by identifying students that might need Tier II instruction. The team digs deeper by giving students informal reading inventories to gauge their individual reading levels. A variety of questionnaires for students, teachers, and parents are used to gather relevant information about each student (Assess).

All of the data gathered is compiled in students' Learning Profiles. Seeing all of the academic information documented in one place and combining it with the personalized learner data he has gathered, Mr. Shapinsky is better able to formulate learning goals.

During meetings with students (and their family members, if they are available), he works with students to write goals (Set Goals) that are relevant to their academic needs as well as being driven by students' desire to make measurable progress. The Intervention Plan outlines how the goals will be met (Instruct) and how progress will be documented (Monitor). Students not only have a say in their academic goals, but are informed of how progress will be measured. Mr. Shapinsky firmly believes that students and their families should be knowledgeable of all phases of ASIM. During his one-on-one meetings, he sets up follow-up meetings with students in nine weeks so they can revisit their Intervention Plans.

▲ RTI and Special Education Eligibility

RTI is much more than a route to eligibility for special education. However, determination of disability is the responsibility of schools under the Individuals with Disabilities Education Act (IDEA), and the legal basis for using RTI to determine a specific learning disability is found in the 2004 reauthorization of IDEA. The law states:

> In determining whether a child has a specific learning disability, a local educational agency may use a process that determines if the child responds to scientific research-based intervention as a part of the evaluation procedures.*

The implication of this language is that, when making eligibility decisions, schools are allowed to use assessments that measure student responsiveness to interventions. However, while the law does grant this flexibility, RTI teams will want to carefully consider a range of specific criteria before qualifying students for special education services. These criteria—to be used as guidelines for specific learning disability determination—are outlined in IDEA. The legislation states that a student qualifying for special education services "exhibits a pattern of strengths and weakness in performance, achievement, or both, relative to age, state-approved grade-level standards, or intellectual development, that is determined by a group to be relevant to the identification of a learning disability, using appropriate assessments."**

These "appropriate assessments" must be consistent with all of the following requirements:

---

*Individuals with Disabilities Education Improvement Act, 2004.
**Ibid.

- A variety of assessment tools and strategies are used to gather relevant functional, developmental, and academic information about the student, including information from the parent

- No single measure is used as a sole criterion

- Technically sound instruments are used to assess the relative contribution of cognitive and behavioral factors, as well as physical or developmental factors

- Assessments do not discriminate on a racial or cultural basis

- Assessments are administered in the student's native language or mode of communication to yield the most accurate information

- Trained, knowledgeable personnel administer the assessments

- Assessments are tailored for specific areas of need

- Assessments are carefully chosen to measure aptitude, independent of physical or other limitations

- The student is assessed in all areas related to the suspected disability, including, if appropriate, vision, hearing, social and emotional status, general intelligence, academic performance, communicative status, and motor abilities

- Assessment tools and strategies result in relevant information to directly help determine the student's educational needs*

Formal policies for making special education determinations within the RTI framework vary depending on location, so always be sure to know and understand your specific local policies and state laws. What does *not* vary is the right to due process and parent participation. If the RTI team suspects a disability, a referral must be made, and parent or guardian consent must be obtained before initiating a special education evaluation. Parents continue to have the right to request a referral for special education evaluation at any time, and they should be given copies of the procedural safeguards and the due process timeline that begins at the time of the parent's consent.

---

*Ibid.

SPOTLIGHT
DEFINING SPECIFIC LEARNING DISABILITIES

A "specific learning disability" means a disorder in one or more of the basic psychological processes involved in understanding or using language—spoken or written. Such disorders may manifest as an imperfect ability to listen, think, speak, read, write, spell, or do mathematical calculations. The term includes such conditions as perceptual impairments, brain injury, minimal brain dysfunction, dyslexia, and developmental aphasia. The term does not apply to students who have learning problems that are primarily the result of a visual, hearing, or motor impairment; an intellectual disability; an emotional impairment; an autism spectrum disorder; or environmental, cultural, or economic disadvantages.

It's important for a multidisciplinary evaluation team to make decisions on special education eligibility. This group will examine multiple sources of relevant data, including all academic achievement measures, medical information, and behavioral factors. Students will be evaluated on an individual basis in all seven of the following key domains—listening, thinking, speaking, reading, writing, spelling, and mathematical calculation—outlined in the definition of a specific learning disability.

▲ To Sum Up

RTI's tenets of student-centered evaluation and formative assessment are not new ideas to middle schools. Identifying academic barriers and using multiple data sources to analyze how best to meet students' needs are methods at the heart of mindful teaching, and as such, have long been an essential part of teachers' regular practice. By combining these positive habits with the framework of RTI, you can make data-founded decisions that serve all learners even more efficiently and more meaningfully.

Identifying academic barriers and using multiple data sources to analyze how best to meet students' needs are methods at the heart of mindful teaching.

As you do so, remember that the assessment processes outlined in this chapter are not one-size-fits-all. Assessment that supports learning is part of effective classroom instruction, and—just like instruction—it should be differentiated. You may need to tailor your assessments to match your school's implementation of RTI and to address the scope and severity of a learner's academic needs. The point of assessment is to drive and support learning, not to get in the way of it.

Learning Profile: Background Information

Student name:	Date of birth: Sex: ☐ M ☐ F
Home phone:	Cell phone (if applicable):
Address:	
City, state, zip code:	

Parent/guardian name:	
Home phone:	Work/cell phone:
Address:	
City, state, zip code:	

Who does the student live with (if not his or her parent/guardian)?

Relationship:

Position of the student in the family:

☐ Only child   ☐ Oldest of ____   ☐ Youngest of ____   ☐ Middle of ____

Language spoken at home:

Hand preference: ☐ Right   ☐ Left   ☐ Both

Have there been previous evaluations (academic, psychological, developmental, and/or other) of the student? If so, please provide results below or attach reports.

Has the student experienced any developmental delays? Explain.

→

Learning Profile: Background Information (*cont.*)

Has the student had major illnesses and/or injuries? Explain.

Does the student have any chronic medical conditions such as allergies? Explain.

What is the student's attendance record? Provide a summary.

Is there any other pertinent family, health, or background information that might be helpful to understand the student's needs (illness of a family member, student has vision or hearing problems, student was premature at birth, student is on medication, etc.)?

Learning Profile: Personalized Learner Data

Student name:

Interests, activities, familial issues, points of pride, feelings regarding school, etc.

Source:

Summary:

Learning preference and thinking style (e.g., visual, auditory, kinesthetic, global, analytical)

Source:

Summary:

Additional learning preferences (verbal/linguistic, visual/spatial, bodily/kinesthetic, logical/mathematical, musical/rhythmic, naturalist, interpersonal, intrapersonal)

Source:

Summary:

Social and behavioral considerations; personality traits that may affect learning

Source:

Summary:

Learning strategies, study skills, and levels of self-management

Source:

Summary:

English language proficiency

Source:

Summary:

Learning Profile: Personalized Learner Data (Student Observation Log)

Student name:

Date and Time	Event

Learning Profile: Screening Results

Student name: _____

Date: _____

Information reviewed:

☐ attendance records

☐ informal reading inventory results

☐ previous grades across subject areas

☐ parent/guardian survey or comments

☐ English proficiency level

☐ writing sample(s)

☐ standardized test scores

☐ student self-inventory

☐ teacher survey or comments

☐ other: ....

Narrative summary:

Learning Profile: Academic Assessment Data
(Summary of Achievement and Ability Test Results)

Student name:

Name of test and area assessed	Date of administration	Student's age at administration	Standard score	Percentile	Notes

Learning Profile: Diagnostic Evaluation Results

Student name:

Summary:

Diagnostic Evaluation Team Members

Name: .... Title: ....

Name: .... Title: ....

Name: .... Title: ....

Name: .... Title: ....

Name: .... Title: ....

Learning Profile: Intervention Plan Form

Student name:

Goal:

Intervention Plan

Title of intervention:

Tier: Intervention setting:

Planned start date: Frequency of implementation:

Person(s) responsible for implementing the intervention:

How will progress be monitored?

How will fidelity of implementation be monitored?

Learning Profile: Progress Monitoring Data

Student name:

Area:	Baseline:	Date:	Score:

Checkpoint 1 Date:	Goal score:	Checkpoint score:	
Checkpoint 2 Date:	Goal score:	Checkpoint score:	
Checkpoint 3 Date:	Goal score:	Checkpoint score:	
Checkpoint 4 Date:	Goal score:	Checkpoint score:	
Checkpoint 5 Date:	Goal score:	Checkpoint score:	
Checkpoint 6 Date:	Goal score:	Checkpoint score:	

Notes:

Area:	Baseline:	Date:	Score:

Checkpoint 1 Date:	Goal score:	Checkpoint score:	
Checkpoint 2 Date:	Goal score:	Checkpoint score:	
Checkpoint 3 Date:	Goal score:	Checkpoint score:	
Checkpoint 4 Date:	Goal score:	Checkpoint score:	
Checkpoint 5 Date:	Goal score:	Checkpoint score:	
Checkpoint 6 Date:	Goal score:	Checkpoint score:	

Notes:

Area:	Baseline:	Date:	Score:

Checkpoint 1 Date:	Goal score:	Checkpoint score:	
Checkpoint 2 Date:	Goal score:	Checkpoint score:	
Checkpoint 3 Date:	Goal score:	Checkpoint score:	
Checkpoint 4 Date:	Goal score:	Checkpoint score:	
Checkpoint 5 Date:	Goal score:	Checkpoint score:	
Checkpoint 6 Date:	Goal score:	Checkpoint score:	

Notes:

Learning Profile: Progress Monitoring Data (Graph)

Student name:

Area monitored:

	Baseline Date	Checkpoint Date	Checkpoint Date	Checkpoint Date	Checkpoint Date	Checkpoint Date

Learning Profile: Documentation of Interventions

Student name: Date:

Title of intervention:

Start date: End date: Time allotted:

Outcome:

Action to be taken:

Notes:

Learning Profile: Observation of Fidelity of Implementation

Student name:	Date:	Time:

Interventionist:	Observer:

Reminder to the observer: The goal of the observation is not to judge or evaluate the teacher; it is to evaluate the degree to which the intervention is being implemented effectively and as designed.

Does the observer have the necessary background knowledge and qualifications to evaluate the effectiveness and fidelity of this particular intervention? ☐ Yes ☐ No

Intervention goal:

Observation of Research-Based Intervention

Title of intervention:

Notes:

Was the intervention implemented as it was designed? Explain.

What was the student's level of engagement during the lesson?

Signature of observer:	Date:

Signature of interventionist:	Date:

Learning Profile: Parent Contact Log

One of the hallmarks of effective collaboration between the school and the home is open communication with parents and guardians. Documentation of your contacts can serve as a way of monitoring your level of communication throughout all stages of each student's learning process.

Student name:

Date/Contact	Notes
Date: Contacted by:	
Date: Contacted by:	
Date: Contacted by:	
Date: Contacted by:	
Date: Contacted by:	
Date: Contacted by:	

CHAPTER

▲ 4

Co-Teaching

RTI requires increased levels of collaboration among those responsible for putting it into practice. In response to this necessity, schools have found it important to change the traditional roles of educators. Teachers can no longer meet the diverse needs of students if they attempt to teach in isolation. In support of RTI implementation, many school districts are incorporating an instructional approach called collaborative teaching, commonly referred to as co-teaching. Broadly speaking, co-teaching can be defined as a partnership between two or more educators who make informed decisions when designing, implementing, and monitoring instruction.[*]

Co-teaching is an inclusive approach that supports classroom teachers, special education teachers, and other staff in meeting the needs of all students, as well as helping in the implementation of RTI. Co-teaching encourages educators to work together and develop a community within and across their classrooms that meets the unique needs of all students. It also increases the likelihood that struggling students will be educated alongside their peers and receive effective instruction within the general education setting.

At the middle school level, co-teaching partners are determined based on the needs of the students, the availability of team members, and the teaming model used in the school. Partners are also assigned based on the needs and expertise of the personnel available to co-teach during a given time frame. Your school and your team will need to tailor your approach based on your resources as well as the needs of students. Fortunately, co-teaching can provide flexibility and responsiveness while fitting into the unique environment of your school.

▲ Co-Teaching in RTI Middle Schools and Classrooms

Co-teaching has the potential to erase boundaries between general and special education. In doing so, it lessens the social stigma associated with pulling students from the general education classroom for specialized instruction. Differentiated instruction and tiered instruction can happen within the general education classroom walls.

The benefits of co-teaching don't end there. Because co-teaching lowers the student-to-teacher ratio, all students—regardless of achievement level—benefit from increased teacher responsiveness. Also, co-teachers model skills they want to see from their students. Collaborative problem solving, cooperation, and communication are essential skills that students are able to see in action on a day-to-day basis.

---

[*]Whitten and Hoekstra, 2002.

The primary objective behind co-teaching is to provide all students with the appropriate support needed to be successful, regardless of the tier in which they are receiving instruction. In a co-teaching system, students who have different instructional needs do not need to be singled out and removed from the classroom to receive specialized instruction. Instead, their instructional needs can be met through the collaborative efforts of a teaching team at each appropriate tier. As a result, learning is less fragmented for students who do need additional support. A separate approach might still be needed from time to time (especially for Tier III support), but the proper use of co-teaching can dramatically increase the amount of inclusion in a middle school.

> Co-teachers model skills they want to see from their students. Collaborative problem solving, cooperation, and communication are essential skills that students are able to see in action on a day-to-day basis.

Like all educators implementing RTI, co-teaching teams use evidence-based strategies and methods at each tier. The movement among tiers is fluid, and the co-teaching model or models used should be chosen to best support the quality of instruction provided to students, particularly students who are struggling and require differentiated Tier I, II, or III services.

▲ Quality Indicators of Successful Co-Teaching

While both general classroom teachers and special education teachers face a variety of challenges associated with co-teaching in middle schools, many research-based guidelines are available that can increase this method's ease of use and its chance of success. To effectively use co-teaching with RTI at the middle school level, educators will take into consideration the quality indicators that support successful implementation. These quality indicators are key factors, identified and supported by research, essential to the overall effectiveness of co-teaching.* These indicators are:

- common planning and reflecting time
- administrative support
- flexibility and spontaneity in teaching
- teaching through differentiated instruction
- teaching to various learning preferences
- balancing theory and practice
- understanding of educational philosophies

Each of these indicators is explored in more detail in the sections that follow.

Common Planning and Reflecting Time

Common planning time is essential for successful co-teaching, and a lack of this time can sometimes lead to the failure of co-teaching. However, by utilizing RTI's teaming framework, teachers can also plan for effective co-teaching. When co-planning time is built into co-teachers' schedules, they have the opportunity to adequately plan so students profit from well-designed lessons, successful collaboration, and effective instruction.

---

*Ibid.

Reflecting time is just as important as co-planning time. Looking back on how lessons were delivered—what is working well and what could be changed—helps build teacher effectiveness. The benefits of planning and reflecting time cannot be overstated. This is especially true in the early stages of partnering. Teachers need time to decide on the most effective co-teaching model (or models) for a given lesson and debrief on the success of the lesson after it is taught. Giving teachers the time and opportunity for this collaborative planning and reflection has the potential to dramatically increase their effectiveness.

TIPS FOR PLANNING AND REFLECTING IN CO-TEACHING TEAMS

- Day-to-day planning can be accomplished face-to-face or through electronic communication. Email and online collaboration websites can be very useful for asynchronous planning, giving teachers freedom to plan together within the busy school day.

- Ask your administrator for additional time at least once each semester to meet face-to-face for an extended period of time (preferably at least a half day) for long-term planning.

- A shared lesson plan format can help you and your co-teachers communicate about lesson objectives, instructional methods, and assessment in a consistent manner. The forms on pages 125–126 offer templates for setting up this shared format.

- Reflecting on the effectiveness of a lesson can be accomplished by a simple conversation, or in a more structured format. For example, documenting your reflections using a Two Plus One Reflection Log (described on page 115; form on page 129) can help you keep track of your thoughts. Using this form, each teacher writes down two aspects of the lesson that went well and one thing that left him or her with questions. You might be surprised by how differently two teachers can view the same experience—or how exciting it is when you perceive the same positive outcomes! Documenting your thoughts about a lesson can be a powerful way to strengthen co-teaching partnerships and become a more reflective practitioner.

- Applaud each other in large and small ways. Offering verbal praise as well as taking the time to write uplifting notes to one another or send a quick text message can go a long way to encourage your mutual efforts.

SPOTLIGHT
ONLINE COLLABORATION TOOLS

Cloud-based systems such as Dropbox, Google Drive, and Wikispaces can make collaboration easier for educators. Many such websites offer tools such as shared space for document storage, customizable editing access, and more. Type *free online collaboration* into your search engine to find a site that fits your needs.

Administrative Support

The second quality indicator, administrative support, is essential to sustaining co-teaching over the long term. Administrators can provide this support in many ways, including by ensuring that teachers are scheduled to plan during the school day; that classrooms of co-teachers are reasonably close to one another; and that information about the co-teaching process is made available to school personnel, parents, and others with a need to know.

In general, if co-teachers do not receive ongoing support and understanding from their administrators, co-planning time will not be a formal or planned part of their school day. Co-teachers who lack this type of administrative support find they have to use personal time to co-plan, and, over time, teachers can become tired of devoting time after school to plan their co-taught lessons. As a result, teachers may co-teach lessons that are not co-planned; deliver lessons that are poorly planned; or return to delivering lessons in isolation. However, when administrators understand how important this quality indicator is to the success of co-teaching, they are likely also to see the importance of building co-planning into the master schedule.

TIPS FOR GAINING ADMINISTRATOR SUPPORT FOR CO-TEACHING

- Ask your administrator to observe an effective co-teaching team within your school or district. Seeing the benefits firsthand may help your administrator understand the benefits of co-teaching in an RTI school.

- Talk to other co-teaching teams around your school system and even around the nation. What are some ways schools similar to yours have worked around time and budget constraints?

- Share helpful co-teaching blogs, listservs, Twitter accounts, and other resources you've found. The tips, advice, and examples you find from these sites will help you and administrators envision the ways co-teaching can benefit your school.

Flexibility and Spontaneity in Teaching

Co-teaching has been referred to as a professional marriage. It requires teachers to be thoughtful about, respectful of, and responsive to the needs of their co-teaching partner or partners, as well as to the needs of their students. As educators plan for and carry out lessons, they will find quality indicator number three—flexibility and spontaneity in teaching—fundamental to their success. Students' behavior, as well as other unplanned or unpredictable situations, often requires teachers to make "in-action" decisions and modify even the best-laid original lesson plans. Flexibility and spontaneity allow teachers to respond productively to these changing circumstances and to adjust lessons according to the needs and responses of the students. Successful co-teaching involves give and take. Give each other the freedom to break from the lesson plan to take advantage of teachable moments and address the needs of your students.

> Flexibility and spontaneity allow teachers to respond productively to changing circumstances and to adjust lessons according to the needs and responses of the students. Successful co-teaching involves give and take.

TIPS FOR INCREASING FLEXIBILITY AND SPONTANEITY

- With your co-teacher or co-teachers, come up with a verbal signal to let each other know that a lesson is not going as planned and that you need to break from the original plan. Using a phrase such as "I think we need to change course" or "I think we may need to steer this boat in another direction" will let your co-teacher in on the fact that you feel a need to alter plans. It's important to trust your partner's instincts. If you end up disagreeing with the choice to change course, talk about it after the lesson when students are not in the room.

- Co-planning backup activities related to students' intervention plans will help you make good use of time if you do need to abandon a lesson or if a lesson does not take as much time as anticipated.

- Identify strategies that take little to no preparation and can be used in various settings. Deborah Corpus and Ann Giddings have called these "desert island" strategies because they can be used anywhere and at any time. Make sure both members of the co-teaching team have knowledge of a variety of these easy-to-use strategies so they can be used spontaneously and seamlessly when needed.

- Give each other permission to take risks and creative approaches to instruction. Expect the process to be messy at times. Good teaching means responding to students' needs, and while you won't always be able to predict or control how a class will react to specific lessons, you *can* control how you respond and adapt to the situation.

Differentiated Instruction and Teaching to Various Learning Preferences

You can further boost co-teaching's effectiveness by implementing the next two quality indicators: teaching through differentiated instruction and teaching to various learning preferences.

These two indicators are closely related. For teachers to successfully differentiate instruction, they must know their students' learning preferences—along with their academic readiness, interests, motivational needs, and thinking styles. Having more than one teacher planning and instructing to meet the needs of the students gives you greater opportunity to familiarize yourself with these qualities, and to focus on the learning strengths of each student.

By working as a team, teachers can corroborate each other's observations and perceptions of students' strengths, needs, and learning preferences.

TIPS FOR DIFFERENTIATING INSTRUCTION AND TEACHING TO VARIOUS LEARNING PREFERENCES

- Talk with your partner about favorite methods for differentiating instruction (such as RAFT assignments, project menus, learning contracts, and so on). Make sure both partners are knowledgeable about each strategy and the rationale for its use.

- Discuss your understanding of learning preferences and what they mean for instruction. Talk about your observations of students and what students' learning styles might be based on how they have responded to previous instruction.

- Make sure you have a class profile accessible to all co-teachers so you can make in-action decisions regarding differentiation and purposeful grouping. Establish a grouping procedure for your co-taught classes, such as the clock grouping strategy (described on pages 51–52).

- Help students figure out their learning preferences and thinking styles.

Balancing Theory and Practice, and Understanding of Educational Philosophies

The final two quality indicators—balancing theory and practice, and understanding of educational philosophies—are vital to establishing a successful co-teaching relationship. With requirements mandating the use of evidenced-based strategies, teachers must know and understand the theories behind the research-based teaching methods and materials they use. Chapter 5 includes more information on research-based teaching. Read the chapter and discuss it with each other. Do evidence-based strategies support your philosophies of education? Talk with your partner about the need to acknowledge that even though a practice is grounded in theory and research, it might not be right for every teaching style or for every group of students.

In addition to considering matters of theory versus practice, co-teachers will benefit from discussing their educational philosophies. This will help them reach a deeper understanding of how each of them teaches and makes decisions about student learning. Teachers don't necessarily have to agree on every point of their educational philosophies. However, they do need to recognize and respect each other's positions and, if necessary, agree to disagree. If agreeing to disagree is not a feasible solution, co-teachers can develop a habit of using the problem-solving form found on page 128. Getting accustomed to this problem-solving process and mindset will help teachers resolve difficult disagreements and develop plans that they are both comfortable with.

TIPS FOR BALANCING THEORY AND PRACTICE AND UNDERSTANDING EDUCATIONAL PHILOSOPHIES

- Discuss with your co-teaching partner how educational theory drives your practice. Do theorists like Howard Gardner, Lev Vygotsky, or Carol Dweck shape your instructional practice?

- Write a one-page summary of your educational philosophy and talk with your co-teacher about common themes. What differs about your philosophies? What is similar? Talk about how your philosophy shapes the way you teach and how you relate to students.

- Choose a professional book to read together. This can promote a shared language surrounding a particular topic and offer an opportunity to discuss theory and practice.

- Subscribe to the same professional journals, listservs, education-related Twitter feeds, and blogs. By talking about the material you read, you can help each other implement the good ideas you learn from various sources.

- If possible, attend a professional conference together.

- Discuss your views on RTI. What do you view as its overarching aim? How does RTI affect your students? Students who are English language learners? Gifted students?

Choreographing the Co-Teaching "Dance"

Schools that address all of these quality indicators are more likely to experience a smooth transition to successful implementation of RTI within the support of co-teaching. In addition, embracing and achieving these indicators will make life better for you as a teacher. You can think of effective co-teaching teams as being similar to famous dancing partners. They design their routines through skilled choreography and then they practice those routines over and over. One partner might rely on the other to take the lead early on in the co-teaching relationship. Eventually, they become more in tune and are able to anticipate each other's next move. Many co-teachers find that stepping on each other's toes from time to time is unavoidable, especially in the early stages. But with practice, the "dance" becomes smooth and quite enjoyable.

▲ Co-Teaching Models

Co-teaching is most successful when teachers understand how to use a variety of co-teaching models to enhance their lessons. Co-teaching teams are able to use these models efficiently so they can move in and out of each one based on their students' needs, and so they can draw reflective and informed conclusions on the success of each lesson. Co-teaching with various models can also help lessons move at a pace that holds student interest and engagement.

The five principal models of co-teaching are:

- complementary teaching
- station teaching
- parallel teaching
- alternative teaching
- shared teaching

The model or models you choose to utilize in a given lesson are driven by that lesson's objectives. Each model has a specific purpose, key attributes, and roles for each co-teacher. In the following descriptions of these co-teaching models, the co-teachers will be referred to as the "lead teacher" and the "support teacher."* The lead teacher is highly qualified in the subject or content knowledge, and is typically the classroom teacher. The support teacher has knowledge of specific learner needs, strategy instruction, and positive behavior supports and is often a special education teacher, intervention specialist, or other support personnel.

Complementary Teaching

Complementary teaching is often used when:

- content is being introduced by the lead teacher to the entire class
- the support teacher is providing academic or behavioral support to small groups or individuals within the large group setting
- co-teaching teams are just beginning to work together
- the support teacher is in the process of learning the content

---

*Dynak, Whitten, and Dynak, 1996.

In the complementary teaching model, the classroom teacher typically assumes the role as the lead teacher and delivers the lesson's content while the support teacher applies strategy instruction to the lesson and finds ways to differentiate instruction. The support teacher may also help with the lesson by monitoring students through close proximity during the lesson to increase participation and engagement in a given activity. The support teacher can also be responsible for keeping the lesson moving at the desired pace. Writing notes on the board while the lead teacher guides a discussion or brainstorming session is an example of using a support teacher to maintain the pace of the lesson while at the same time employing a visual method to reinforce ideas.

This model is most widely used by co-teachers at Tier I. It can, however, be misused—especially if the quality indicators previously discussed are not fully understood. One common example of misuse is a scenario in which the lead teacher teaches and guides the lesson while the support teacher "drifts" without a designated, pre-planned role or specific purpose. The end result is that the support teacher takes on a subordinate role, acting as a classroom assistant or paraeducator to the lead teacher. To prevent this outcome, you and your co-teacher can take steps such as ensuring you have co-planning time, identifying students who may need additional support and monitoring throughout the lesson, and planning for both of you to actively participate in the lesson's delivery.

The reason for choosing complementary teaching over other models is based primarily on the individual strengths of the co-teachers. If the support teacher does not have the content knowledge of the subject matter, then complementary teaching is most appropriate. The key attributes of complementary teaching are that the support teacher has knowledge in differentiated instruction, diverse learning styles, evidence-based strategies, and positive behavior supports, while the lead teacher has specific content knowledge. The skills of both teachers complement one another, resulting in a collaborative environment and effective lesson. By the end of a semester of co-teaching, the support teacher will typically have gained substantial working knowledge of the content, while the lead teacher will have broadened his or her knowledge of differentiation, evidence-based strategies, and grouping procedures. It is at this point that the team can comfortably begin using additional models.

▲ **Figure 4.1: Co-Teaching Activities**

If the lead teacher is doing this:	The support teacher can be doing this:	Benefits to students in RTI classrooms:
• Presenting new information to the class • Explaining a new concept	• Modeling note-taking • Filling in a graphic organizer on a board or visual projector	• Use of visual representations to support understanding

If the lead teacher is doing this:	The support teacher can be doing this:	Benefits to students in RTI classrooms:
• Collecting or reviewing homework	• Taking attendance • Checking in with students (asking how they're doing, how class is going, and so on)	• Increased instructional time • Increased personal attention to students
• Explaining directions • Responding to questions • Modeling the first problem	• Distributing papers • Writing down instructions or a model problem on the board or visual projector • Periodically asking clarifying questions of the lead teacher	• Increased instructional time • Use of visual representations to support understanding
• Providing direct instruction to the whole class or checking for understanding with a large, heterogeneous group of students	• Providing one-on-one support as needed • Checking for understanding with individual students or a small group • Using proximity control for behavior management	• Increased differentiated instruction • Increased instructional time • Errors and misconceptions are caught quickly • Increased personal attention to students
• Facilitating student learning during project-based instruction with a large, heterogeneous group of students	• Working closely with students in need of more teacher direction and targeted support	• Increased differentiated instruction • Errors and misconceptions are caught quickly • Increased personal attention to students
• Administering an assessment with a large, heterogeneous group of students	• Administering an assessment with a small group of students • Reading parts of the assessment aloud	• Testing accommodations provided to students in need of a small group environment
• Preparing lessons aligned to standards in the core curriculum	• Providing suggestions for modifications and accommodations for diverse learners • Preparing alternate lesson plans for intervention groups • Considering enrichment opportunities	• Increased differentiated instruction

Source: Adapted from Murawski, W.M., and L.A. Dieker. "Tips and Strategies for Co-Teaching at the Secondary Level." *Teaching Exceptional Children,* 36:5, 52–58 (2004).

▲ **Figure 4.2: Complementary Teaching Classroom Picture**

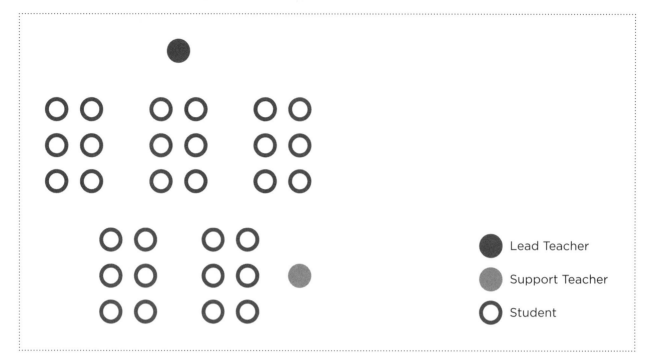

RTI in Action

COMPLEMENTARY TEACHING

At Illiopolis Middle School, Mr. Ahmed is a special education (support) teacher for the seventh-grade team at Tier I. He has a seating chart for the social studies class he co-teaches with Ms. Aiden, the social studies (lead) teacher. Mr. Ahmed uses his seating chart to take attendance and handle student issues concerning previous absences and makeup work. Meanwhile Ms. Aiden greets students and sets the tone of the classroom for the next hour. While Ms. Aiden begins the lesson, Mr. Ahmed circulates the room and makes notes on the seating chart, indicating students' level of participation, understanding of the content, and work completion. At the end of the lesson, if time permits, the co-teachers reflect on the lesson, compare their observations using their Two Plus One Reflection Logs (page 129), and prepare for the next day of class. If time is limited and one or both teachers are due in another class, they make a copy of the notes taken by Mr. Ahmed during class for further reflection and planning at a later time.

SPOTLIGHT
TWO PLUS ONE REFLECTION LOGS

The Two Plus One approach to reflection is a powerful way to help co-teachers think about a lesson and compare their observations and opinions. Using this method, co-teachers use reflection logs (page 129) to record what went well with co-taught lessons, as well as ways in which they could be improved.

When considering a lesson, each co-teacher lists two highlights of the lesson—the "plusses." Then each co-teacher writes down one thing he or she might want to change and how the lesson may have gone differently if the team had approached it in a different way. After recording these thoughts, co-teachers review their notes together, comparing and contrasting their viewpoints.

The point of the Two Plus One Reflection Log is to communicate the positives of a lesson and to raise questions and concerns about how things might have gone better, not to provide definite answers. Rather, Two Plus One provides a starting point for co-teachers to affirm successful teaching, talk through issues, and arrive at possible solutions as a team. It also challenges you and your partner to continually reflect on what works for your students. Daily logging is especially helpful in the beginning of new partnerships. As your partnership with your co-teacher strengthens, you may only feel the need to use the log from time to time.

Station Teaching

The purpose of station teaching is to break a lesson objective into small chunks to promote the learning of specific content. The underlying principle of this method is that if the information is taught in smaller lessons, students are less likely to feel overwhelmed and are more likely to comprehend and retain the content. Station teaching can also be used to review content if students need to revisit previously taught material in a new way.

In station teaching, the lesson is segmented into mini lessons and taught at stations designed by the teachers. Students are strategically grouped and circulate to each station throughout the period, the next day, or several days depending on the length of the lesson. In this model, the lead teacher has the overall content knowledge of the lesson or the "big idea" and assigns the co-teacher or co-teachers stations to develop and teach based on their knowledge and strengths. While co-teachers simultaneously teach their stations, all teachers work together to monitor the lesson's overall outcome.

Two of station teaching's key attributes are the effective use of multiple teachers' strengths, and the strategic grouping of students for better retention of content. The stations are developed using differentiated instruction and are designed to offer multiple approaches to the material. For example, if students are grouped by learning preferences, then each station will be differentiated to address the needs of visual, auditory, and kinesthetic learners. Other grouping strategies may include student interests, thinking styles, and skill sets. Station teaching allows the co-teaching team to use a variety of activities. This model also gives students an opportunity for physical movement that can help keep middle school students engaged and alert during long block-scheduled classes.

▲ **Figure 4.3: Station Teaching Classroom Picture**

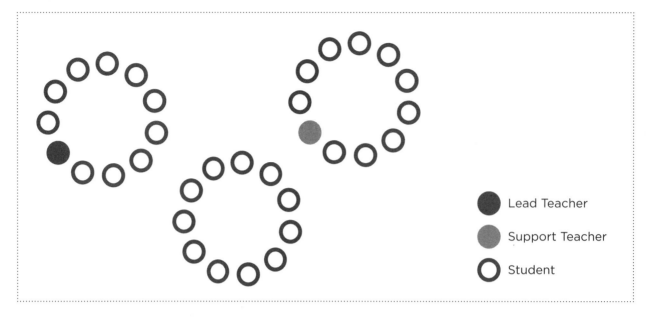

Lead Teacher

Support Teacher

○ Student

RTI in Action

STATION TEACHING

Mr. Lee and Ms. Alexander are preparing their students for an upcoming science test by setting up three review stations in their classroom. Students will spend 30 minutes in each station. Mr. Lee is leading a station devoted to peer-paired note review. At his station, he meets with eight students at a time. He pairs these students and has them review each other's notes while also adding to their own notes and discussing the material with each other. Once they are partnered and on-task, Mr. Lee checks in on another station. This station has students taking a pretest on computers. While this is designed as an independent station, Mr. Lee still checks in with students to answer their questions if needed. As students take the test, they receive immediate feedback from the computer that lets them know how they are performing.

Meanwhile, Ms. Alexander leads a station of her own. She is working with another group of eight students in a review session. She checks their understanding of key material and answers questions they have about the content. She finds that using a small-group format for the question-and-answer session encourages students to ask more questions; in turn, discussing the content in a more intimate forum gives her a better sense of students' grasp of the material. In fact, this is one of the main reasons that Mr. Lee and Ms. Alexander chose station teaching for the review session. Additional benefits are the varied instructional approaches available within the stations. Students are able to work individually, in pairs, and in small groups. Plus, the rotation from station to station offers a useful opportunity for students to periodically move around the classroom.

SPOTLIGHT
WORKING WITH CLASSROOM AIDES

Classroom aides are valuable members of the RTI and co-teaching team, and their support can be invaluable. Two key characteristics of a successful co-teaching partnership with a classroom aide are a high level of instructional support and the clear communication of each team member's instructional responsibilities.

Classroom aides sometimes have limited knowledge and experience with research-based instructional methods (although this is not always the case). If classroom aides are working with students, teachers and administrators must be sure these aides are trained in the instructional methods required for a given lesson. Also, if a lesson requires the implementation of a research-based program, training is also essential—even though the aide isn't delivering a whole-group lesson in the front of the classroom. Due to time restrictions, on-the-job training might be necessary. Modeling, demonstration of lessons while offering explanations, and instructional videos are all training methods that can be accomplished during the busy school day.

RTI calls for increased individualized and small-group instruction to meet students' needs. Classroom aides can have a very meaningful role within this instructional format.

Parallel Teaching

The purpose of parallel teaching is to lower the student-to-teacher ratio, so each teacher is able to work more directly and intensely with a smaller group of students. In this model, both teachers understand the content and are capable delivering the information. A common reason for choosing this model is that teachers want to boost the number of student responses (less teacher talk, and more student input). The lead teacher and support teacher collaboratively plan and organize the content of the lesson, divide the class into two groups, and individually facilitate the lesson.

▲ **Figure 4.4: Parallel Teaching Classroom Picture**

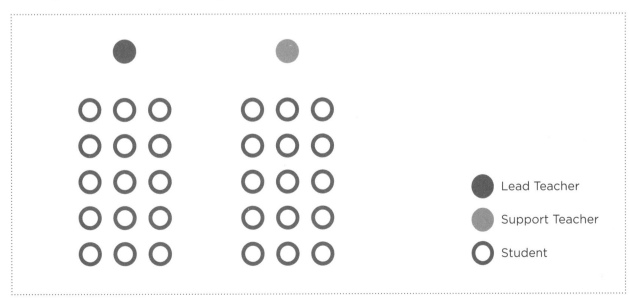

● Lead Teacher

● Support Teacher

○ Student

If time allows, the two parallel groups can get back together as a class to discuss the content and prepare for the next class session. This is a perfect opportunity to summarize key points in the lesson and check for understanding. Following the delivery of the lesson, the teachers reflect together about their individual groups and examine any student needs for additional instruction.

The key attribute of parallel teaching is that both teachers (lead and support) know the content to the extent that they can effectively facilitate the lesson without support. In this model, teachers can closely monitor students' responses because of the reduced number of students per group. Students can be grouped in a variety of ways, including heterogeneously or by learning preference. Parallel teaching may be useful for activities such as test review, student discussion, role playing, peer tutoring, or student presentations.

Alternative Teaching

The purpose of using alternative teaching is to support students who need "pre-teaching" so they are ready for a given lesson or to support those who did not master the content of a main lesson when it was first taught. Alternative teaching typically happens before and/or after the main lesson, and generally takes place at Tier II and Tier III. In this model, the lead teacher instructs the main lesson to the whole group, and the support teacher works with individuals or with a small group of students to pre-teach, reteach, supplement, or deepen instruction. This type of co-teaching requires step-by-step planning to ensure that the logistics and goals of pre-teaching or reteaching can be fully achieved. In addition, both teachers must have adequate content knowledge for one teacher to reteach or pre-teach a group while the other provides broader instruction to the rest of the students.

Planning and executing alternative teaching involves three main steps:

- **Step 1:** Teachers identify students who need to review the content prior to the main lesson so they can fully participate in the class lesson; students who

▲ **Figure 4.5: Alternative Teaching Classroom Picture**

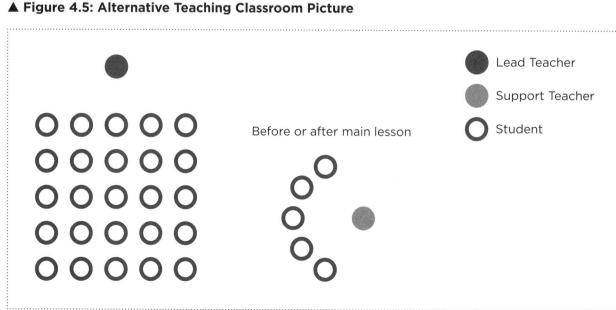

need to be retaught; and/or students who need a supplemental discussion or activity.

- **Step 2:** The lead and support teacher make decisions together about the content of the lesson and agree on the appropriate structures for alternative, remedial, or enrichment lessons to increase student learning and success.

- **Step 3:** The support teacher meets with selected students to pre-teach content before the main lesson. Once the lesson has been taught, co-teachers will determine which students have not mastered the content and need reteaching using a different approach.

Using the support teacher to respond to student needs in a very explicit way is a key benefit of alternative teaching.

Alternative teaching's core elements include:

- pre-assessing students to ensure they have the background knowledge needed to successfully engage in the lesson

- pre-teaching students who do not have the background knowledge to complete the lesson

- conducting ongoing monitoring during the main lesson

- reteaching material to students who did not fully understand the material taught, and conducting ongoing progress monitoring during reteaching

Shared Teaching

Shared teaching involves both co-teachers having content knowledge of the subject matter and the determination that students will benefit from observing a high level of collaboration between instructors. Shared teaching is a good model to use when whole-group instruction is determined to be the most effective means of delivering the content and when co-teachers' roles are easily interchangeable as they teach the lesson. In addition to its other benefits, shared teaching is a good way to keep lessons moving at a pace that keeps learners engaged.

In this model, teachers jointly plan, deliver, and assess the lesson. They are able to spontaneously and fluidly exchange lead and support roles during the lesson. Throughout, they use modeling strategies such as turn-taking, question-asking, effective communication, and problem solving. At the same time, teachers use in-action reflection to spontaneously react to each other and to students.

To carry out successful shared teaching both teachers:

- share the planning and instruction of students in a coordinated fashion

- have equal knowledge of the content

- possess a shared philosophy of classroom instruction

- believe effective instruction to all students in the class is critical

While it has many benefits, shared teaching is probably the most challenging approach to successfully implement, as it demands a high level of trust, flexibility, and communication. It can easily be misused to result in complementary teaching or tag teaching (in which one teacher delivers instruction while the other completes a task unrelated to the lesson and then they switch places). Most often, new co-teaching teams do not start with this type of approach, since they first need time to build their relationship. However, if teams have trust and common knowledge of content, over time, they can effectively move to this model. Once mastered, shared teaching can be very powerful.

▲ **Figure 4.6: Shared Teaching Classroom Picture**

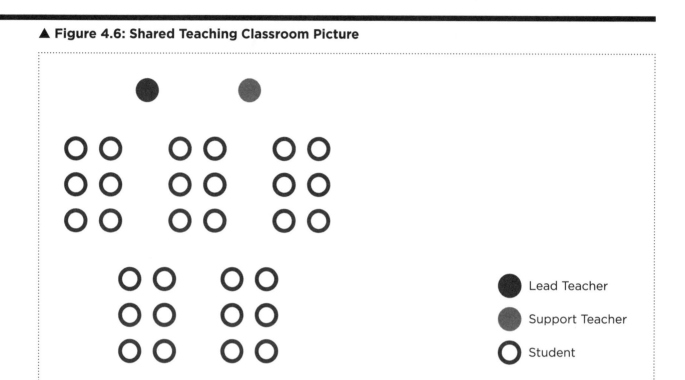

▲ **Figure 4.7: Examples of Using Co-Teaching Models at Each RTI Tier**

Model	Tier I	Tier II	Tier III
Complementary	Lead teacher presents lesson content while support teacher models a strategy used in the lesson or provides some form of additional teaching support.	Lead teacher works with a small group of students on content while support teacher circulates the room monitoring and documenting students' work.	Lead teacher teaches content to the large group while support teacher works with individuals or small groups of students.
Station	Lead and support teacher(s) develop and lead stations while students rotate to each station. Independent-study stations can also be used to complete tasks such as computer work, journal writing, silent reading, and revision.	Lead and support teacher(s) develop and lead stations while students rotate to each station. Stations have been developed to help students needing additional support, as well as assisting students who need to be challenged. Students rotate to stations assigned based on individual student need.	Lead and support teacher(s) develop and lead stations while students rotate to stations in assigned groups. Students who are struggling with content are assigned (typically in very small groups) stations providing intense remediation until students are working at grade level.
Parallel	Lead and support teacher plan lesson together using the same objectives. They divide the class into two groups, and each teacher teaches one of the groups.	Lead and support teacher plan lesson together using the same objectives. They split the class into two groups. Each teacher teaches one of the groups. Grouping may be determined by student needs.	Lead and support teacher plan lesson together using the same objectives. They split the class into groups and differentiate instruction by group or individual. The support teacher will have a small number of students to provide more explicit instruction.
Alternative	Lead teacher teaches the main lesson alone or through co-teaching one of the other four models. Prior to the main lesson, co-teachers determine if any students need pre-teaching of the lesson content, and/or after the main lesson they determine if any students (in need of Tier II or III support) would benefit from reteaching or extension.		
Shared	Co-teachers plan, teach, and evaluate the lesson together.	Not applicable	Not applicable

▲ **Figure 4.8: Key Points of Co-Teaching***

Model Name	Lead Teacher Role	Support Teacher Role	Purpose	Key Attributes
Complementary	Lead teacher has content knowledge	Support teacher provides strategy instruction or other support	Content is being introduced by the lead teacher while the support teacher provides support to small groups or to the large group through strategy instruction, modeling the use of a strategy, or proximity control	• Draws on the strengths of each teacher • Provides inclusive instruction through large-group instruction • Activates background knowledge for all students • Uses evidence-based strategies and performance assessment
Station	Lead teacher has content knowledge and big idea for lesson	Support teacher develops and teaches small groups in work stations	Breaks down the lesson objective into small segments or chunks lesson to promote the learning of specific content	• Takes a complex idea and breaks down the learning into more manageable short lessons • Allows for grouping based on a variety of student strengths or needs • Provides inclusive instruction through small-group instruction • Draws on unique strengths of each teacher

Model Name	Lead Teacher Role	Support Teacher Role	Purpose	Key Attributes
Parallel	Lead teacher has content knowledge for the lesson	Support teacher has content knowledge for the lesson	Lowers the student-to-teacher ratio so that each teacher is able to work more directly and intensely with a smaller number of students	• Teachers plan the lesson together and teach separately to lower the student-to-teacher ratio • Parallel groups allow teachers to group students based on needs
Alternative	Lead teacher has content knowledge and teaches lesson	Support teacher implements support activities for small groups or individuals before and after the formal lesson	Supports students who are not ready to participate in the main lesson and helps students who did not master the main lesson's content	• Draws on the strengths of each teacher • Activates background knowledge for students in need • Teaches students differently from the formal lesson • Repeats and reinforces information from the formal lesson
Shared	Lead teacher has content knowledge for the lesson	Support teacher has content knowledge for the lesson	Models teamwork for students while delivering content that is best suited to whole-group instruction	Teachers plan the lesson together and teach together modeling effective communication, problem solving, trust, and respect

*Whitten and Sheahan, 2010.

▲ The Importance of Using Multiple Co-Teaching Models

Although this chapter has presented information about co-teaching approaches in separate sections, the models can often be used in combination, and you're likely to find benefits from blending the models. No single approach is inherently preferable to another. Your choice of co-teaching model in each case will be driven by your lesson objective, your strengths and those of your co-teacher, the content knowledge you and your co-teacher have, and the level of support your students need across the tiers. Throughout a lesson, co-teachers may plan to weave in and out of several models. For example, co-teachers may begin a lesson with complementary teaching while introducing a graphic organizer used for notes during the main part of the lesson. Next they present the main part of the lesson using station teaching with students grouped by learning preferences. Lastly, they bring the lesson to a close using shared teaching to summarize and review the content from the graphic organizer. Fluid movement in a lesson using multiple models to fit a specific lesson is part of the co-teaching "dance" described earlier in the chapter. A solid, shared knowledge of all the co-teaching models will help orchestrate the movement of this dance.

▲ To Sum Up

Co-teaching provides students with more opportunities to participate successfully in a differentiated classroom across all three RTI tiers. It also gives teachers the necessary support to meet their students' individual needs, and helps keep lessons moving at the proper pace to encourage and increase student engagement. Through collaborative lesson planning, observing each other teach, and reflecting on the success of lessons and student learning, teachers are continually engaging in honing their practices. By combining a variety of teaching strategies and co-teaching models, teachers in RTI classrooms can create effective lessons and inclusive learning environments to help students at every tier succeed.

Tier I Lesson Plan

Date:	Co-teachers:

Content area:

Lesson objectives:

Co-teaching model(s) *(check the appropriate box or boxes)*

☐ Complementary ☐ Alternative ☐ Station

☐ Parallel ☐ Shared

Lesson Preparation	Co-Teachers' Responsibilities
Materials needed:	
Other:	

Lesson Plan	Co-Teaching Model(s)
Introduction:	
Instruction:	
Guided practice:	
Independent practice:	
Assessment:	
Closure:	

Room Arrangement	Notes

Tier I & II Lesson Plan

Date: _____ Co-teachers: _____

Content area:

Lesson objectives:

Co-teaching model(s) *(check the appropriate box or boxes)*

☐ Complementary　　☐ Alternative　　☐ Station

☐ Parallel　　☐ Shared

Lesson Preparation	Co-Teachers' Responsibilities
Materials needed: Tier I　　　　　　Tier II	

Lesson Plan	Co-Teaching Model(s)
Introduction: Tier I　　　　　　Tier II	
Guided practice: Tier I　　　　　　Tier II	
Independent practice: Tier I　　　　　　Tier II	
Assessment: Tier I　　　　　　Tier II	
Closure: Tier I　　　　　　Tier II	

Room Arrangement	Notes

Using the Problem-Solving Process for Co-Teaching

This collaborative problem-solving form can be used with your co-teacher when you encounter a specific issue, or on a regular, predetermined basis, such as once every two weeks, three times per semester, or whatever schedule makes sense for you. Especially in the early stages of a co-teaching partnership, develop a habit of using this form routinely. Even if major problems or disagreements don't crop up frequently, walking through the process will help you and your co-teacher(s) strengthen your relationship as well as your teaching.

The problem-solving process consists of five steps: Identify, Analyze, Brainstorm, Develop, and Follow Up. Each time you use this process, set aside enough time to thoughtfully consider each area and to discuss your perspectives with each other. Use the form to document your thoughts and ideas in each of the five steps, with each teacher filling out his or her own copy of the form, and keeping these forms in your records. This will help you identify common areas of difficulty, review your progress and your development as a team, and improve your ability to anticipate problems before they arise.

Identify the problem or concern.
In this section, each teacher individually defines the problem in writing.

Analyze the problem or concern.
Compare what you've each written and discuss any differences in the way you've each identified the key concern. Work to resolve differences. Together, redefine the problem in writing. Use language that you both agree is clear and accurate.

Brainstorm for solutions.
Together, consider multiple ways of resolving the issue. List all ideas on the form and discuss the possible solutions.

Develop an action plan.
Using the list you've brainstormed together, independently prioritize the list by numbering the ideas from most to least important in your view. Discuss how each of you prioritized the ideas and determine if you can agree on the top action plan to implement. This may end up being a blend of several of your ideas. Write down the action plan and make a few notes about how you intend to implement it.

Follow up.
Set a date for your next problem-solving meeting. At that time, you'll discuss whether you each feel the plan you developed is working and whether you view the problem as having been resolved or whether further action needs to be taken.

Problem-Solving Process for Co-Teaching

Date:	Teacher name:	Content area:

Co-teaching partner(s):

Identify the problem or concern.

Analyze the problem or concern.

Brainstorm for solutions.

Develop an action plan.

Follow up.
We will meet again to discuss our progress on ....
(date)

Two Plus One Reflection Log

Lesson date: Teacher name: Content area:

Co-teaching partner(s):

1. One highlight of the lesson:

2. A second highlight of the lesson:

Plus One *(concern or problem observed)*:

CHAPTER 5

Research-Based Teaching

Strong instruction grounded in research is essential to all tiers of RTI—from the classroom teaching of all students to the intense and strategic interventions at Tier III. Even with decades of educational research on pedagogical best practices, teaching remains both an art and a science. Truly masterful teaching makes use of proven practices but is still flexible. Having a keen awareness of students' needs and providing responsive instruction based on that knowledge is at the heart of RTI. This chapter offers you a wealth of research-based instructional methods, strategies, and programs that support the RTI model and strengthen instruction across all content areas.

▲ Evidence-Based Instructional Methods and Universal Design for Learning

Before addressing individual teaching strategies designed for meeting specific learning needs through differentiated instruction, it's helpful to look at some proactive instructional methods that can be used across content areas in the middle school setting. These practices form the basis of the strategies appearing later in the chapter and fit into the framework of universal design for learning (UDL). As discussed in Chapter 1, UDL calls for the use of proven practices that are flexible enough to accommodate a wide range of learners. Key principles of UDL include student choice and lessons that present information in diverse ways.

The methods outlined in this chapter are aligned with universal design for learning, and have been carefully selected based on research findings. These strategies have been demonstrated to be effective in multiple content areas with students of diverse backgrounds. For more information on the instructional methods listed here, see the References and Resources section on pages 203–208.

RTI, differentiated instruction, and universal design for learning are best viewed not as separate initiatives, but as necessary and complementary approaches. All three begin and end with the same belief: Students benefit from an education that is matched to their academic readiness, interests, and learning profiles. When teachers design instruction in a way that is multisensory, varied, relevant, and exploratory, and which places students at the center, they are best prepared to address the academic and developmental needs of middle school learners.

Set Learning Goals

Working with students to set goals can help focus their academic efforts and is a critical element of motivation. Goal setting provides direction and focus for learning, and is key to the ASIM approach discussed in Chapter 1 (see page 6). For most educators, the Common Core State Standards will be a starting point for writing more personalized learning goals with students. Begin by making sure that students understand the relevant standards in broad terms. Then add personalization based on individual preferences and specific learning needs. Be sure that teachers *and* students are able to articulate the relevance of each goal and how it relates to multiple content areas. This is key for middle school students, who tend to be driven by the knowledge that they are working toward something pertinent and meaningful to their lives. Letting students influence goal setting can be a powerful motivating factor.

After learning goals are set and have been written down in measurable terms, it's important to provide students with timely feedback on how they're doing. Focus on how individual students are progressing toward their own goals, rather than how their performance compares to that of other students. Recognizing students' effort as they work toward their goals will go a long way toward healthy academic motivation and teaching students the relationship between effort and achievement.

The What to Try When charts in this chapter (beginning on page 142) identify common areas of challenge for middle school students. The statements about these areas of difficulty can be personalized and reworded into goals. For example, a student may need to "develop research skills" (page 147). This can be reworded into a goal that reads: "I will develop research skills by generating questions, gathering relevant information, and using and citing multiple sources of data." When asked about this goal's relevance, the student would ideally be able to express how inquiry and research are lifelong strategies that will help her continue to be a self-motivated learner.

Provide Strategy-Based Instruction

Goal setting is particularly effective in combination with strategy-based instruction. Without guidance and assessment, many students struggle to accurately determine how well they have mastered new material. In fact, learners often overestimate what they know and the depth of their knowledge. Harold Pashler and his colleagues call this the "illusion of knowing," and it is especially common among students who have learning disabilities. Strategy instruction focuses on methods that improve metacognition—an awareness of one's own thinking and knowledge—until the use of these strategic methods becomes habitual and automatic.

There are many ways to teach students how to use these strategies. One approach that has been proven especially effective with middle school students is the Self-Regulated Strategy Development Model. This model is designed to ensure that all key aspects of strategy instruction are addressed. It involves the following steps.

1. Introduce the strategy and discuss prior knowledge students may have about it, if any.

2. Lead the class in a discussion of the strategy, including its purpose, for whom it is designed, and its expected benefits.

3. Model the strategy.

4. Help students begin to memorize the strategy by reviewing it and by restating the strategy to their peers.

5. Pair students and have them practice the strategy until all learners are able to perform it independently. Provide multiple opportunities for practice as students move toward self-directed use of the strategy.

6. Direct students to use the strategy on their own.

When students can self-regulate their learning (set goals, self-instruct, self-monitor, and provide themselves with positive reinforcement), they are able to make greater academic gains.

Incite Curiosity and Activate Prior Knowledge

How teachers prepare their students for learning is of utmost importance. For instance, using props or other visuals can create curiosity and get students excited to learn. Another method is to use discussion to bring out what students already know about a topic, since introducing new material within the context of previously known information helps students make meaningful connections. Following are several effective ways to activate student knowledge, incite curiosity about new information, and set the stage for learning.

- **Student-generated questioning.** Questions can help students form context around what they are learning or are about to learn. When students come up with their own questions and concerns about a particular topic, they activate their prior knowledge while at the same time framing a relevant discussion around new information. These "pre-questions" help students identify what they don't yet know, and thus need to learn. Questioning can also be used to establish why a particular topic is important and relevant. Asking students to generate their own questions about a topic and helping them seek out the answers creates a powerful and authentic form of learning.

- **Cueing.** Cues (sometimes called provocations) give students clues about what they are about to learn or experience. You can provide these in an introduction that provokes thought about a topic and precedes more complete discussion of new material. Cues can alert students to what they might already know about the topic, create interest and a sense of curiosity about it, and prepare them to learn more.

- **Advance organizers.** Advance organizers offer students a preview of key information in the form of an outline. This is a technique best employed when teaching complex information. You can share organizers with students before lessons to prepare them to learn about a particular topic. Advance organizers in the form of note outlines can also free students from having to write copious notes, allowing them to focus more fully on the lesson.

Well-designed questions, cues, and advance organizers will focus on what is most important in overall understanding of a topic, as opposed to details and obscure facts. The goal of this teaching method is to help students realize and analyze what they already know about a topic, and to generate curiosity in them to learn more. This approach can be especially helpful for learners who like to understand big-picture context before taking in new information, but it will benefit all students.

Design Multiple Opportunities to Learn Content

After introducing new material, effective instructors revisit that content in unique and meaningful ways while helping students deepen their understanding at every pass. Of course, educators also know that boredom and lack of motivation can be the potential pitfalls of using "skill and drill" instruction, and repetitive practice lessons are best used sparingly. However, studies consistently show that exposing students to key concepts and reexposing them to the same content weeks or months later promotes learning. To avoid disinterest, this reexposure can be accomplished in creative ways. Using a variety of instructional methods, such as small-group dialogue and project-based learning, is a good way to hold the interest of all learners. Another tactic is to incorporate the use of technology, such as video viewing and Web-based research, so that students have some control over the amount of repetition they experience, according to their needs, before moving on to the next topic.

Other common and long-used methods for encouraging students to revisit information are quizzing students and assigning homework. Both have been shown to be strong motivators of student study, as they incentivize students to revisit information on their own in largely self-directed ways. While questions around the effectiveness of quizzing and homework are raised periodically, studies continue to indicate that they are effective in reinforcing learning, particularly in secondary school. With all of this in mind, it's important to assign quizzes and homework with a great deal of thought and careful planning. Homework, for example, will cover and build upon the information taught in class, and students should be able to complete it independently or with minimal support. It's also critical for teachers to provide specific and timely feedback on student work.

In all contexts, activities assigned for student practice should give learners the opportunity to reexamine content and extend their thinking about a topic. This often requires that you plan for various and creative forms of practice, as spacing learning over time will help students extend their knowledge base. The art of teaching comes in planning reexposure to content in such inventive ways that students' motivation to reencounter information is not diminished.

SPOTLIGHT
MULTISENSORY INSTRUCTION

Combining verbal explanations, visual representations, and hands-on learning in the classroom is one engaging way to meet the needs of students with various learning styles. Using multiple means of representation is also a powerful way to communicate new material to students. At the same time, it gives you varied opportunities to revisit content. Allowing students to demonstrate their knowledge through multiple means of expression is a key principle of universal design for learning.

Promote Higher-Level Thinking

Students of all ages benefit from being challenged by questions and activities that promote higher-level thinking, as shown in the upper levels of Bloom's Taxonomy (Figure 5.1, on the following page). In a middle school setting, the cognitive development of adolescent students makes it particularly important for educators to nurture the ability to think abstractly and from different perspectives. Encouraging students to examine ideas from multiple points of view helps them think critically and develop well-reasoned arguments. After students have acquired basic knowledge about a certain concept, teachers can engage them in thoughtful discussion, problem solving, and analysis. The following list presents a variety of methods for stimulating higher-level thinking.

- Have students create metaphors and analogies about a topic or idea.
- Ask learners to question and evaluate the motivations of people or organizations.
- Ask students open-ended "why" and "how" questions, instead of multiple-choice or yes/no questions.
- Ask students to generate and test hypotheses on a subject.
- Encourage learners to connect abstract and concrete concepts (including real-life situations).
- Ask students where certain information comes from and what or who might be influencing that information.
- Ask students to identify similarities and differences between two or more concepts, ideas, historical figures, works of literature, or other topics of study.
- Ask students to consider and discuss "what if" scenarios: Instead of X happening, what if Y happened?
- Discuss solutions to problems and brainstorm other potential ways these problems might be solved.
- Ask students why certain information is significant.
- Encourage students to think out loud and make their thinking known so they can demonstrate the reasoning behind their conclusions. (In your teaching, model this on a regular basis as well.)

▲ **Figure 5.1: Bloom's Taxonomy**[*]

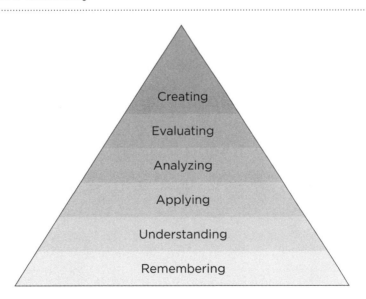

*Anderson, L.W., and D.R. Krathwohl (eds.). *A Taxonomy for Learning, Teaching, and Assessing: A Revision of Bloom's Taxonomy of Educational Objectives.* New York: Longman, 2001.

Use the Gradual Release of Responsibility Framework

The Gradual Release of Responsibility Framework is an approach that moves from a teacher-directed instructional model to cooperative learning and, ultimately, to independent application of material by students. This method is supported by cognitive science, research on master teachers, and proven instructional procedures. It artfully combines a variety of instructional tools to meet the needs of learners at different stages of academic readiness. The four main components of the framework follow, with descriptions of teachers' roles and responsibilities at each stage. In these descriptions, "I" refers to the teacher, while "you" refers to students.

- **Focus Lessons (I do it).** Teach focus lessons in order to establish a purpose for learning the new material, model the thinking process, and explain new concepts.

- **Guided Instruction (We do it).** During the guided instruction phase, meet with small groups, providing practice and feedback based on learner needs. Encourage students to ask questions and share their thoughts about the material.

- **Collaborative Learning (You do it together).** In this phase, students interact with peers to enhance and deepen their thinking.

- **Independent Learning Tasks (You do it alone).** At this stage, build in opportunities for students to work with the material on their own. This helps them become more self-directed. This individual practice time is needed to gain confidence in completing tasks independently.

These shifts in instructional focus must occur purposefully and carefully to ensure student understanding. When teachers know the method well and have a thorough knowledge of their students, the Gradual Release of Responsibility Framework offers an excellent opportunity to differentiate instruction in combination with RTI.

SPOTLIGHT
A WORD ABOUT EXPLICIT INSTRUCTION

Longstanding pedagogical debates about student-initiated learning versus explicit, teacher-directed instruction have resulted in strong feelings about its use in the classroom. Explicit instruction is a highly structured, teacher-centered instructional model that emphasizes thoroughly planned lessons that break down learning into steps. Explicit instruction also involves delivery of information and continuous modeling. The initial lesson consists of fast-paced instruction, followed by guided practice and reduced support until a student demonstrates mastery of the material.

Ideally, explicit instruction is not used in isolation. Student-initiated learning is also critically important and deserves a key place in middle school classrooms. With that said, explicit instruction *is* highly effective for developing specific skills, and is well suited to students who need teacher guidance in grasping new material at Tier II or III, or for short lectures at Tier I before moving on to student-directed self-study. When used in these instances, explicit instruction can be very successful in combination with more student-initiated approaches such as the Gradual Release of Responsibility Framework.

With this combined approach, all students in the classroom—including those at different tiers—don't necessarily have to move through the stages at the same time.

Integrate Project-Based Learning

Project-based learning is a student-directed instructional method in which learners work collaboratively to investigate, solve problems, and reflect on their learning. Students design, plan, and carry out projects centered on specific research questions or areas of interest. This process is related to the inquiry-learning and problem-based learning methods, but involves the production of a presentation, publication, or other product through which students communicate what they have learned. The teacher's role is to serve as a facilitator and to deepen students' thinking about topics by asking questions. Keeping students accountable to their work plans is also a responsibility, especially if students are new to project-based learning. Guiding students through developing and following work plans that include timelines for project completion can be part of the process.

Project-based learning can take many different formats, but the essential components follow.

QUESTION DEVELOPMENT

1. Provide students with a context for the project. What broader themes will students' projects explore or address? How is this connected to what the class is studying?

2. Ask students to generate questions related to the theme. You may need to help students reshape and strengthen their questions. Questions that follow these two criteria typically make for strong projects:

   - The question does not have an easy answer.
   - The question has significance in the real world.

COLLABORATIVE RESEARCH

3. Place students in heterogeneous collaborative groups (two to four students per group) based on similar areas of inquiry.

4. Instruct students to discuss what they know about their topics, set learning goals, and conduct preliminary research to further refine their questions.

5. Give students time during class to conduct serious research. Make sure that they are using a variety of credible sources.

PRODUCT DEVELOPMENT

6. Help students reflect on the research process and discuss the answers different groups reached, as well as any additional questions that may have been raised.

7. Have groups brainstorm and discuss ideas for products. These could include posters, presentations, electronic books, podcasts, or digital slideshows to communicate what they have learned. Groups may choose to focus on a single idea or create multiple products.

8. Instruct students to begin working on their products with the mindset that multiple drafts are expected and valuable. Encourage them to seek feedback from you as they develop these drafts.

9. Have groups practice their presentations, workshop their writing, or otherwise share the products of their collaboration with peers. Ask them to provide one another with feedback, and to use this information to refine the product until the final version is complete.

DISSEMINATION

10. Encourage students to disseminate the information they've gathered to a wider audience by communicating their findings to a group that was not involved with the project (such as parents or another class).

Creating a work plan that incorporates these steps is a good class activity that serves to outline the process of completing a project. The Buck Institute for Education (www.bie.org) is a great resource for classroom project ideas and tips for carrying out the initial planning stages. Project-based learning is a large undertaking, but it meshes with a number of common RTI goals as well as Common Core State Standards, including those relating to time management, goal setting, collaborative problem solving, and following work plans.

RTI in Action

At the end of the school year's first semester, Mr. Brady—a sixth-grade social studies teacher at Eastlane Middle School—reflected on his instruction and his students' level of engagement during class time. He felt that there had been a good balance of teacher direction, student collaboration, and independent work time. He worked with learners who needed specific interventions on a regular basis while the rest of the class was working independently. For instance, with one small group, he specifically targeted the use of academic vocabulary in conversation and in writing. Mr. Brady also found that he frequently needed to give mini-lessons on syllabication and offer explanations of word parts and their meanings. This need is one that might easily have been overlooked if Mr. Brady hadn't had the opportunity to work with these students in small groups.

While Mr. Brady never felt as though he had quite enough time to connect with *every* student, *every* day, he used peer collaboration to support all learners. Mr. Brady also found that his students were most engaged when they were allowed to have greater choice, whether that meant selecting from several ways to convey their understanding, the opportunity to research their own questions about a topic, or other options.

One area Mr. Brady felt still needed strengthening was the frequency with which he discussed students' individual learning goals, especially for those learners who had intervention plans. Looking ahead toward the next semester, he planned to focus on these goal discussions with all students, but especially those needing extra support.

SPOTLIGHT
THE FLIPPED CLASSROOM

Flipping the classroom is an instructional approach that takes into account and makes use of the rich supply of free information available on the Internet. Flipping the classroom involves students watching lectures or instructional videos as homework—on their own time and at their own pace. This allows them to watch and rewatch as often as needed until they are comfortable with the content. Class time is used for topical collaborative activities, discussion, or hands-on problem solving. The teacher acts as the facilitator and is available to answer students' questions and promote engagement. Because explicit instruction is given outside of class time, the teacher is available to work with small groups (especially those needing Tier II support) in the classroom. Middle school students will likely need guidance in their development of self-directed learning, so it is important to start slowly instead of diving headfirst into flipped learning.

The following resources are a sample of the Web-based resources that can be used to flip the classroom.

Khan Academy (www.khanacademy.org)

Khan Academy features instructional videos for students of all ages. The site can be used in a variety of ways, including as a study tool for flipping the classroom, or as a way for students to learn, measure their own progress, and work toward individualized goals at their own pace. Topics vary. Videos are 5 to 10 minutes in length.

MIT + K12 (k12videos.mit.edu)

Developed in collaboration with the founder of Khan Academy, MIT + K12 similarly features educational videos. Produced by MIT students for a K–12 audience, these videos focus on science, technology, engineering, and math. Videos are 5 to 10 minutes in length.

TED-Ed (ed.ted.com)

An extension of the well-known TED Talks, TED-Ed lessons are recorded by educators and professionally animated. Videos cover many topics and are organized by theme. The site also provides quizzes, open-ended questions, and supplementary resources. Videos are 2 to 20 minutes in length.

Wonderopolis (wonderopolis.org)

Every day this website posts a new "wonder" in the form of a question, followed by a video as well as text and resource links. The website is searchable, so students can easily find wonders that have been previously posted. Students can also submit their own ideas for wonders to be included on the website.

A flipped classroom acknowledges that teachers are no longer the classroom's sole sources of knowledge and information. Educators' roles have changed, and will continue to evolve as access to information through technology increases. This doesn't mean that content-area expertise is no longer valid or necessary in the 21st-century classroom. In-person resources remain hugely valuable. In addition, teachers' skills as facilitators and expertise in creating collaborative environments are more important than ever. Today's educators must establish a climate where students can come together and create, solve problems, and communicate in meaningful ways. That role remains true regardless of whether students receive foundational information in the form of reading, experimentation, video viewing, or traditional lecture.

▲ Research-Based Strategies and Programs

As is true of all instructional methods, it's important that interventions in place at your school be grounded in solid evidence. Some users of RTI demand that every intervention be subjected to rigorous research and stamped with an official seal of approval. While this type of academic research is indeed valuable, direct teacher experience and research are also indispensable.

Ultimately, it's up to your state, district, and local policies to determine what can officially qualify as an intervention when a student is being considered for special education services. However, remember that eligibility is only one aspect of RTI. Interventions can and should be implemented for *all* students as a means of differentiating instruction.

SPOTLIGHT
STRATEGIES VS. PROGRAMS

In this chapter, you'll see some **programs** included among **strategies**. Programs are generally larger in scope, often commercially produced, and may call for broader or more systematic implementation. Each program is denoted by an asterisk* next to its title.

This section provides you with information on strategies and programs aimed at developing effective habits for academic success across all content areas and tiers. These strategies are geared for middle school students, but the habits instilled are also applicable to personal and professional life outside of school. When teaching any new strategy, implement a scaffolding method that includes modeling the strategy, providing guided practice using the strategy, and then giving students the opportunity to independently apply the strategy.

In choosing which strategies and programs to include in this book, we've highlighted learning skills and instructional approaches that apply across many or all subject areas. You'll see that some strategies focus on math or science, but that most have broad utility. In addition, we've included strategies addressing inquiry, research, critical thinking, self-management, and learning strategies—all key skills that middle school students are developmentally prepared to use and expand, and which will help them succeed in the rest of their education and beyond.

You'll also note that many strategies focus on literacy development. In order to make gains in literacy, reading instruction needs to take place all day long and be the job of all teachers. In turn, these strengthened reading skills will help students in all content areas, and will prepare them for the more advanced texts they'll encounter in high school. Furthermore, it is every teacher's responsibility to provide books that build students' knowledge about specific content, engage their interest and intellect, and are written at their reading level.

Explicitly teaching reading strategies helps students become more skillful at interpreting, understanding, and analyzing text in *all* subject areas. Because students have different styles of learning and reading, they will find strategies that work best for their personal styles. While a specific strategy may support the strengths of one student, the same strategy may prove to be difficult or monotonous to another. This is the reason for explicitly teaching a variety of strategies and giving students the chance to reflect on the most effective and beneficial strategies for them. With your guidance and with the benefit of self-reflection, students will become increasingly aware of the strategies that provide them with the appropriate level of support. Encourage students to consider questions such as:

- Is this strategy something I already do or don't do as a reader?
- Does this strategy help me better understand the text?
- How might I use this strategy with texts from other subject areas?

You'll also see that the strategies and programs in this chapter focus on instruction. This is, of course, just one facet of RTI. Conducting assessment practices, holding team meetings to discuss students' progress, calling home, and providing students with technology tools can also all be part of intervention plans for students. However, an intervention plan focuses above all on instructional interventions. Many of the strategies in this chapter make use of small-group instruction, but some involve peer tutoring, computerized instruction, and other instructional approaches.

> In choosing strategies and programs, we've highlighted learning skills and instructional approaches that apply across subject areas. In addition, we've included strategies addressing inquiry, research, critical thinking, self-management, and learning strategies—key skills that middle school students are developmentally prepared to use and expand, and which will help them succeed in the rest of their education and beyond.

This is by no means an exhaustive list of every strategy and program. It is, however, a carefully chosen and varied selection of techniques and tactics to get you started and inspired. The What to Try When charts can help you select appropriate interventions. These charts can also be customized (using forms included in this book's digital content) to include additional strategies in which you are trained and use on a regular basis. You and your team may want to add to the charts together as a way of compiling resources and sharing knowledge and expertise about interventions. The information you bring together in these charts—for example, which colleagues are able to provide training on particular interventions—can offer an opportunity for professional development without ever leaving the school building.

The What to Try When charts list common academic problems and suggestions for which strategies or programs (denoted with asterisks) may most effectively address various learning challenges. During RTI meetings, pick several potential strategies from each academic area before determining which might work best based on students' academic goals, interests, and learning strengths. These charts are broken down into the following categories:

- Word Recognition
- Reading Fluency
- Reading Comprehension
- Language and Vocabulary Development
- Writing to Communicate
- Inquiry and Research

- Critical Thinking
- Self-Management and Learning Strategies

As you explore these charts and the strategies that accompany them, remember that no instructional strategy or program will promote student success every time. Student needs will vary and interventions may not always lead to the results you hope to reach. Yet every small success moves students forward and gives you information you can use in the future.

▲ Word Recognition

What to try when a student does not recognize affixes or syllabication patterns in words:

Strategy or Program	Page Number
Fountas & Pinnell Leveled Literacy Intervention System*	158
Pattern Sorts	172
REWARDS®*	184

What to try when a student over-relies on phonics to read words:

Strategy or Program	Page Number
Audio-Assisted Reading	151
Fountas & Pinnell Leveled Literacy Intervention System*	158

▲ Reading Fluency

What to try when a student reads with an improper rate (either too quickly or too slowly):

Strategy or Program	Page Number
Audio-Assisted Reading	151
Fountas & Pinnell Leveled Literacy Intervention System*	158
Read-Aloud	179
Read Naturally®*	180
SCUBA-Dive Into Reading	184

What to try when a student reads with little prosody (struggles with expression and proper phrasing):

Strategy or Program	Page Number
Audiobooks	152
Joke Books	165
Read-Aloud	179
Read Naturally®*	180
Readers Theatre	180

▲ Reading Comprehension

What to try when a student struggles to make inferences:

Strategy	Page Number
QAR	177
REAP	182
Subtext Strategy	190

What to try when a student needs help understanding text structure:

Strategy or Program	Page Number
Possible Sentences	174
READ 180®*	181
Summarizing by Drawing	191
THIEVES	194

What to try when a student has limited comprehension of historical, technical, or scientific texts:

Strategy	Page Number
TWA + Plans	196

What to try when a student does not grasp the main ideas or draw conclusions from the text:

Strategy or Program	Page Number
Annotating Text	150
READ 180®*	181
Text Rendering	193
TWA + Plans	196

What to try when a student has difficulty seeing the author's point of view:

Strategy	Page Number
QAR	177
Think Pair Share	56
TWA + Plans	196

▲ Language and Vocabulary Development

What to try when a student has difficulty identifying patterns in language:

Strategy	Page Number
Literature Circles	168
Sentence Building, Elaborating, and Pruning	186

What to try when a student does not use context to determine the meaning of words and phrases:

Strategy	Page Number
Frayer Model	158
Interactive Word Wall	163
LINCS + VOC	168

What to try when a student needs to strengthen knowledge of roots and affixes:

Strategy	Page Number
Interactive Word Wall	163
Word Sorts	199

▲ Writing to Communicate

What to try when a student needs to improve his or her understanding of the writing process:

Strategy or Program	Page Number
Brainstorming	154
The Process Approach	175
Reverse Outlining	183
6 + 1 Trait® Writing*	187
Thinking and Self-Questioning	195
TWA + PLANS	196

What to try when a student has difficulty writing opinion pieces on topics or texts:

Strategy	Page Number
Forced Freewriting	157
RAFT	178
Thinking and Self-Questioning	195

What to try when a student struggles to convey ideas and information clearly:

Strategy or Program	Page Number
6 + 1 Trait® Writing*	187
TAG (Writer's Workshop)	192
Thinking and Self-Questioning	195
TWA + PLANS	196

What to try when a student needs help writing narrative pieces:

Strategy or Program	Page Number
6 + 1 Trait® Writing*	187
TAG (Writer's Workshop)	192

What to try when a student's writing lacks structure:

Strategy or Program	Page Number
Kinesthetic Writing, of Sorts	165
Sentence Building, Elaborating, and Pruning	186
6 + 1 Trait® Writing*	187
TAG (Writer's Workshop)	192
TWA + PLANS	196

▲ Inquiry and Research

What to try when a student seems to lack intellectual curiosity:

Strategy	Page Number
Interview Grids	164
SQ3R	188
Students as Problem Solvers	189
WebQuests	198
Working Backward	200

What to try when a student needs to develop research skills (generating questions; gathering relevant information by using and citing multiple sources; presenting findings; emphasizing salient points):

Strategy	Page Number
Interview Grids	164
SQ3R	188
Web-Based Bookmarks	198
WebQuests	198

▲ Critical Thinking

What to try when a student needs help evaluating information from differing perspectives:

Strategy	Page Number
Conflicting Texts and Quotes	156
How Do You Know?	161
Interactive Read-Aloud	162
Take a Side	193

What to try when a student does not evaluate the soundness of reasoning:

Strategy	Page Number
Conflicting Texts and Quotes	156
Interactive Read-Aloud	162
PROVE-ing What You Know	176
Take a Side	193

What to try when a student needs to develop stronger metacognitive and/or self-reflective skills:

Strategy	Page Number
CRA	156
How Do You Know?	161
Interactive Read-Aloud	162
PROVE-ing What You Know	176

▲ Self-Management and Learning Strategies

What to try when a student needs help setting goals:

Strategy or Program	Page Number
AVID*	153
Beyond SMART	153
Goal-Setting Protocol	159
KWL-Plus	167

What to try when a student has difficulty with time management:

Strategy or Program	Page Number
AVID*	153
High-Preference Strategy	160
Making Choices	170
PIRATES	173

What to try when a student needs help initiating a task and following work plans:

Strategy	Page Number
Goal-Setting Protocol	159
Making Choices	170
Self-Talk	185

What to try when a student lacks test-taking strategies:

Strategy	Page Number
Making Choices	170
PIRATES	173
Self-Talk	185

What to try when a student needs to improve note-taking skills:

Strategy	Page Number
CALL UP Note-Taking	154
Structured Note-Taking	189

What to try when a student lacks effective study skills:

Strategy	Page Number
Anticipation Guide	150
Mnemonic Devices	171
Self-Talk	185

What to try when a student needs to increase academic motivation:

Strategy or Program	Page Number
Anticipation Guide	150
AVID*	153
Beyond SMART	153
KWL-Plus	167
Self-Talk	185

Annotating Text

Area Addressed: *Reading Comprehension*

Strategy Summary

Annotating text is a useful strategy for students who need to improve their skills in self-questioning and their level of interaction with the text. This strategy also promotes conversation about shared reading.

Steps

1. Before reading the text (such as a book chapter, short story, poem, or essay), provide each student with four or five sticky notes.

2. Instruct students to write out questions about the text on the sticky notes during their reading of the text and to place the sticky notes next to the parts of the reading that triggered their thoughts.

3. After students have finished the reading and filled all of their sticky notes, form groups of three to five students. Give groups time to discuss the text and the questions students documented on the sticky notes.

4. Instruct students to explain to their group the parts of the text that triggered their questions and to read their questions. Group members should have an opportunity to explain their thoughts about each question, answering it from their own perspectives.

5. If a group isn't able to answer a question, members should pursue the issue further by seeking additional resources they can use to draw conclusions about the text.

Teacher Tips

- Students may need help drafting substantive questions that do not have simple answers or answers that can be found directly in the text.

- Make sure that each student has text that matches his or her independent reading level.

Probst, R. "Tom Sawyer, Teaching, and Talking." In *Adolescent Literacy,* K. Beers, R.E. Probst, and L. Rief (eds.). Portsmouth, NH: Heinemann, 2007.

Anticipation Guide

Area Addressed: *Self-Management and Learning Strategies*

Strategy Summary

Anticipation guides are teacher-created materials that activate students' prior knowledge of content. This strategy also supports student engagement, comprehension, and assessment of information learned.

Steps

1. Select a text, video, or other piece of content that fits into your unit of study or lesson objectives.

2. Develop an anticipation guide to prepare students for learning. The following parameters will help you craft strong guides:

- Use a series of statements from the text or video to which a student is asked to respond. What is the student's opinion about the statements? Do they have personal connections to the selected text? What questions does the selected text raise for the student?

- Include statements with varying degrees of difficulty.

- Include statements that will challenge students' thoughts and opinions and require them to think critically about their answers.

3. Have students complete their anticipation guides to the best of their ability, using critical thinking to respond to each point.

4. Read, watch, or study the content information.

5. Have students return to the anticipation guide and consider what they've learned. Invite them to:

- reevaluate their original responses to the guide's questions

- choose to maintain or change their positions, filling out a second guide to show any changes in their thinking based on what they've learned

Teacher Tips

- Anticipation guides can be used to build interest and excitement for learning. They are also helpful in showing students the relevance of the material they are learning.

- By varying the complexity of the statements, anticipation guides can be differentiated to meet students' needs.

Kozen, A.A., R.K. Murray, and I. Windell. "Increasing All Students' Chance to Achieve: Using and Adapting Anticipation Guides with Middle School Learners." *Intervention in School and Clinic,* 41:4, 195–200 (2006).

Audio-Assisted Reading

Areas Addressed: *Word Recognition/Reading Fluency*

Strategy Summary

In this strategy, students listen to a selection of text that has been recorded by a fluent reader.

Steps

1. Students will have their own copies of the text so they can follow along with the audio recording, tracking each word the reader says.

2. When the entire passage has been heard, each student will choose a particular section to practice reading aloud.

3. Cue the recording to that particular section.

4. Students will practice reading their chosen sections along with the recording. They will continue this step until they achieve fluency and can read the section independently.

5. Each student will individually read the section to the teacher. The teacher listens to the reader and offers feedback based on word recognition and fluency, relating the feedback to the student's goals. If working with a small group of students, the students who are not working one-on-one with the teacher could practice in pairs during this time.

Teacher Tips

- Monitor students as they listen to the recording to ensure they are on task. Choose recorded readings that are at students' instructional level, and that are read at a pace all students will be able to follow. Finally, be sure that the recording has clear sound and that it plays at a suitable volume.

- This strategy can be used for one-on-one support or in a small-group setting.

- In a group setting, separate students who may distract each other.

- Research supports the use of this strategy with English language learners.

Eldredge, J.L. "Increasing the Performance of Poor Readers in the Third Grade with a Group-Assisted Strategy." *Journal of Educational Research,* 84(2), 68–76 (1990). More information about the use of recorded book as an intervention with middle school students can be found at www.recordedbooks.com/pdf_brochures/school /intervention_guide.pdf.

Audiobooks

Area Addressed: *Reading Fluency*

Strategy Summary

You can use audiobooks to promote interest in reading and to model reading prosody. Prosody is the extent to which a reader can read aloud in a way that sounds like natural speech, conforming to the rhythms, cadences, and flow of spoken language. Commercially produced audiobooks are usually read by trained orators and professional actors. In addition to being engaging to listen to, they offer a rich opportunity to improve sight word recognition and, therefore, to increase reading fluency. Try integrating audiobooks in the follow ways:

- **Classroom listening centers.** Allow students to listen to audiobooks during sustained silent reading time or free time.

- **Book clubs.** Allow students who might not be reading at grade level to independently listen to books on CD or on MP3 players so they can participate in book club discussions with their peers.

- **Teasers.** Introduce students to new books by playing the first chapter for the whole class. Listening to a book's opening may encourage some students to pick up the book on their own and read it independently.

- **Take-home packs.** Let students check out audiobooks from the classroom and take them home for listening and reading on their own time.

Teacher Tips

- This strategy can be used with fiction or nonfiction books.

- Encourage students to read along while listening by tracking the text with tracking tools or their fingers.

- Audiobooks can be found at most public libraries; downloaded from websites such as itunes.com, audible.com, and recordedbooks.com; or purchased at bookstores.

- Offer enough choices so that students can select audiobooks based on their interests.

- Research supports use of this strategy with English language learners.

Esteves, K.J., and E. Whitten. "Assisted Reading with Digital Audiobooks for Students with Reading Disabilities." *Reading Horizons Journal,* 51:1, 21–40 (2011).

AVID*

Area Addressed: *Self-Management and Learning Strategies*

Program Summary

AVID is a program aimed at preparing students for college and closing the achievement gap. The acronym stands for Advancement Via Individual Determination. The program uses WICOR (writing, inquiry, collaboration, organization, and reading) as its foundation. The program also focuses on self-advocacy, social skills, and student engagement. The fundamentals taught through the AVID program—such as strategies for improving organization, time management, and goal setting—can be applied to all content areas.

Teacher Tips

- The AVID program can be implemented school-wide.
- AVID offers professional development opportunities such as training and workshops. Visit www.avid.org for more information.

Swanson, M.C. "Advancement via Individual Determination: Project AVID." *Educational Leadership*, 46:5 (1989).

Watt, K., C.A. Powell, and I.D. Mendiola. "Implications of One Comprehensive School Reform Model for Secondary School Students Underrepresented in Higher Education." *Journal of Education for Students Placed at Risk*, 9:3, 241–259 (2004).

Beyond SMART

Area Addressed: *Self-Management and Learning Strategies*

Strategy Summary

Teachers may be familiar with developing SMART goals for themselves and for students. A SMART goal is Specific, Measurable, Attainable, Relevant, and Time-Bound. You can go beyond the SMART basics to develop goals that focus more on individual needs and take into account learners' identities, desires, challenges, and feelings. This more holistic system of goal setting helps students understand how their SMART goals are relevant to their lives.

To go beyond SMART, after you've set a SMART goal, talk with the student about how that goal will benefit him or her in the future. This can be as basic as having a conversation with the student. It is, nevertheless, essential in helping the student see how the goal is relevant to his or her future growth and development. Especially for middle school students, seeing real-life context and useful applications can help maintain and increase motivation.

Teacher Tips

- Include your students in SMART goal setting by helping them identify each part of the goal (its specificity, measurability, and so on). After a discussion about the goal's significance, revise it if needed.

Day, T., and P. Tosey. "Beyond SMART? A New Framework for Goal Setting." *Curriculum Journal*, 22:4, 515–534 (2011).

Brainstorming

Area Addressed: Writing to Communicate

Strategy Summary

Brainstorming can be done as a collaborative process or individually. Use the following ideas to help students break the idea logjam.

1. **Freewriting.** Set a time limit or word count limit and have students spontaneously write until the limit is reached. Explain that in this process the writer does not judge the writing but simply writes as rapidly as possible, capturing any thoughts that come to mind on the topic. Afterward, have students review their freewriting to pick out any ideas, terms, or phrasing that might be incorporated into a writing assignment.

2. **Listing.** Each student selects a topic or theme based on an idea or key term connected to the writing assignment. Students then independently brainstorm lists of items that might relate to their topics. Finally, after a certain amount of time has elapsed, students review their lists to select items that might be useful in the assigned composition, or which trigger additional writing ideas.

3. **References.** Each student jots down key ideas or terms from the writing assignment. He or she then browses through various reference works (dictionaries, encyclopedias, specialized reference works on specific subjects, and so on) looking for entries that trigger useful ideas. Students can also try a variation of this strategy by typing assignment-related search terms into online search engines.

Teacher Tips

- This can help students generate topics for writing assignments and uncover new ideas. These can be saved for future writing topics.

- Each student could select a series of key terms or concepts linked to the writing assignment. Writers then brainstorm using the framework of a simile: "___ is like ___." The student plugs a key term into the first blank and generates as many similes as possible, and repeats this process with additional terms and ideas for further brainstorming.

University of North Carolina at Chapel Hill. "Brainstorming," *The Writing Center,* writingcenter.unc.edu /faculty-resources/tips-on-teaching-writing/in-class-writing-exercises (accessed June 16, 2014).

CALL UP Note-Taking

Area Addressed: Self-Management and Learning Strategies

Strategy Summary

Based on research from the University of Kansas Center for Research and Learning, this strategy is designed to be used by students while taking notes in class. This strategy helps students pay closer attention and be more focused on what is being discussed during class time. CALL UP is an acronym that stands for the following note-taking steps.

Steps

1. **Copy** from the board.

   - Listen and look for cue words or phrases that help you identify main ideas.
   - Copy the main ideas down on the left side of your paper, next to the margin. Underline these main ideas.

2. **Add** details.

   - Listen and look for pertinent details and add them to your notes.
   - Write down these details about one inch to the right of your paper's left-hand margin. Mark a line (-) in front of each detail.

3. **Listen** for questions and write them down.

   - Listen to the questions the teacher and students ask.
   - Write down a question if it helps your understanding.
   - Put a "Q" in front each question.
   - Indent each question under the main idea, about an inch from the margin (like the details).

4. **Listen** for answers and write them down.

   - Listen for the answer to each of the questions you've recorded. Write down these answers.
   - Put an "A" in front of the answer.
   - Indent each answer under the main idea.

5. **Utilize** the text.

   - Later, use your textbook to review and understand information.
   - Read or reread the main idea and details from the text as you've recorded them in your notes.

6. **Put** it in your own words.

   - Write the information you've learned in your own words as part of your notes.
   - Write your statements under the main idea. In the margin, record the page numbers where you found the information so you can easily reference it later.

Teacher Tips

- When students are learning this strategy, model it for the group a few times and help students memorize the steps. If desired, you can also offer feedback the first few times students use CALL UP Note-Taking to help them get accustomed to the process.

- To differentiate for students who need more or less support, use this strategy in tandem with a graphic organizer.

Czarnecke, E., D. Rosko, and E. Fine. "How to CALL UP Note-Taking Skills." *Teaching Exceptional Children,* 30, 14-19 (1998).

Conflicting Texts and Quotes

Area Addressed: Critical Thinking

Strategy Summary

This strategy gives students the opportunity to consider multiple sides to an issue, and helps them think through their rationale for how they form their opinions.

Steps

1. Choose two or more texts or quotes that conflict with each other. Examples include different interpretations of the same set of data, differing historical accounts, opinion articles, and so on.

2. Pair students to discuss the conflicting texts or quotes. Ask students to decide which side they agree with and why. Partners may or may not agree, but all students must choose a side and spend some time discussing the reasons for their views.

3. Once students have had time to explore the ideas in pairs, form two larger groups (or more, depending on how many sides to an issue exist), placing students with those who share the same views. These groups are not likely to be equal in size.

4. Each group collaborates to develop an argument supporting their point of view. When each group has created a clear and succinct position, have each group elect one or two members to lead a discussion. These discussion leaders will explain how their group's members interpreted the text or quote, provide clear explanations of their group's position, and describe the reasoning behind it.

5. Give groups the chance to respond to one another's views. This might mean asking for clarification, providing counterarguments, or fleshing out certain points. You may want to provide a set amount of time for these responses.

6. Following the discussion, ask all students to write brief reflections discussing whether they changed their minds about the conflicting text or quotes, and why or why not.

Teacher Tips

- Model respectful debate and disagreement for students. The goal of this strategy is not necessarily for students to convince or persuade each other, but to spark productive discussion and give students a chance to hear and consider different points of view.

- If there are only two sides to consider, this strategy can be combined with Take a Side (page 193).

Adapted from *Academic Conversations: Classroom Talk That Fosters Critical Thinking and Content Understandings* by Jeff Zwiers and Marie Crawford. Portland, ME: Stenhouse, 2011.

CRA

Area Addressed: Critical Thinking

Strategy Summary

CRA is an acronym standing for Concrete, Representational, and Abstract. The CRA strategy was originally designed to support learning of abstract mathematical concepts through concrete and representational teaching. However, its steps can be generalized to fit other content areas, as well.

Steps

1. Identify a key abstract concept in your lesson or unit of study to discuss with the class.

2. Match abstract ideas with appropriate concrete and representational depictions. For example, when studying math, you might start with the concrete (physical manipulatives such as blocks) and move to the representational (a drawing or diagram) and the abstract (numbers and symbols only). In other areas of study, you might choose to move in the opposite direction, taking an abstract concept such as bravery and depicting it representationally (through a symbol of bravery such as a lion, for example) and concretely (through a detailed written account or role play of a person being brave). While the "concrete" part of CRA is often not literally physical when this strategy is used outside of math, thinking about an abstract concept in these multiple ways will help students develop their critical thinking and analytical skills.

3. Ask students to explain their thinking and the connections between concrete, representational, and abstract concepts and ideas.

Teacher Tips

- CRA is a flexible strategy that can be used for any abstract concept that can be represented in a concrete way.

- CRA can be challenging initially. However, with practice, the process of making abstract concepts more concrete will help students build understanding and will give them tools to approach complex content that may be unfamiliar or intimidating at first.

Witzel, B.S., P.J. Riccomini, and E. Schneider. "Implementing CRA with Secondary Students with Learning Disabilities in Mathematics." *Intervention in School and Clinic,* 43:5, 270–276 (2008).

Forced Freewriting

Area Addressed: *Writing to Communicate*

Strategy Summary

The idea behind this strategy is that if students write freely, keeping their pencils moving for a set amount of time, they will document their thoughts, ask questions, and formulate an opinion about a text in a free-flowing, spontaneous, and productive way.

Steps

1. Begin the activity by instructing the students to listen to an oral reading of thought-provoking text. The selected text can be an article, poem, excerpt from a book, or essay. The passage should take no longer than 10 minutes to read aloud. Explain to students that they just need to listen at this point, and that they will have a chance to respond after the passage has been read.

2. After the reading, tell students to write down any thoughts, questions, or connections to other texts or events that came to their minds. In a forced freewrite, the only rule is that the pencil or pen needs to keep moving. Give students 10 minutes for the freewrite.

3. Following the freewrite, place students in groups of three to five. Ask each student to share a thought or question that came out of the freewriting experience and discuss it with the group.

4. Finally, ask students to write their opinion of or response to the text in a one- to three-paragraph paper.

Teacher Tips

- During the freewrite, students can write in narrative form or use notes, thinking maps, or other organizers to document their thoughts, questions, and connections.

- This activity can be modified for many different subject areas to encourage writing across the curriculum.

Probst, R. "Tom Sawyer, Teaching, and Talking." In *Adolescent Literacy,* edited by K. Beers, R.E. Probst, and L. Rief. Portsmouth, NH: Heinnemann, 2007.

Fountas & Pinnell Leveled Literacy Intervention System*

Areas Addressed: Word Recognition/Reading Fluency

Program Summary

Originally designed for students in the early grades, the Fountas & Pinnell Leveled Literacy Intervention System (LLI) has now been extended to the upper grades. LLI is a small-group, supplementary intervention program designed to help teachers provide daily, small-group reading instruction for students. Lessons address multiple areas of literacy development including word recognition, reading fluency, vocabulary, and comprehension.

Teacher Tips

- This commercially produced program is designed to be used with small groups of students who need intensive support to achieve grade-level competency. When using this program, choose the system designed for a student's reading level, not necessarily his or her grade level. If there is a large discrepancy between reading level and grade level, it is important to be sensitive to the fact that texts might not be high-interest. If this is the case, make sure students have access to high-interest books written at their reading level during silent reading time or at other points during the day.

- English language learners can also benefit from LLI.

- A summary of the research base for Leveled Literacy Interventions can be found at www.heinemann.com/fountasandpinnell/research/LLI_3_8_ResearchBase.pdf.

Manset-Williamson, G., and J.M. Nelson. "Balanced, Strategic Reading Instruction for Upper-Elementary and Middle School Students with Reading Disabilities: A Comparative Study of Two Approaches." *Learning Disabilities Quarterly,* 28:1, 59–65 (2005).

Frayer Model

Area Addressed: Language and Vocabulary Development

Strategy Summary

The purpose of this strategy is to increase students' skills in word analysis while building vocabulary. The Frayer model is a graphic organizer that prompts students to describe and elucidate the meaning of a word or concept in a lesson or unit of study. The model consists of four squares that students fill in with the following information in the following order:

- **Upper Left:** A definition of the term in the student's own words
- **Upper Right:** A description of the term's essential characteristics
- **Lower Left:** Examples of the term or concept
- **Lower Right:** Non-examples of the term or concept

Steps

1. Explain to your class how to use the Frayer model graphic organizer. Model the type and quality of desired answers when providing this explanation.

2. Select a list of key concepts or words from a reading selection. Write this list on the board and review it with the class before students read the text.

3. Divide the class into peer pairs. Assign each pair one of the key concepts or words and have them read the selection carefully to define this concept or word. Have the pairs work together to complete the four-square organizer for their concepts.

4. Ask the pairs to share their conclusions with the entire class. Use these presentations to review the entire list of key concepts or words.

Teacher Tips

- Look online for examples of the Frayer model in use.
- This activity can be modified for many different subject areas.
- The emphasis of this strategy is on increasing lesson-related vocabulary while also broadening understanding of concepts embedded in the text.

Frayer, D., W.C. Frederick, and H.J. Klausmeier. *A Schema for Testing the Level of Cognitive Mastery.* Madison, WI: Wisconsin Center for Education Research, 1969.

Goal-Setting Protocol

Area Addressed: *Self-Management and Learning Strategies*

Strategy Summary

This protocol was originally designed by Jay Davis for National School Reform Harmony, to be used school-wide. However, it can also be implemented at the classroom level. This strategy would be most useful at the beginning of a unit of study, or when embarking on a major class project that incorporates both small groups and individual work.

Steps

1. Make sure that students understand the basic overview of the study unit or project, and how the goal-setting protocol will interact with it. Remind students that this protocol's structure ensures that individual goals and group goals are both being met.

2. Have students independently brainstorm lists of goals that align with the relevant project or unit of study. The goals should relate to group work and also to students' individual learning needs. This independent brainstorming time is also a good opportunity for students to create a list of reading that relates to the project.

   #### Individual Goals

   - *Example:* One of my personal goals is to learn the firsthand stories of Holocaust survivors.

Group Work Goals

- *Example:* One of the group goals is to collaborate to create a timeline of World War II.

Reading Topics

- *Example:* I would like to read *The Diary of Anne Frank* as well as fictional books set during World War II.

These three categories should also be written on a whiteboard or other surface visible to the whole class, heading three separate columns. Encourage students to list as many things as they can in each column during their solo brainstorming.

3. Place students in three-person groups and give them 15 minutes to discuss their brainstormed lists, with each person talking for about 5 minutes. If desired, students can revise or extend their own lists of goals after listening to their peers.

4. Have each student write one individual goal on the board with his or her name next to it. Students can list their ideas for group goals and topics from their reading lists, as well. Students can once again revise their lists if this step has sparked new ideas. Ask students to indicate which group goals interest them most by placing a dot and their initials on the board next to their preferred ideas.

5. Create groups based on shared interests and complementary goals. Help students craft project guidelines to indicate individual student responsibilities (based on individual goals) as well as shared group goals.

Davis, J. "Goal Setting Protocol," *National School Reform Faculty,* www.nsrfharmony.org/protocol/doc /goal_setting.pdf (accessed June 17, 2014).

High-Preference Strategy

Area Addressed: *Self-Management and Learning Strategies*

Strategy Summary

This strategy focuses on students' preferred and/or most easily completed problems in mathematics. The purpose of using the high-preference strategy is to ease students into tasks to increase their completion of work and to maximize the time they have to complete given tasks. Over time, this helps students gain confidence and build their problem-solving skills, even when they encounter tasks that are more difficult or unwelcome.

1. Determine students' high-preference math problems.

   a. Observe students during math.

   b. Notice which problems they are doing and which they are skipping.

   c. Conference with students and discuss their high-preferred and low-preferred problems.

2. Develop practice work that includes both high-preferred and low-preferred problems. Be sure to provide two or three high-preference problems before presenting low-preference problems.

3. Instruct students to complete all problems as promptly as possible.

4. Once student work is complete, provide feedback.

Teacher Tips

- For a given task, design high- and low-preference problems that are similar, such as high-preferred addition problems alongside non-preferred addition problems.

- Collect frequency data and determine task complete rate (total number of problems correct divided by the time) to determine if strategy is useful for each student. Monitor this task complete rate over time and make adjustments according to student progress.

Banda, D.R., R.M. Matuszny, and W.J. Therrien. "Enhancing Motivation to Complete Math Tasks Using the High-Preference Strategy." *Intervention in School and Clinic,* 44:3, 146–150 (2009).

How Do You Know?

Area Addressed: Critical Thinking

Strategy Summary

This strategy involves explicitly teaching students the powerful process of inference—combining prior knowledge with textual clues to draw logical conclusions.

Steps

1. Explain to students that they are going to learn a new way to understand text by making inferences.

2. Model the strategy by reading a section of text aloud and stopping at a place where an inference could be made and would be productive.

3. Ask a question that prompts students to infer relevant information. For example, "How do you think this character would feel about [a related current event in the news]?"

4. When students respond, challenge them to explain their rationale by asking, "How do you know?" You can follow up with related questions such as, "Does the author say that outright? What clues in the text did you use to draw that conclusion?"

5. When students are familiar with the strategy, ask them more open-ended questions. Rather than asking for a target answer, say, "Are there any inferences you can make in this paragraph?" Again, follow up by asking students to talk about their thought process. "Explain how you made those connections."

Teacher Tips

- Before introducing this questioning strategy, preselect quality texts to identify types of inferential connections that could be made.

- Student discussions about their inferences provide opportunities for English language learners to hear peers' language and consider different views and ways of thinking.

Richards, J.C., and N.A. Anderson. "How Do You Know? A Strategy to Help Emergent Readers Make Inferences." *The Reading Teacher,* 57:3, 290 (2003).

Interactive Read-Aloud

Area Addressed: *Critical Thinking*

Strategy Summary

In their book *Planning and Managing Effective Reading Instruction Across the Content Areas*, Deborah Corpus and Ann Giddings explain the benefits of the interactive read-aloud strategy for students through grade eight. Depending on how teachers frame their questions, this strategy can be used to address many potential areas of difficulty, such as language and vocabulary and reading comprehension. Whatever the area targeted, Interactive Read-Aloud will *always* call for critical thinking on behalf of students. The following steps define the lesson planning logistics for each stage of an interactive read-aloud. Pick and choose from these questions to put together a list that fits your class and your students, and use these questions before, during, and after reading, and also when revisiting the text.

Before you share the read-aloud, what will you do to engage students' interest and curiosity? Will you

- pose a problem?
- do a picture walk?
- set up a graphic organizer?
- provide an emotional hook of some kind?

During the read-aloud, what will you do to keep the students engaged? Will you

- use "turn and talk" at key points?
- stop to fill in a graphic organizer?
- pose questions or ask for responses?
- make connections to knowledge from other sources related to the book?
- have students participate by reading a refrain?
- have students sketch what they are visualizing?

After you finish reading, what will you do to be sure the message has stuck? Will you

- complete a graphic organizer?
- have students do a quick-write?
- make connections to what students have learned or will learn in the content areas?
- share related materials?
- play a game using the information from the text?
- chart the reading strategies used during the reading?
- add to a running review of new information about the content area or the reading processes studied in class?

Teacher Tips

- Customize each interactive read-aloud based on your instructional objectives, the text, and the individual needs of your students.

- A quick-write, as suggested in the "After Reading" activities, is an exercise in which you ask students to freewrite for a short time—fewer than 10 minutes—in response to an open-ended question or prompt related to the reading.

- Consider connecting the "After Reading" activities to the "Before Reading" activities. For example, if you lead students in an anticipation guide (page 150) at the pre-reading stage, come back to it after the reading has ended.

- When using a "turn and talk," simply ask students to turn to someone nearby and briefly talk about the topic or question being covered in class.

Adapted from *Planning and Managing Effective Reading Instruction Across Content Areas* by Deborah Corpus and Ann Giddings. Copyright © 2010 by Deborah Corpus and Ann Giddings. Reprinted by permission of Scholastic Inc.

Interactive Word Wall

Area Addressed: Language and Vocabulary Development

Strategy Summary

The interactive word wall strategy is aimed at expanding and deepening vocabulary. Words can be displayed on an actual wall, dedicating different wall space to different classes. Or you can create a digital "wall" using Web applications such as Padlet.com or software such as PowerPoint. To implement an interactive word wall in your classroom, use the following steps as a guide.

Steps

1. **Establish background knowledge.** First, students must determine their current level of vocabulary knowledge. Ask each student to choose which of the following three statements applies to his or her knowledge of each word.

   - I have never seen this word.
   - I have seen this word, but I don't know what it means.
   - I have seen this word and it has something to do with [fill in blank].

2. **Explore the word further.** As needed, have students look up the word's definition in a dictionary (standard or online). Prompt students with guiding questions about the usefulness of the word; multiple meanings or connotations it might have; the word's prefixes, suffixes, identifiable roots; and so on. For additional exploration, group students and assign different words to each group. Each group prepares a definition, synonyms, antonyms, and examples of assigned word(s). If desired, students can also draw pictures next to the words to help them remember meanings.

3. **Apply the word to real situations.**

   - Group members brainstorm real-life situations or contexts related to the word.
   - Use the target word in sentences about these real-life scenarios.

4. **Present findings to the class.**

   - All groups reconvene as a whole class to explain their discussion and findings.
   - Display group work (definitions; lists of synonyms and antonyms; sentences using the words; drawings illustrating the words) on the word wall.

- Extend each group's findings with group discussion about the words.

Teacher Tips

- This strategy can be used in all content areas, including math, science, and foreign languages.

Harmon, J., K. Wood, W. Hedrick, J. Vintinner, and T. Willeford. "Interactive Word Walls: More than Just Reading the Writing on the Walls." *Journal of Adolescent & Adult Literacy,* 52:5, 398–408 (2009).

Interview Grids

Area Addressed: *Inquiry and Research*

Strategy Summary

The Interview Grids activity is a way for students to gather information from peers and to develop, practice, and strengthen their paraphrasing skills. Using a matrix similar to the one depicted as follows, students move around the classroom talking with other students. For example, if your class is studying early civilizations, your interview grid could be filled out in the following way:

- Explain the factors that influenced the movement of people, goods, and ideas and the effects of that movement on societies and regions over time.

- Compare the availability of resources versus the scarcity of resources and their effects on the migration and settlement of people.

- Argue why the needs of early man did or did not result in the development of technology.

All of the prompts will require students being questioned to reflect and think critically about the answers, rather than simply reporting basic information. Examples that work well are prompts that begin with words and phrases such as compare and contrast; explain; argue; and so on.

Student Name	Explain . . .	Compare _____ and _____	Argue why . . .
Lia			
Paolo			
Kristen			

After 20 to 30 minutes have passed, have students meet in small groups and share the information they've collected. Restating classmates' thoughts about and understanding of a topic relevant to a unit of study helps all students solidify their own knowledge base, think in new ways about what they're learning, and gain insight into the research process.

Teacher Tips

- Teach students to monitor their tone of voice and body language when reporting back to their small group, making sure that they are being respectful of one another's viewpoints.

- Model how students can effectively connect their findings as they report by using terms such as "on the other hand," "similarly," "based on data I collected," and so on.

Adapted from Academic Conversations: Classroom Talk That Fosters Critical Thinking and Content Understandings by Jeff Zwiers and Marie Crawford. Portland, ME: Stenhouse, 2011.

Joke Books

Area Addressed: *Reading Fluency*

Strategy Summary

Joke books can be a fun way to increase fluency, and specifically prosody (reading with expressiveness, appropriate inflection, and natural flow). To use joke books as a way to improve prosody, have each student choose a joke and read it. Next, have the student identify what he or she sees as the source of the joke's humor. Have a conversation about why the humor works, acknowledging that humor is highly subjective and that people have different senses of humor. Finally, have the student reread the joke, changing emphasis if necessary to focus on humorous words or to improve the joke's timing.

Teacher Tips

- Discuss both the joke itself and the student's delivery of the joke. The Two Plus One Reflection Log (page 129) could be used to privately offer constructive feedback, with the student filling out one log and the teacher filling out another, followed by a brief meeting to discuss both sets of comments.

- Talk to students about how punctuation can guide delivery and affect a reader's voice, word emphasis, timing, and expression. Consider how these changes can impact a joke's effectiveness.

- As an extension of this strategy, set up a class "Comedy Hour." Have students practice their jokes in preparation for the Comedy Hour. This practice will naturally incorporate repeated reading, which helps build fluency.

Ness, M. "Laughing Through Rereading: Using Joke Books to Build Fluency." *Reading Teacher,* 62:8, 691–694 (2009).

Kinesthetic Writing, of Sorts

Area Addressed: *Writing to Communicate*

Strategy Summary

This strategy, developed by Kirstin Bittel and Darrek Hernandez, focuses on kinesthetic learners and the writing process used to document science experiments. The strategy works by segmenting the writing process using a flipbook and sentence starters. This approach ensures that all parts of the experiment are documented for the teacher to evaluate, and also helps students work on sentence variation.

Steps

1. Before constructing the flipbook, provide students with sentence starters or brainstorm starters as a class and list them on the board. Students can then include these in

their flipbooks under the appropriate flaps. Examples of sentence starters for a science lab might be:

- Today's objective was . . .
- For example, . . .
- Scientists often use _____ as a way to determine _____.
- Today in the lab we . . .
- To gather our evidence, we . . .
- I measured . . .
- We calculated . . .
- For example . . .
- I learned . . .
- I discovered . . .
- In conclusion, I found . . .

2. To make the flipbooks, give students three half sheets of paper and have them lay the sheets on top of each other, vertically oriented. Students shift the top sheet of paper down so its top edge is an inch or so lower than the top edge of the middle sheet. Repeat with the middle sheet, so its top edge is an inch or so below the top edge of the bottom sheet. Fold the stack of papers from the bottom, folding upwards along a horizontal line about an inch below the middle of the top sheet of paper, so that when folded the top sheet's bottom edge is about an inch below its top edge. Then staple along the fold.

3. Instruct the students to label the flaps of the flipbook as follows:

- Top flap: Scientific conclusion
- 2nd flap: What was the objective?
- 3rd flap: Briefly, what did you do?
- 4th flap: What evidence do you have?
- 5th flap: What did you learn?
- 6th flap: Sample conclusion

4. Under flaps 2 through 5, have students list appropriate sentence starters that could be used to answer each question. (Students don't all need to use the same starters.) Under the 6th flap, have them write a sample conclusion paragraph that exemplifies strong writing. If desired, you can create this sample as a whole class before using the flipbooks. Students can then refer to this model as they write their own conclusions after each experiment.

5. As students carry out an experiment in class, they will make notes on their findings. At the close of the experiment, they can use the flipbook's questions and sentence starters to craft a well-written conclusion summarizing their investigation and its findings.

Teacher Tips

- This strategy can be adapted to other content areas, including math and foreign languages.

Bittel, K., and D. Hernandez. "Kinesthetic Writing, of Sorts." *Scientific Scope*, 29:7, 37–39 (2006).

KWL-Plus

Area Addressed: Self-Management and Learning Strategies

Strategy Summary

KWL-Plus is a strategy that helps students organize information as they read to support better comprehension and retention. KWL-Plus is an acronym that stands for:

Knowledge: What do I already know about this topic?

Want: What do I want to learn?

Learn: What have I learned?

Plus: At each step, students make notes about the topic and categorize details based on related ideas. For example, if the topic being studied is a group of animals, categories might include *habitat, diet, behavior*, and so on. These categories could be provided by the teacher or chosen by the students. After reading, students summarize what they have learned.

Once they are familiar with the strategy, students can use KWL-Plus independently or in small groups to organize their notes and increase their comprehension of text. As they're getting familiar with this strategy, you can offer them support and feedback by carrying out the following steps as a whole class.

Steps

1. On the board or overhead, create three columns under the headings K, W, and L.

2. Activate students' prior knowledge about the topic of study, and write student responses on the board under the K column.

3. Initiate the Plus component by asking students to categorize information from the K column.

4. Have students ask themselves what they want to know. Write their questions under the W column.

5. Prior to reading the text—either as a group or independently—choose stopping points for discussion. Tell students to listen or look for answers to their questions.

6. At each stopping point, students discuss the questions answered and any other new information learned.

7. Once you've completed the reading, categorize information in the L column by using categories from the K column and additional categories as needed.

8. To further organize students' thoughts about the topic, create a graphic outline or display of information using the categorized information from the L column.

9. Number the categories in all of the columns in order of importance and have students use this information to summarize the text out loud or in writing.

Teacher Tips

- Students can use the KWL-Plus strategy in peer pairs, in flexible groups, or as a whole group.

- KWL-Plus can be applied to all content areas.

Headly, K.N., and P.J. Dunston. "Teachers Choose Books and Comprehension Strategies as Transaction Tools." *The Reading Teacher,* 54:3, 260–268 (2000).

LINCS + VOC

Area Addressed: *Language and Vocabulary Development*

Strategy Summary

This teaching strategy brings together two tools which, in combination, help students visualize and organize information as a way of increasing vocabulary. The memory enhancement techniques associated with the combination of these two approaches encourage students to use prior knowledge, keyword mnemonic devices, and visual imagery to create vocabulary-building study cards.

Steps

1. At the beginning of a lesson or unit of study, identify new vocabulary words from related text and list these words on the board. Have students write each word on the top front half of an index card.

2. Instruct students to find each new word in the lesson's text and copy down an exact sentence used in the text on the bottom front half of the card.

3. Have students consult "experts" to learn each word's definition. This might mean talking with a friend who is familiar with the word, asking a teacher the word's meaning, or using another source. Students will then write down these definitions on the top back half of their index cards.

4. Instruct students to compose short stories to remind themselves of each word— without using the word itself in the story. They will write these stories down on the bottom back half of their cards. If desired, students can also draw simple pictures next to their stories as an additional reminder of the relevant word's meaning.

5. Have students self-test daily using the cards until they are able to easily use the words in context.

Teacher Tips

- This activity can be completed by the whole class, small groups, or individuals.

- Students can practice using the vocabulary cards individually, in pairs, or in small groups.

- Encourage students to use their vocabulary cards as cues during writing exercises related to the lesson or unit of study.

Billmeyer, R., and M.L. Barton. *Teaching Reading in the Content Areas: If Not Me, Then Who?* Alexandria, VA: ASCD, 1998.

Ellis, E.S. *The LINCS Vocabulary Strategy.* Lawrence, KS: Edge Enterprises, 2000.

Literature Circles

Area Addressed: *Language and Vocabulary Development*

Strategy Summary

Literature Circles are a guided approach to student-led discussions of both nonfiction and fiction literature. The strategy brings together groups of three to five readers who gather to discuss what they have read. Initially, students take turns at specific "jobs" to guide discussion and practice the application of key reading comprehension strategies. After they have learned these strategies for analyzing and discussing text, the jobs can be phased out to allow for a more free-flowing discussion.

Steps

1. Select four or five different texts of similar length, and present them to the class.

2. Let students submit their first, second, and third choices of texts. Place students in groups of three to five, depending on class size, based on students' interest in the books presented.

3. Divide each text into equal parts.

4. Schedule one class day for reading each section of the text, and one day for discussing each section. Continue this rotation until all parts of the text have been read and discussed. Depending on how much class time you want to use, you may also assign students to read the text at home, and only hold the discussion in class.

5. The following jobs are assigned to members of the group for each discussion day and rotate throughout the course of the strategy so each student has an opportunity to do each job. Assign jobs on or before each reading day (whether reading takes place in class or at home) so that students can keep their roles in mind as they read.

   Depending on student needs, content area, and chosen texts, you may not use all of these jobs with your class. You can also create your own, based on comprehension strategies you are teaching. Explain each job to students before using the strategy. Sample jobs include:

   - *Discussion Director:* This student is responsible for developing questions regarding the text and asking these questions of fellow group members to keep the discussion flowing.

   - *Vocabulary Master:* This student is responsible for identifying and defining new or interesting words.

   - *Literary Luminary:* This student is responsible for highlighting and explaining key events or important information.

   - *Connector:* This student is responsible for making connections between the text being read and other readings, current events, and/or group members' prior experiences.

   - *Illustrator/Mapper:* This student is responsible for creating a visual representation of a key event or other information from the text.

6. On reading days (whether in class or at home), students read the text and prepare for the discussion based on their individual jobs. On discussion days, students focus on their specific jobs as they carry out a discussion on the reading.

Teacher Tips

- Students can help determine the jobs used in the Literature Circles activity based on what they find challenging or interesting about reading new texts.

- Monitor group discussions and provide feedback as needed. If a group is not discussing the text appropriately, you may need to sit in and model leadership skills at keeping the discussion on track, respectful, and productive. You could also assign a student to take this role.

- Follow-up or extension activities can be developed after the entire text has been read. These might include role plays, visual projects, written reports, presentations, creative writing inspired by texts, or other projects.

- The effectiveness of Literature Circles hinges on its replication of authentic book clubs in ways that motivate learners by giving them choice, agency, and responsibility—choice of books, personal response through discussion, and a responsibility to contribute to the discussion.

- To read more about implementing Literature Circles, see *Literature Circles: Voice and Choice in Book Clubs and Reading Groups* by Harvey Daniels (Stenhouse Publishers, 2002).

Daniels, H. "What's the Next Big Thing with Literature Circles?" *Voices from the Middle,* 13:4, 10–15 (2006).

Making Choices

Area Addressed: *Self-Management and Learning Strategies*

Strategy Summary

Making Choices provides opportunities for students to make decisions about their own work, which is effective in minimizing inappropriate behaviors, strengthening appropriate responses, and increasing levels of engagement for students. Above all else, this strategy gives students the power to make choices and effectively manage themselves in the classroom. Consider the following opportunities for students to make choices in the classroom:

- **Select when to begin a task.** Provide the overall due date for task completion, but give the students the option to start working on the task immediately or to delay the start date. This will teach students time-management skills and help them determine how they work best.

- **Choose to take short breaks from the task.** Set the total amount of time allocated for the task and allow the students to set a schedule within that timeframe that includes breaks with specific time limits.

- **Select the materials or tools used to complete task.** Have students make lists of the materials and tools they feel they need to complete the task.

- **Select the order in which to complete the task's steps.** Depending on the needs of your students, provide a list of steps needed to complete the task and allow the students to put the steps in the correct order, or provide the students the task and have them break it down into steps themselves.

- **Select a peer or peers with whom to work on the task.** Have each student list three classmates with whom he or she would like to work. Try to give students their first choice if possible and reasonable.

- **Select where in the room to complete the task.** While students are identifying their timelines, ask them also to include the location where they will complete the task.

- **Select methods or strategies to use in completing the task.** Provide a list of potential strategies or methods from which students might choose to successfully complete their task.

Teacher Tips

- If desired, you can create a menu of choices for students in advance.

- Consider and plan for different thinking styles and learning preferences when planning choices.

- Students will need guidance when first implementing this strategy. Make sure the stakes are low and they do not have a significant impact on their overall grade if they make mistakes. Then you can gradually increase the level of responsibility and the level of consequences.

Jolivette, K., K. McCormick, and J. Stichter. "Making Choices—Improving Behavior—Engaging in Learning." *Teaching Exceptional Children,* 34:3, 24-29 (2002).

Mnemonic Devices

Area Addressed: *Self-Management and Learning Strategies*

Strategy Summary

Many types of mnemonic devices can be used to support learning, studying, and memorization. Follow these key steps to successfully guide your students in the use of mnemonic devices.

Steps

1. Identify students' memory challenges and/or deficits.

2. Distinguish curriculum areas where mnemonics can be used to enhance memory.

3. Discuss and model mnemonic strategies with students.

4. Evaluate the effectiveness of the strategy.

5. Conference with students after they've had several chances to use their mnemonic devices. Talk about what worked well and what could improve.

6. Help students learn ways to generalize mnemonic strategies to varied tasks and different content areas.

7. Continuously monitor students' use of their mnemonic devices, and evaluate how effective the strategies are. Work with students to improve strategies as necessary.

Types of mnemonic devices include the following. Explain and show examples of each type to students.

Letter Strategies

- Acronym: Create a word or words by merging the first letters of a series of words. For instance, ROY G. BIV is a common mnemonic to remember the order of colors in a rainbow (or the visible spectrum): Red, Orange, Yellow, Green, Blue, Indigo, Violet.

- Acrostics: Use the first letter of each word in a sentence to represent information to be remembered. For instance, an acrostic to remember the names of the eight full-fledged planets in order from the sun could be: "My Very Educated Mother Just Served Us Nachos" (Mercury, Venus, Earth, Mars, Jupiter, Saturn, Uranus, and Neptune).

Keywords

- In the keyword method, students choose words that are associated in one way or another with the target information to be remembered. This method ties new information to prior knowledge, and increases the concreteness and meaningfulness of the newly acquired information. It can be used in the following steps:

  1. *Sound:* Students choose keywords that sound similar to the target terms and are concrete enough to be easily pictured.

2. *Scenario:* Students imagine scenarios incorporating the keywords in a concrete way, either in an image, a sentence, a sequence of events, or similar.

3. *Retrieval:* Students retrieve the target information by thinking of the keywords and recalling the visual or sentence and what is happening in the scenario.

Teacher Tips

• Mnemonic devices can be used in a variety of settings: whole group, small groups, or one-on-one intervention.

• This strategy can be easily used in any content area.

Kleinheksel, K.A., and S.E. Summy. "Enhancing Student Learning and Social Behavior Through Mnemonic Strategies." *Teaching Exceptional Children,* 36, 30–35 (2003).

Pattern Sorts

Area Addressed: *Word Recognition*

Strategy Summary

This teaching strategy helps students recognize common patterns in words.

Steps

1. List a variety of words that share common patterns such as vowel digraphs, affixes, Greek and Latin roots, and so on.

2. Ask students what these words have in common.

3. Have the students do an open sort or a closed sort. In an open sort, students sort the words without being provided with specific categories, while in a closed sort they place the words in predetermined categories.

4. Once the words have been sorted, discuss their common features. For example, they might share a root, such as in the words *destruction, constructed,* and *instructive.* Ask students to consider what this information can tell them about the words' meaning or use. This analysis of word parts and patterns is helpful for word recognition and vocabulary development.

Teacher Tips

• This activity can be done to review previous patterns that have been introduced in combination with a newly introduced pattern.

• Students can complete the pattern sort in pairs, in small groups, or as a whole class.

Gillet, J., and M.J. Kita. "Words, Kids, and Categories." *The Reading Teacher,* 32, 538–546 (1979).

Templeton, S., F. Johnston, D. Bear, and M. Invernizzi. *Words Their Way: Word Sorts for Derivational Relations Spellers.* Boston: Allyn and Bacon, 2009.

PIRATES

Strategy Summary

The PIRATES strategy is one of the many components of the Strategic Instruction Model (SIM), an instructional system designed by Deshler and Schumaker. PIRATES is a test-taking strategy, and its letters form an acronym standing for the following steps to help students complete tests independently and successfully:

Steps

1. **Prepare**

   - Prepare to succeed.
   - Write your name and the word PIRATES on your test paper.
   - Make decisions about managing your time and about the order in which you'll work on the test.
   - Make positive statements to yourself about the test, such as "I can do this."

2. **Inspect**

   - Inspect the instructions.
   - Read all instructional text carefully.
   - Underline key words.

3. **Read, Remember, and Reduce**

   - Read all questions and choices.
   - Remember what you studied in preparation for this test.
   - Reduce the number of possible answers by eliminating the ones you know are incorrect.

4. **Answer or Abandon**

   - Answer all questions that are known.
   - Abandon questions that you're unsure about.

5. **Turn Back**

   - Go back to abandoned questions.
   - Reread the abandoned questions and the possible answers (if it's a multiple-choice test).

6. **Estimate**

   - Answer questions for which you now know the answers after further reflection.
   - Make your best guess at answers to questions you're still unsure about.

7. **Survey**

   - Look over the whole test.
   - Make sure every question is answered.
   - Make sure all your answers are neat and legible.

Teacher Tips

- Model and practice the PIRATES strategy with students before gradually releasing responsibility and having students use this approach independently.

- As needed throughout the semester or school year, periodically review the PIRATES steps, especially before major standardized tests.

Deshler, D.D., J.C. Lancaster, P.E. Lancaster, and J.B. Schumaker. "The Efficacy of an Interactive Hypermedia Program for Teaching a Test-Taking Strategy for Students with High-Incidence Disabilities." *Journal of Special Education Technology,* 21:2, 17–30 (2006).

Possible Sentences

Area Addressed: *Reading Comprehension*

Strategy Summary

The purpose of this strategy is to improve students' understanding of text and key concepts presented within the text, and to give students practice in using vocabulary to make predictions about content. Introduce this strategy by explaining and modeling how to make possible sentences using the following steps.

Steps

1. Choose six to eight words from the text that may be difficult for students. List these words on the board.

2. Choose an additional four to six words from the text that may be more familiar to students and list these on the board, as well.

3. Define all of the listed words. If possible, let students do this by using their background knowledge.

4. Have students (individually or in small groups) develop sentences using at least two of the listed words in each sentence. Write all contributed sentences on the board.

5. Ask students to read the text to confirm, modify, or extend the information on the board.

6. After reading, revisit the original sentences and revise as needed. As needed, add any new information to the listed words and definitions.

7. Have students use the revised list as the basis for creating summaries of the content. Talk about how identifying new terms can help them predict what they will learn from a text.

Teacher Tips

- Students can implement this strategy before and after reading text.

- This strategy can be scaffolded for individual students or small groups of students based on the background knowledge they bring to the activity.

- This strategy can be modified for many different subject areas to encourage writing and vocabulary use across the curriculum.

McLaughlin, M., and M. Allen. *Guided Comprehension: A Teaching Model for Grades 3–8.* Newark, DE: International Reading Association, 2002.

The Process Approach

Area Addressed: Writing to Communicate

Strategy Summary

This strategy models a three-stage process of writing research papers, reports, and other compositions:

1. The planning stage

2. The draft stage

3. The evaluation and revision stage

Model this three-phase process often in groups before students practice independently.

Steps

1. **Selection.** Introduce the planning stage by selecting the topic and type of compositions students will write, which might include descriptive, compare and contrast, or opinion papers.

2. **Prewriting.** Work with students to brainstorm ideas that could appear in their compositions. Prewriting can involve examining what students already know about a topic, making a plan for research, or arranging ideas in a visual way. Explain to students that even though they will be writing individual papers, the collaborative brainstorming session is meant to generate ideas and form the basis of their prewriting plans. Summarize the brainstormed ideas and list them on the board. Model self-questions such as: "Can I give an example of this? Does the reader need to know more about this? What would be the best way to order these pieces of information?"

3. **Supporting information.** Prompt students for information that will support the ideas the group has listed. This information will include facts, details, reasons, examples, and so on. Highlight the main ideas that are formulated.

4. **Prewriting plan.** Discuss ideas generated in Step 2 and fleshed out in Step 3. Guide students to ask themselves questions such as, "What am I going to say about this?" and to take notes on their answers. Remind writers that all comments can be clarified or restated later. These questions and answers should help students identify frameworks and approaches for their writing.

5. **Teacher-directed group draft (optional).** Using the prewriting plan, work with students to write a draft composition on the board. This step is only recommended for the first time you are using the process approach. Students can then apply changes to their individual "first pass" papers based on lessons learned from the group draft.

6. **The first pass.** Introduce the draft stage, at which point students will begin writing their own individual papers. Emphasize that this will be the "first pass" at developing ideas and structure, and that students don't need to worry about striving for perfection at this stage.

7. **Critical analysis.** Introduce the evaluation and revision stage. Have students read their compositions as if for the first time. Have them use the questions and answers raised by this step to revise their drafts.

8. Editing. Model self-questioning to help students assess their final drafts. Good questions include: "Does the way I organized the information make sense? Does this paper help the reader better understand my topic? Is my paper free of technical errors such as grammatical and spelling mistakes?"

Teacher Tips

- Modeling this strategy will help students begin to use the process on their own as they plan and write papers across content areas.

- Students at all levels will benefit from this strategy's flexible, practical routine of planning, writing, and reviewing compositions.

Vallecorsa, A.L., R.R. Ledford, and G.G. Parnell. "Strategies for Teaching Composition Skills to Students with Learning Disabilities." *Teaching Exceptional Children*, 13, 52–55 (1991).

PROVE-ing What You Know

Area Addressed: Critical Thinking

Strategy Summary

PROVE-ing is a strategy developed by David Scanlon and designed to support students in retelling, explaining, and defending their understanding. PROVE also guides students to seek additional information about concepts they don't fully understand. PROVE is an acronym that stands for Present, Reveal, Offer, Verify, and Express.

Steps

1. **Present:** Present the knowledge I will prove.

   This step cues the student to begin his or her inquiry by stating a proposition or hypothesis.

2. **Reveal:** Reveal information to support my knowledge.

   This step asks the student to provide a rationale statement behind the proposition, explaining his or her thinking.

3. **Offer:** Offer evidence to support my knowledge.

   This stage supports the "R" step by requiring the student to give further information or details demonstrating that the proposition is correct and why.

4. **Verify:** Verify my knowledge.

   This step asks the student to provide an explanation or example that supports the "R" step, but is taken from resources other than the student's own knowledge.

5. **Express:** Express my knowledge in a summary statement.

   This stage requires the student to create a new statement that takes into consideration any new information the student discovered through inquiry and research in the preceding steps. This new information may have either supported or challenged the student's original statement, and therefore the "E" step may confirm *or* refute the initial proposition.

Teacher Tips

- With frequent use, this strategy will help students learn to self-monitor for their own understanding and decide when to go through the PROVE steps independently.

- You may choose to add a component to "V" step by asking students to defend their knowledge when faced with challenge or debate.

- If necessary, while students are still familiarizing themselves with this strategy, create a handout or poster listing the PROVE steps.

- Review this strategy regularly to support students' recall of steps.

- You may want to have students record their progress and findings through each step. They can then use these notes to study, self-assess, organize reports, or prepare for debate.

Scanlon, D. "PROVE-ing What You Know: Using a Learning Strategy in an Inclusive Class." *Teaching Exceptional Children,* 34:4, 48–54 (2002).

QAR

Area Addressed: *Reading Comprehension*

Strategy Summary

This strategy helps students understand various questioning techniques and how to comprehend text in various ways and at multiple levels.

Steps

1. **Questions:** Begin by introducing students to the four question types:

   - *Right There.* These are questions with answers that can be found "right there" in the text.

   - *Think and Search.* These questions require the reader to derive the answer from more than one sentence, paragraph, or page.

   - *Author and You.* These questions require the reader to connect his or her prior knowledge with the text to come up with the answer. These questions are more inferential in nature.

   - *On Your Own.* These questions require the reader to apply background knowledge and may not even require reading the actual text in order to answer the question correctly.

2. **Answers:** Ask students to answer different types of questions after reading a passage. Have students identify the types of questions and discuss the different strategies they may use to answer each question.

3. **Relationships:** Have students write their own questions relating to the passage. Make sure students use all four of the question types and that the questions they ask make connections to many different parts of the passage.

Teacher Tips

- Partners or teams can write questions for each other to answer.

- Students could be asked to highlight or underline where they found "Right There" and "Think and Search" answers.

Raphael, T.V. "Teaching Question-Answer Relationships, Revisited." *The Reading Teacher,* 39:6, 516–522 (1986).

RAFT

Area Addressed: *Writing to Communicate*

Strategy Summary

This strategy is aimed at helping students understand the role and purpose of a writer, learn how to target a certain audience with their writing, consider how to use different formats of written composition, and think about how to frame different topics.

Steps

Introduce this activity by talking with students about how developing a strong sense of purpose in writing and knowing your audience are important parts of writing to communicate. Explain that students will use the following ideas and questions to write informational papers from a creative point of view. At the same time, the RAFT exercise is a good starting point for students to think about the power of writing, and how they can use different ways to frame their compositions for different audiences or purposes.

RAFT is an acronym standing for: Role, Audience, Format, and Topic. Have students take notes as they consider these concepts and as they ask and answer the following questions. They can then use those notes to plan, compose, and craft their papers.

1. **Role**

   What role are you taking on as a writer? In addition to writing from their personal perspectives, students can experiment with adopting different points of view such as that of an inanimate object, a star athlete, or a concerned community member.

2. **Audience**

   To whom are you writing? If you are an inanimate object such as a computer keyboard, perhaps you are writing to your typist. If you are a concerned community member, perhaps you are writing to the town council. How might your point of view change the way you write?

3. **Format**

   In what format are you writing? Formats might include editorial columns, fan letters, or diary entries. Again: How does the format change the way you approach the writing?

4. **Topic**

   What are you writing about? What message are you trying to convey with your writing?

After students have used these notes to write their papers, talk about the process. How did this strategy change the way they approached the writing? Were they happy with the results? Why or why not? What did they learn from this exercise, and how can they apply that knowledge to other writing tasks?

Teacher Tips

- Complete a RAFT paper as a whole class before asking students to do so independently.
- If desired, find examples of RAFT papers online and share them with your students as they're getting familiar with this strategy.

- RAFT papers are an effective means for differentiation, as they have many built-in opportunities for customization. Some components may need to be consistent among all students in your class based upon your lesson objectives, but the RAFT strategy is an excellent opportunity to build in student choice.

Santa, C., L. Havens, and B. Valdes. *Project CRISS: Creating Independence Through Student-Owned Strategies,* Dubuque, IA: Kendall Hunt, 2004.

Read-Aloud

Area Addressed: Reading Fluency

Strategy Summary

A teacher-led read-aloud is a general practice aimed at improving students' language and literacy skills. It is one of the best ways for students to hear fluent reading and also gain an appreciation for books and reading. In addition, integrating the read-aloud strategy into multiple content areas offers an opportunity for students to understand content in a different way, and can lead to dynamic classroom conversations.

Steps

1. Reading could come from a chapter book, article, classroom text, or poem. It can serve one or more of the following purposes:

- Building students' background knowledge
- Prompting discussion about the topics and themes of the reading
- Providing students with interesting vocabulary words and examples of strong writing
- Assuring that students hear fluent reading

2. During and after a read-aloud, students do one or more of the following:

- Pay attention to illustrations, if applicable. How do students think the visuals help with their interpretation of the text?
- Answer teacher-posed questions that aid understanding. The teacher will invite students to look for narrative themes or, if relevant, visual motifs.
- Make predictions about what will happen next within the text, and explain the rationale for their thinking.

Teacher Tips

- Try reading historical fiction aloud to help students move beyond a literal comprehension of historical fiction to a deeper and more critical understanding of historical fiction's meaning and interpretation.
- *The Read Aloud Handbook* by Jim Trelease is a wonderful resource that provides research behind reading aloud to students and gives practical tips for teachers (as well as parents) using read-aloud strategies.

Albright, L.K., and M. Ariail. "Tapping the Potential of Teacher Read-Alouds in Middle Schools." *Journal of Adolescent & Adult Literacy* 48:7, 582–591 (2005).

Readers Theatre

Addressed Area: *Reading Fluency*

Strategy Summary

Readers Theatre incorporates repeated exposure to a text while giving students an authentic means for practicing reading with expression, at an appropriate pace and volume, and in meaningful phrases.

Steps

1. Choose a book for your students to read. Select one that can easily be adapted to a script format. Many fiction texts will naturally fit into this format, but nonfiction such as history and biography can also work well.

2. Assign character roles to as many students as possible to involve all students in some way.

3. Give students time to rehearse their parts while infusing appropriate tone, pace, and volume.

4. Explain that each student must assume his or her character by trying to speak like that character. Encourage students to decide how their characters will talk based on context and clues from within the book. (And again, remember that "characters" *can* be real figures from history, depending on your text.)

5. Control the content and difficulty of the text selected and which roles are assigned to each student. Students with learning difficulties can easily participate in this activity by taking on less demanding roles.

6. If some students do not end up with character roles, you can assign them to facilitate sound effects or provide narration.

7. You can monitor students' active engagement, fluency, and expression as a form of assessment for this strategy.

Teacher Tips

- Both fiction and nonfiction can be adapted to Readers Theatre scripts.

- This strategy promotes reading fluency, comprehension, and motivation.

Martinez, M., N. Roser, and S. Strecker. "I Never Thought I Could Be a Star: A Readers Theatre Ticket to Fluency." *The Reading Teacher,* 52, 326-333 (1999).

Read Naturally*

Area Addressed: *Reading Fluency*

Program Summary

Read Naturally is a commercially produced program aimed at improving reading for students at all grade levels. The following information provides an overview of the program, specifically as it pertains to developing reading fluency.

Steps

1. Each student sets a reasonable, achievable fluency goal based on his or her baseline scores and in comparison with the program's norm reference charts.

2. Start with an unpracticed "cold reading" of a student-selected passage from their targeted levels. Students set a timer for one minute to assess themselves on the passage. As they read, they keep track of the words they don't know or stumble over (by putting up a finger or making a light pencil mark underneath the problem word). At the end of one minute, students make note of how many words they read and subtract all the marked words or "errors," leaving the total wcpm (words correct per minute). They then graph this initial, unpracticed wcpm score on a bar graph using a colored pencil.

3. Students practice reading the same passage three or four times along with a fluent model. This model can come from an audio recording or a trained reader.

4. Students read the text independently again. A timer is set for one minute and students read the text several times until they reach their predetermined goal level.

5. The student reads the passage for one minute, and this time the teacher keeps track of errors. At the end of one minute, the total number of errors is subtracted from the total number of words read. The student "passes" if three criteria are met: (a) the wcpm score meets or exceeds the predetermined goal, (b) three or fewer errors were made, and (c) the student read the passage with correct phrasing and attention to punctuation. When students "pass" a text, they move on to another passage at the same level; if the goal is not met, they continue practicing this same text. After passing, students graph their new scores on the same bars as their original, unpracticed scores, using different colored pencils. (If you prefer, students can also do this graphing on computers.)

6. Students continue reading passages of equivalent difficulty for approximately 10 to 12 texts. At that point the teacher examines the data on the student's graph to decide what step to take next. The student may move up or down a level.

Teacher Tips

• It can be helpful to encourage students to point to the text with tracking tools or their fingers to follow along as they read.

• Computerized programs such as Read Naturally do not replace teaching instruction, but they can serve as valuable supplements.

• More information regarding Read Naturally can be found at www.readnaturally.com.

Hasbrouck, J., C. Ihnot, and G. Rogers. "Read Naturally: A Strategy to Increase Oral Reading Fluency." *Reading Research and Instruction*, 39, 27–37 (1999).

READ 180*

Area Addressed: *Reading Comprehension*

Program Summary

READ 180 is a computerized program designed for students needing Tier II or III support in the area of reading comprehension. It includes leveled paperback books for independent reading, audiobooks with corresponding text for supported reading, and resource books designed to address reading comprehension. Progress monitoring is built into the program. The recommended instructional period is 90 minutes and comprises direct instruction from a teacher, small-group rotations, and a wrap-up period.

Teacher Tips

- READ 180 does not replace instruction from a qualified reading teacher. This supplemental program is designed to be used only with students who might benefit from extra time spent reading and responding to text, not as a one-size-fits-all reading program.

- For more details, visit read180.scholastic.com.

Institution of Education Sciences. "What Works Clearinghouse Intervention Report: Adolescent Literacy—READ 180," ies.ed.gov/ncee/wwc, October 2009 (accessed June 16, 2014).

REAP

Area Addressed: *Reading Comprehension*

Strategy Summary

REAP is an acronym that stands for Read, Encode, Annotate, and Ponder. This strategy is useful when reading a text for information. It can also be used to make inferences by drawing logical conclusions based on evidence from the text. Teach this strategy through modeling the following steps.

Steps

1. **Read** to discover the writer's message.

   Begin by having students read simply to get an overall understanding of what the author is saying in the text. This is an important skill to teach students because it's the first step in comprehending text. If students do not understand the author's message, they will not progress in their reading comprehension skills or building of information.

2. **Encode** the message by putting it into your own language.

   Ask students to rephrase the message using their own words. It's important for each student to put the author's words into language he or she can understand. Many students do not have the vocabulary of an established author, and there are likely to be some words in the text that they don't understand. Part of reading is increasing vocabulary, so it may be beneficial for students to connect meaning to the unfamiliar words.

3. **Annotate** by writing the message in notes for yourself or to share with others.

   Instruct students to write small messages (in the margins or on sticky notes) throughout the text to discuss with their peers. Usually different students will view the same text differently, and meaningful discussion can arise from sharing these views on what the author meant.

4. **Ponder** the message.

   Teach your students to process what they're reading by asking themselves, "What did the text mean to me? How can I relate my personal experiences to it?" During this step, students look back through the reading and think about it again, pondering the message and information. Often, by looking back and summarizing an entire reading, students will pick up details they missed on the first read. By summarizing, students are mentally organizing the text for easy retrieval.

Teacher Tips

- During the "encoding" step, have each student create a personal vocabulary list. Every time a student encounters a new or unfamiliar word, he or she adds it to the vocabulary list, along with a meaningful definition. Students will use these lists during exercises in written expression. They can refer to their personal vocabulary lists to enhance their writing.

- This strategy can be used in combination with Think Pair Share (page 56). Have students use REAP first, and then follow up with a Think Pair Share of the information.

- This strategy can be generalized to multiple content areas.

Eanet, M.G., and A.V. Manzo. "REAP: A Strategy for Improving Reading/Writing/Study Skills." *Journal of Reading,* 19:8, 647–652 (1976).

Reverse Outlining

Area Addressed: *Writing to Communicate*

Strategy Summary

This strategy is designed for students to use once they have written their first drafts of a paper. Reverse outlining will help writers determine if their drafts will meet the assignment's criteria. It will also help students identify areas that need expanded analysis or support, and will reveal whether papers need more structure or organization. Walk students through the following steps to create a reverse outline.

Steps

1. Go through the paper and number every paragraph.

2. Begin constructing the outline by looking at the topic sentence of each paragraph. Ask yourself if it clearly describes the paragraph's main idea. If a paragraph's topic sentence provides a succinct version of the paragraph, add this topic sentence to the outline in numerical order as a summary for that paragraph. If it does not clearly summarize the paragraph, write a one-sentence summary to express the main point of the paragraph and put that in the outline.

3. Once you have summarized every paragraph and placed all summaries in your outline, review your outline and make sure that each item relates to the main point of your paper. Cut any paragraphs that are not on topic. Add to paragraphs that need more support. As you read through your outline, determine if you need additional paragraphs to enhance your paper.

Teacher Tips

- Explain to students that many writers come up with new ideas when viewing compositions from the vantage point of reverse outlining. At this point, writers can make productive decisions about whether to keep, cut, or expand certain paragraphs in the draft.

- Encourage your students to think critically about organization. When reading the reverse outlines, do they see that their writing follows a logical sequence? Are any of the topics repetitive? If necessary, encourage them to make strategic choices for rearranging their papers on a paragraph-by-paragraph basis, or to add or delete paragraphs to improve organization.

University of Wisconsin. "Reverse Outlines: A Writer's Technique for Examining Organization," *The Writer's Handbook,* writing.wisc.edu/Handbook/ReverseOutlines.html (accessed June 16, 2014).

REWARDS*

Areas Addressed: Word Recognition/Reading Fluency

Program Summary

REWARDS is an established program that was originally designated for early grades and has now been extended to include upper grades. REWARDS is a multisyllabic word reading strategy developed by Anita Archer. It has been proven effective in helping students break words into manageable, decodable chunks; read long words in content-area textbooks; read accurately, quickly, and with confidence; increase oral and silent reading fluency; and improve comprehension skills as decoding and fluency increase. Over time, these overt strategies are faded into covert strategies. The REWARDS program is most often used at a Tier II level responding directly to students who lack advanced word-recognition skills and who read at a slower rate than their peers.

Teacher Tips

- This commercially produced program is effective for adolescent students who are struggling. It is to be used with small groups of students who need intensive support. The program is a powerful short-term intervention.

- This program can support any core curriculum and offers flexible options for implementation.

- English language learners can also benefit from REWARDS.

- For more information, visit www.soprislearning.com/literacy/rewards-program /response-to-intervention.

Archer, A.L., M.M. Gleason, and V. Vachon. *REWARDS Reading Excellence: Word Attack and Rate Development Strategies: Multisyllabic Word Reading Strategies.* Langmont, CO: Sopris West, 2000.

Vachon, V., M.M. Gleason, and A.L. Archer. *REWARDS for Secondary 6–12 (Intervention).* Langmont, CO: Sopris West, 2007.

SCUBA-Dive into Reading

Area Addressed: Reading Fluency

Strategy Summary

SCUBA-D is an acronym representing six different cues for students to use when encountering unfamiliar or difficult words while reading. This strategy uses context clues, phonics, and dictionary skills to help students identify difficult words in classroom materials and homework assignments. Students are taught to use the following steps to increase their reading fluency.

Steps

1. **S: Sound** It Out

   Look at the letters and say the letter sounds. Start at the beginning of the word and move to the end.

2. **C: Check** the Clues in the Sentence

   Think about the meaning of the other words in the sentence and use that context to guess a word that could fit in place of the unknown word.

3. **U: Use** Main Idea and Picture Clues

   Ask yourself what the story, paragraph, and reading is primarily about. Look for clues to this information in the title, first sentence, headings, and pictures.

4. **B: Break** Words into Parts

   Look for the smaller pieces or parts of the unfamiliar word that can help you figure out the whole word. These smaller parts might be found in the beginning, middle, or ending of the word.

5. **A: Ask** for Help

   If the first four steps don't help you figure out the unknown word, ask a classmate or teacher for help.

6. **D: Dive** into the **Dictionary**

   Look up the word and use the letters in parentheses next to the word to figure out what the word sounds like. If available, electronic dictionaries can be helpful.

Teacher Tips

- It can be helpful to encourage students to use SCUBA-D for independent reading.
- This strategy can be used for reading both fiction and nonfiction.
- Encourage students to memorize this strategy, and give them opportunities to practice using it.

Cheng, L., and G. Salembier. "SCUBA-Dive into Reading." *Teaching Exceptional Children*, 29:6, 68–70 (1997).

Self-Talk

Area Addressed: Self-Management and Learning Strategies

Strategy Summary

Self-talk is a behavior management strategy that helps curb impulsive behavior and encourage self-control for students in middle school settings. When using this approach, begin by developing key phrases that match students' goal behaviors. Students then memorize and use these phrases, which will help guide them through complex or challenging tasks or situations. For example, self-talk phrases might include, "Think before I speak" or "Listen before I speak." Once students are familiar with self-talk, they can start to develop their own key phrases, with support and feedback as needed. The following steps are used to teach this strategy and work toward students' independent use of self-talk.

Steps

1. Ask student to say a chosen key phrase aloud.
2. Ask student to whisper the phrase.
3. Ask student to move only his or her lips while "saying" the phrase.
4. Ask student to mentally say the phrase, without moving his or her lips.

Teacher Tips

- This strategy is especially effective in conjunction with school-wide and class-wide positive behavior supports that you already have in place.

- Consider formal and informal language in developing phrases. Ideally, self-talk will feel natural to students and will be easy to remember, while also being focused and precise.

Garrick-Duhaney, L.M. "A Practical Approach to Managing the Behavior of Students with ADD." *Intervention in School and Clinic*, 38:5, 267–279 (2003).

Sentence Building, Elaborating, and Pruning

Areas Addressed: Writing to Communicate/Language and Vocabulary Development

Strategy Summary

This strategy calls students' attention to patterns in language and explores how writing can be more vivid, while also helping students build, elaborate, or (if necessary) prune sentences in their writing.

Steps

1. **Building**

   The sentence-building activity teaches students about sentence structure by starting with a basic sentence such as "Ava yelled" and building upon it to include more details, based on prompts such as how, where, and why. See the following chart for an example.

	Who/What	Does/Is	How?	Where?	Why?
Basic	Ava	yelled			
Elaboration	Ava	yelled screamed rooted cheered applauded shouted	enthusiastically loudly passionately	at the basketball game	to encourage her team to cheer on her team

2. **Elaborating**

   Students elaborate on their basic sentences to learn about sentence structure and to expand their vocabulary. Students also experiment with manipulating and reframing sentences by moving phrases around while keeping the meaning intact.

3. **Revising**

   Students revise their basic sentences into a variety of sentences by moving around the sentence parts and using different words and phrases. For example:

   - At the basketball game, Ava yelled enthusiastically to encourage her team.

   - Ava rooted passionately to cheer on her team at the basketball game.

4. Pruning *(optional)*

Pruning a sentence involves trimming away information. Take a complex sentence and work backward to remove the how, where, and why, so that you are left with the basic sentence. By pruning sentences, students learn about the necessary elements of clear writing and how to edit their written work.

Teacher Tips

- After completing the strategy, invite students to evaluate which of the revised sentences appeals to them the most and explain why. What did using this strategy teach them?

- This strategy fits well into the Gradual Release of Responsibility Framework (page 136).

Adapted from Carolyn Hood (2007), as cited in *Academic Conversations: Classroom Talk That Fosters Critical Thinking and Content Understandings* by Jeff Zwiers and Marie Crawford. Portland, ME: Stenhouse, 2011.

6 + 1 Trait Writing*

Area Addressed: Writing to Communicate

Program Summary

6 + 1 Trait Writing is a research-based program produced by the Northwest Regional Educational Laboratory. It defines the following seven key characteristics to create a common vision of strong, well-crafted writing.

- **Ideas**

   The *ideas* of a piece of writing are its overall message or theme, as well as the details, which must be well-chosen to interest the reader and enrich the writing. When considering the ideas trait before writing, it's also important to think about the scope of the topic covered in a piece. The ideas discussed should be narrow enough to be effectively covered within the piece, but still interesting, with room to explore.

- **Organization**

   Organization is the structure of a piece and the flow of one idea to the next. Good writing has clear, logical organization that is easy to follow. Well-organized writing also makes sure the reader isn't left with loose ends or unresolved questions.

- **Voice**

   Voice is the most subjective of the traits, and the most difficult to define. A writer's voice comes through with a unique or distinctive tone. It gives the writing personality and flair. Voice is what gives readers the sense that they are listening to a real person.

- **Word Choice**

   Word choice is the careful selection of language. Choosing words purposefully will result in vigorous, colorful writing that is also clear and precise. Strong word choice lends texture and vibrancy to writing without making a piece overwritten or unnecessarily complex.

- **Sentence Fluency**

   Sentence fluency is writing's flow, rhythm, and ease of reading. A piece with strong sentence fluency includes a variety of sentence structures and lengths, and omits places where the reader stumbles or gets confused.

- **Conventions**

  Conventions are writing's technical and mechanical aspects. These include grammar, spelling, punctuation, and usage.

- **Presentation**

  Presentation is how a piece of writing appears on the page or screen. This includes the neatness of the handwriting, if applicable, or the clear and aesthetically pleasing formatting of a document. It may also include the clarity of visuals such as infographics, and the effective use of text organizers such as headers and bulleted lists. Presentation is the "+ 1" piece of the 6 + 1 traits, because while it is important, it is not as critical as the other traits.

Teacher Tips

- Each trait can be integrated into the steps of the Process Approach (page 175)—planning, drafting, revision, and editing. With practice, students will be able to apply these traits to their writing in all classes and subject areas.

- In addition to being a teaching strategy, the 6 + 1 Traits can be an assessment method. When used for assessment, the traits are translated to a rubric format. See educationnorthwest.org/traits/traits-rubrics for more information on rubrics.

Culham, R. "6 + 1 Trait Writing." *Northwest Regional Educational Laboratory* (2005).

Jarmer, D. et al. "Six-Trait Writing Model Improves Scores at Jennie Wilson Elementary." *Journal of School Improvement* (2000).

SQ3R

Area Addressed: *Inquiry and Research*

Strategy Summary

SQ3R stands for Survey, Question, Read, Recite, and Review. This strategy incorporates preview, predicting, and establishing a purpose for reading.

Steps

1. **Survey.** Have students survey the text by looking at key features such as the title, headings, subheadings, pictures, bold print, and key words.

2. **Question.** Ask students to think about what they now know about the text based on the survey. Given what they've learned, have students write down questions they have that they think might be answered by reading the entire passage.

3. **Read.** Have students read the passage.

4. **Recite.** Ask students to recite or write the answers to the questions they wrote in step 2.

5. **Review.** Have students review what they learned from the reading and apply that new knowledge to another context. This review could involve creating a poster that visually represents the information, participating in a group discussion about the topic, or summarizing the information in a written report.

Teacher Tips

- Use SQ3R repeatedly until the process becomes internalized by students.
- This strategy can also be used for informational reading comprehension.

Martin, M.A. "Student's Application of Self-Questioning Study Techniques: An Investigation of Their Efficiency." *Reading Psychology,* 6, 68–83 (1985).

Structured Note-Taking

Area Addressed: *Self-Management and Learning Strategies*

Strategy Summary

The structured note-taking strategy is used to support students' comprehension of information taught and learned in all content areas. Explain and model the following steps for the class before having students use them independently.

Steps

1. Draw a vertical line approximately 2 inches from the left side of a piece of paper.
2. Label the narrow left-hand column "Main Ideas."
3. Label the wide right-hand column "Details."
4. While reading a selected text, write big ideas, key terms, and other core information from the text in the "Main Ideas" column.
5. In the "Details" column, write down additional thoughts and information pertaining to these main ideas.
6. At the bottom of the page, synthesize the main ideas and details to write a brief summary about the reading.

Teacher Tips

- Use instructional time to teach and model this note-taking strategy.
- Use notes recorded by students to facilitate discussion and reflection on content taught and learned.

Fisher, D., N. Frey, and D. Williams. "Seven Literacy Strategies that Work." *Educational Leadership,* 60, 70–73 (2002).

Students as Problem Solvers

Area Addressed: *Inquiry and Research*

Strategy Summary

This strategy supports students in developing problem-solving skills through research and inquiry. It allows students to become independent problem solvers by researching the strategies different people use to solve problems. Students can learn from studying people who have solved the same, similar, or different math problems.

Steps

1. Students find people to research. Research subjects could include peers or adult role models.

    *   Encourage students to research people whom they think are likely to have different problem-solving abilities from themselves. Encourage students to talk to their parents, grandparents, teachers, and other adults in their lives.
    *   Determine which math problems to present to different people. These can be generated by the class or by individual students.

2. Expand the problem-solving process to other subjects. Have students take detailed notes on how each person they talk to solves the problem, and how approaches vary from subject to subject. For example, do some people get frustrated with difficult problems while others stay calm? Do some people work better by talking through the problem out loud, while others need to have space and quiet?

3. Students share with the class what they learned.

4. The teacher takes notes on student presentations.

5. Students are encouraged to apply the strategies they learned from their research of the work of others.

Teacher Tips

*   Depending on the types of problems being studied and solved, you could use the "fishbowl" method to model solutions for your whole group. In this technique, one person acts as the model while the rest of the group observes. Be sure student models show and explain their work as they progress through the problem.

Miller, C. "Student Researched Problem Solving Strategies." *Mathematics Teacher*, 93:2, 136–138 (2000).

Subtext Strategy

Area Addressed: *Reading Comprehension*

Strategy Summary

This strategy is for students to go beyond the literal text and to make stories personal by putting themselves in the story.

Steps

1. Select a text for students to "act out." Choose something with a variety of characters and plenty of room for interpretation and inference. Lead students in using the illustrations, if available, to make predictions about the text before reading it aloud to the group.

2. Explain to students that they are going to act out the story, but with a twist. Rather than reciting dialogue directly from a script, students will describe what their characters are thinking and feeling.

3. As you read the text, pause at appropriate points to give students a chance to talk briefly about what their characters are thinking and feeling.

4. After students are familiar with the strategy, divide them into groups and give each group a stack of sticky notes and a scene from the book. Students write down what their characters were thinking or feeling and put the sticky notes in appropriate spots in the reading. At this point, students can expand on what they said during the read-aloud. Students can use these notes as cues when they carry out the next step.

5. Finally, have students perform their scenes in front of the class, acting out their subtexts—their characters' thoughts, feelings, and desires.

Teacher Tips

• Using this strategy will help students make connections to characters that go beyond a quicker or more surface-level read.

• Students will reach a deeper understanding or empathy for characters.

• While this strategy fits naturally with fiction texts, it could also be applied to some nonfiction readings, such as history or social studies texts.

Clyde, J. "Stepping Inside the Story World: The Subtext Strategy: A Tool for Connecting and Comprehending." *The Reading Teacher,* 57:2, 150–160 (2003).

Summarizing by Drawing

Area Addressed: Reading Comprehension

Strategy Summary

This strategy involves creating visual representations to summarize text, particularly text that covers a complex topic or includes many details. Once students are comfortable with the strategy, they can apply it to a variety of subject areas and classes.

Steps

1. Provide students with an informational passage at the appropriate reading level. Readings used in this strategy could be topical articles, sections taken from science or social studies textbooks, or other relevant material.

2. Have students read the passage silently, or read it aloud together as a group.

3. Instruct students to create images depicting the main points of the reading passage. The visual representations students produce could show an overall synthesis of what the text was teaching, or could depict a more detailed sequence of events.

4. Ask students comprehension questions about the passage and have them answer using only their pictures for guidance.

Teacher Tips

• The visuals that students create can take many forms. They might be timelines, charts, drawings, or other informative depictions. Encourage students to choose the formats that they think will best help them understand and remember the content.

• These pictures can become study guides that students use throughout a lesson or unit of study. Linking students' pictures to the content being studied can work as a mnemonic device that students have created on their own.

- This strategy works particularly well with texts delivering a lot of information that students need to remember.
- If desired, students could create their graphics using computer programs or online tools.
- To extend this strategy, group students and ask them to compare and contrast the ways each of them depicted the information.

Elliot, J. "Summarizing with Drawing a Reading-Comprehension Strategy." *Science Scope,* 30, 23–27 (2007).

TAG (Writer's Workshop)

Area Addressed: *Writing to Communicate*

Strategy Summary

This strategy helps students learn how to give constructive feedback after reading or listening to a classmate's writing. The most effective way to implement this strategy is in a writer's workshop format. Form workshop groups that are no larger than four students per group. Use your knowledge of students' strengths, needs, and personalities to determine the composition of each group. Workshop groups helps writers by giving them suggestions on how and where to add more details to strengthen their writing, while also letting them know what already works well and what readers enjoyed. The TAG acronym reminds the listener and reader to:

1. **Tell** what he or she liked.

2. **Ask** questions.

3. **Give** ideas (offer suggestions to improve the piece).

Following are several sample questions students can ask and suggestions they can make during a writer's workshop conference:

- Is there anything that is hard to understand?
- Where could more information be added?
- Tell what *you* liked best about the story.
- What was the problem or conflict? How was it solved? Would there be other ways to solve it?
- What part do *you* think needs more work?

Teacher Tips

- Have students provide each other with their feedback in the order of the letters in TAG. You may want to require students to provide at least three likes and three suggestions for improvement.
- Model the TAG procedure for students by telling them what you liked, asking relevant questions, and giving ideas that might help students expand or clarify their writing.
- As needed, you can sit in on workshop groups and model the TAG procedure.

Marchisan, M.L., and S.R. Alber. "The Write Way: Tips for Teaching the Writing Process to Resistant Writers." *Intervention in School and Clinic,* 36:3, 154–162 (2001).

Take a Side

Area Addressed: Critical Thinking

Strategy Summary

Take a Side helps students justify their thinking and back up their reasoning. Begin by describing the strategy and indicating a real or imaginary continuum in the classroom. Explain that this continuum represents the range of perspectives on an issue. Students may not choose the exact middle of the range, but if they are *near* the middle, they must have a solid reason for being there. Continue this strategy using the following steps.

Steps

1. Present two sides of an issue or topic.

2. Have students privately write down their positions and identify which side of the issue they are on. Once everyone has had a few minutes to consider their views, instruct each student to walk to the point on the continuum representing his or her position.

3. Ask students to explain to those near them why they are standing where they are on the continuum.

4. Next, have some students move to the opposite side of the continuum and engage in respectful debate with their peers. Advise them to make a case for their side while keeping an open mind.

5. Reconvene as a group and have students report on what they learned from the experience. Do they see things differently than they did before? Have they gained any insight? Has their position strengthened? Changed? Why or why not?

Teacher Tips

- When creating your classroom continuum, you could simply point to two walls and identify them as opposing viewpoints, or you could use tape or paper to create a physical line on the floor.

- Before beginning this activity, discuss your goals with the class. Make sure students understand that the idea is not to argue with their peers, but to evaluate the soundness of their own (and others') reasoning, and to listen to and consider multiple perspectives.

Adapted from Wilhem (2002), as cited in *Academic Conversations: Classroom Talk That Fosters Critical Thinking and Content Understandings* by Jeff Zwiers and Marie Crawford. Portland, ME: Stenhouse, 2011.

Text Rendering

Area Addressed: Reading Comprehension

Strategy Summary

This strategy helps students clarify and expand their thinking about informational texts by breaking these texts into small parts, highlighting significant pieces, and discussing them with peers.

Steps

1. Place students in small groups. Explain that this activity will help them identify how they are interpreting a reading's salient points, and also give them a chance to consider how and why other students have similar or different understandings and "take-aways" from the same text.

2. The first round of this activity requires each student to share one *sentence* from the document that he or she thinks is most significant.

3. In the second round, each student shares one *phrase* that he or she thinks is particularly important.

4. In the third round, each student shares a *word* that he or she thinks is very significant.

5. Still in small groups, students discuss what they heard from each other, how individuals' translation (or rendering) of the text varied, and what these different interpretations reveal about the text. Call students' attention to the similarities and differences in their sentences, phrases, and words.

6. Finally, students share and discuss any new insights about the reading, either still in their small groups or as a whole class.

Teacher Tips

- A student from each small group can document the phrases and words that group members choose, or the teacher can list them during a whole-class discussion. These lists can be revisited later to review content or to link the reading to other topics.

- After the first time you use this activity with a class, bring it to a close with a debriefing about the overall process of text rendering.

- This strategy can be used to bridge a reading with a class discussion or to generate questions.

National School Reform Faculty. "Text Rendering Experience," www.nsrfharmony.org/protocol/doc/text _rendering.pdf (accessed June 16, 2014).

THIEVES

Area Addressed: Reading Comprehension

Strategy Summary

This strategy activates prior knowledge, and its steps serve as an advance organizer for the text. When introducing the strategy to students, explain that THIEVES is an acronym for the following steps of breaking down and analyzing a reading. Have students ask themselves the questions associated with each letter of the THIEVES acronym and use the answers to enhance their understanding of the text.

Steps

1. Title.

   The title is the first look into a reading Ask yourself: What do I think I will be reading about? What do I already know about this topic? How does it relate to preceding chapters or other readings?

2. **Headings.**

   Headings are the gateway to general subject areas within the reading. Ask yourself: Does this heading tell me anything? Does it give me clues about what I am going to be reading? Can I turn this heading into a question that is likely to be answered in the actual content?

3. **Introduction.**

   The introduction provides the framework for the text. Ask yourself: How does the first paragraph introduce what I will be reading? Do I have any prior knowledge on this subject?

4. **Every** first sentence in a paragraph.

   Preview the text by reading the first sentence of each paragraph.

   Ask yourself: What do I think each paragraph will be about? How do I think the information in this reading is organized?

5. **Visuals** and **vocabulary**.

   Perusing photographs, charts, graphs, maps, or tables provides an insight into reading. Ask yourself: How much does the text explain the visuals? How do the captions help me better understand the meaning of the visuals? Does the text include a list of key vocabulary terms and definitions? Are important words in bold type and defined? Do I know what these key words mean?

6. **End**-of-the-reading questions.

   These questions can be a clue to important points and critical concepts in the text. Ask yourself: What information do I learn from the questions? Where are potential answers to the questions located within the text?

7. **Summary.**

   Give attention to the conclusion of the reading and summarize your thoughts at the end of the reading, highlighting the most critical concepts addressed in the text. Ask yourself: What is the most important information addressed in this chapter? What will best help me remember this information?

Teacher Tips

- This strategy is readily applicable to a wide range of content material.
- This activity can be done individually, in pairs, or in small groups.

Manz, S.L. "A Strategy for Previewing Textbooks: Teaching Readers to Become THIEVES." *The Reading Teacher,* 55:5, 434–435 (2002).

Thinking and Self-Questioning

Area Addressed: Writing to Communicate

Strategy Summary

This strategy is designed for individual use while planning, drafting, and editing compositions. It gives students a chance to organize their thoughts and consider approaches to a composition before, during, and after writing.

Steps

Before students start to write, have them plan by asking themselves the following four questions.

1. **Who am I writing for?** This question helps students determine their purpose in writing their compositions, and consider how to match their ideas and style to their audience.

2. **Why am I writing this?** This question will help generate ideas and help writers consider how best to frame their writing.

3. **What do I know about my topic?** This question helps students activate background knowledge and apply it to their compositions. It can also spark new ideas about how to approach the topic.

4. **How can I group my ideas?** This question helps students consider different ways to structure their papers and choose an organizational strategy best suited to their goals for the writing.

During drafting, writers take ideas they've gathered during the planning stage and adapt those ideas to fit their audience and purpose. After first drafts are complete, writers ask themselves these follow-up questions to guide their revision.

1. **Does everything make sense?** Is the organization clear? Are there places where a reader might get confused?

2. **Did I accomplish my plan?** Are there any ideas I generated during prewriting that I didn't follow up on or that still need work?

When these questions have been answered, students can implement their editing plans to add, delete, substitute, and modify their ideas.

Teacher Tips

- Model this strategy for students on a regular basis. It may take some time and practice for students to internalize the process.

- To extend this strategy, give students sample papers to analyze. As they read through the samples, have them ask the questions listed previously and consider what they like about the samples and what they might have done differently.

Englert, C.S., T.E. Raphael, L.M. Anderson, H.M. Anthony, and D.D. Stevens. "Making Strategies and Self-Talk Visible: Writing Instruction in Regular and Special Education Classrooms." *American Educational Research Journal*, 28:2, 337–372 (1991).

Gillespie, A., and S. Graham, "Evidence-Based Practices for Teaching Writing," *Better: Evidence-Based Education*, education.jhu.edu/PD/newhorizons/Better/articles/Winter2011.html, 2011 (accessed April 20, 2014).

TWA + PLANS

Areas Addressed: *Reading Comprehension/Writing to Communicate*

Strategy Summary

TWA + PLANS is a two-part strategy that brings together reading comprehension and writing skills. The TWA section of this strategy focuses students' attention on understanding before, during, and after reading informational text. The PLANS portion is focused on demonstrating comprehension through writing.

Steps

While reading, students use the TWA acronym to build comprehension. TWA stands for the following steps.

1. **Think:** Think before you read.
   - Think about the author's purpose.
   - Think about what you want to learn.
2. **While:** Think while you read.
   - Think about linking knowledge within what you're reading, and also connecting what you're learning to what you already know.
   - Reread sections of the text if you lose your way.
3. **After:** Think after you read.
   - Think about the main idea or ideas of the text.
   - Summarize information that you have learned.

When students begin to write about the text they've read, they move on to using the PLANS strategy. PLANS stands for the following steps.

1. **P: Pick** goals for the writing you're about to do. Are you writing to inform? To persuade?
2. **L: List** ways to achieve your goals.
3. **A: And**
4. **N:** Make **notes** on the reading in preparation for beginning to write about it.
5. **S: Sequence** your notes in a way that is clear, organized, and logical.

Once students have gone through the TWA and PLANS steps, they are prepared to begin writing.

Teacher Tips

- Teach and model the steps of this strategy when you are first introducing TWA + PLANS to students.
- If desired, you can provide students with a graphic organizer to help direct their notetaking.
- Teach and guide students to use the PLANS strategy in combination with their notes from the TWA strategy to analyze what they've read and to put their thoughts into clear, organized writing.
- When your students are new to this strategy, you may want to create cards or posters of the TWA + PLANS acronyms to remind them of the steps.

Mason, L., K. Snyder, D. Sukhram, and Y. Kedem. "TWA + PLANS Strategies for Expository Reading and Writing: Effects for Nine Fourth-Grade Students." *Exceptional Children,* 73:1, 69–89 (2006).

Web-Based Bookmarks

Area Addressed: *Inquiry and Research*

Strategy Summary

By using Web-based bookmarks, content instruction can be easily extended to the Internet. Carefully chosen Web-based bookmarks provide students with assistance, structure, and support while researching content online.

Steps

1. Prior to instruction, go online and bookmark sites that have content and instruction applying to your lesson or learning objectives and that are appropriate for students.

2. Introduce each new Web-based activity to students. Explain that even though you have bookmarked credible websites, it is still important for students to be watchful for clues or information that might reveal an author's or organization's point of view. When conducting online research, students should document information relevant to their research questions or projects, and at the same time work to distinguish between fact, opinion, and reasoned judgment presented in online text.

Teacher Tips

- Use Web-based bookmarking to support content area instruction and to provide additional information in various formats beyond the textbook.

- Students do more and more research online today, but their sources are not always reliable. Extend this activity by assessing sites together and giving students information on how to determine a site's value and reliability.

Forbes, L.S. "Using Web-Based Bookmarks in K–8 Settings: Linking the Internet to Instruction." *The Reading Teacher,* 58:2, 148–153 (2004).

WebQuests

Area Addressed: *Inquiry and Research*

Strategy Summary

WebQuests are inquiry-based learning experiences that incorporate multiple online activities, tasks, and websites for students to use as they conduct research and explore content. A WebQuest is an engaging task that makes use of the Web and its resources to engage students in higher-level thinking skills. This technological strategy complements and supports all areas of content.

Before starting your first WebQuest, familiarize students with the following key components of a WebQuest. If helpful, you could even walk through one WebQuest as a group.

- **Introduction:** Every WebQuest should begin with a brief written overview familiarizing students with the WebQuest and its overarching theme.

- **Task:** The outcome and goal of the WebQuest. This task should be clearly and precisely stated, and will relate to a topic within your curriculum or your lesson goals. A WebQuest task could be solving a research problem; writing a paper; preparing a presentation; or many other activities. Strong tasks will require students to process, evaluate, and transform the information they find online, not just summarize it.

- **Process and Resources:** The process is the series of steps students will take to move through the WebQuest toward completion of the task. The resources are the links they will use along the way. Be sure all links are active.

- **Evaluation:** Explain how students' performance on WebQuests will be evaluated. This might be through a scoring rubric or other means.

- **Conclusion:** Revisit what students have learned and accomplished. You may choose to extend WebQuests through class discussion, written reflection, or other activities.

Teacher Tips

- Many ready-to-use WebQuests are available online, and you can also craft them yourself. Visit webquest.org to begin looking for WebQuests that fit your needs, or to find out more about creating your own.

- WebQuests require and strengthen the use of higher level-thinking skills including synthesis, analysis, problem solving, creativity, and judgment.

- Students can complete WebQuests independently, in pairs, or in small groups.

- You can use screen-reading software to support struggling readers and help them use WebQuests.

- To make WebQuests more accessible, especially when you are introducing the strategy to students, you can use them in conjunction with other research-based strategies such as graphic organizers.

Skylar, A., K. Higgens, and R. Boone. "Strategies for Adapting WebQuests for Students with Learning Disabilities." *Intervention in School and Clinic,* 43:1, 20–28 (2007).

Word Sorts

Area Addressed: Language and Vocabulary Development

Strategy Summary

This strategy helps students understand relationships among words by having learners sort words according to common features.

Steps

1. Choose ten to twenty content area words or words for a selected text, lesson, or unit of study. Have students write the words on index cards.

2. Arrange students in groups to identify and discuss similarities and differences between the words.

3. Have students conduct a closed sort or an open sort with an emphasis on the meaning of the words.

   - **Closed Sorts**

     Students sort the terms according to given categories that you have predetermined. Categories may vary significantly depending on the content area. For example, if the closed sort is being used for math-related vocabulary, categories may include ideas such as two-dimensional shapes, three-dimensional shapes, and angles. For a composition or literature class, categories could include parts of speech; words with multiple meanings; number of syllables; and words with prefixes or suffixes.

- **Open Sorts**

  Provide students with words to be sorted and have them create as many categories for these words as possible. Provide guidance and suggestions as needed.

Teacher Tips

- Students can perform word sorts individually, in pairs, or in small groups.

- Word sorts can be adapted to almost any subject matter.

- For an added challenge during closed sorts, teachers can introduce new words related to the categories, or even include words that have no relation to any of the given categories, and ask students to determine where these words should be sorted.

Greenwood, S. "Content Matters: Building Vocabulary and Conceptual Understanding in the Subject Areas." *Middle School Journal*, 35:3, 27–34 (2004).

Working Backward

Area Addressed: *Inquiry and Research*

Strategy Summary

The purpose of problem solving is not always just to find the solution but also to determine different ways to reach an answer. Working backward is a math strategy that promotes inquiry and problem solving.

Steps

1. Provide students with a problem and its solution.

2. Help students connect the problem with the solution by working through a problem-solving process such as:

   - identify the problem

   - analyze the problem

   - brainstorm for solutions

   - pick the best solution

3. Pair students and ask them to explain to each other one way the problem could be solved as well as other ways, if any.

4. Bring the group back together for discussion. Did students have different ideas? Did they learn to look at the problem in a different way after hearing others' thoughts on how to solve it? How is it helpful to talk through problem-solving approaches with others?

Teacher Tips

- You can easily differentiate this strategy by providing students or pairs with different problems and solutions, depending on learners' academic readiness.

- This strategy works well in a context of peer pairing or other styles of flexible grouping.

- Working backward promotes critical thinking and use of higher-level thinking skills.

Shellard, E.G. "Helping Students Struggling with Math." *Principal*, 84, 40–43 (2004).

A Final Word

As a middle school educator, you already juggle many responsibilities, demands on your time, and day-to-day challenges. We know there are times when implementing and using RTI must seem daunting. But remember: You and your colleagues are already using many of the skills and techniques that make up RTI's foundation. High-quality instruction that responds to students' unique needs is at RTI's core. So when you care about your students as individuals and when you use your knowledge of learners' strengths and needs to guide them toward success, you are enacting key principles of RTI.

It's true that RTI can be misunderstood or oversimplified, which can sometimes result in mountains of paperwork and one-size-fits-all interventions that don't do justice to your students' needs and strengths. But the strategies, tips, and tools we've laid out in these pages will help you work with your fellow educators to implement thoughtful assessment, goal setting, and progress monitoring using collaborative planning and problem solving, all while keeping student learning and support at the center of your work.

We hope this book helps you and your colleagues implement an RTI model that works for you and your middle school—one that honors learner differences and makes productive use of the knowledge, expertise, and professional judgment that you and your fellow educators bring to the table. We're happy to be part of the effort to make learning joyful and meet learner needs. We wish you well on the journey!

Kelli J. Esteves
Elizabeth Whitten

References and Resources

▲ References

Aronson, E., and S. Patnoe. *Cooperation in the Classroom: The Jigsaw Method*. London: Pinter & Martin, 2011.

Bandura, A., C. Barbaranelli, G.V. Caprara, and C. Pastorelli. "Self-Efficacy Beliefs as Shapers of Children's Aspirations and Career Trajectories." *Child Development*, 72, 187–206 (2001).

Batsche, G., J. Elliott, J.L. Graden, J. Grimes, J.F. Kovaleski, D. Prasse, D.J. Reschly, J. Schrag, and W.D. Tilly III. *Response to Intervention: Policy Considerations and Implementation*. Alexandria, VA: National Association of State Directors of Special Education, 2005.

Baumann, J.F., E.C. Edwards, E.M. Boland, S. Olejnik, and E.J. Kame'enui. "Vocabulary Tricks: Effects of Instruction in Morphology and Context on Fifth-Grade Students' Ability to Derive and Infer Word Meanings." *American Educational Research Journal*, 40:2, 447–94 (2003).

Bear, G., and W.A. Proctor. "Impact of a Full-Time Integrated Program on the Achievement of Nonhandicapped and Mildly Handicapped Children." *Exceptionality*, 1, 227–238 (1990).

Bender, W.N. *Response to Intervention: A Practical Guide for Every Teacher*. Thousand Oaks, CA: Corwin Press, 2007.

Bittel, K., and D. Hernandez. "Kinesthetic Writing, of Sorts." *Scientific Scope*, 29:7, 37–39 (2006).

Bouck, E.C. "Co-Teaching . . . Not Just a Textbook Term: Implications for Practice." *Preventing School Failure*, 51:2, 46–51 (2007).

Brandt, R. *Powerful Learning*. Alexandria, VA: ASCD, 1998.

CAST. *Universal Design for Learning Guidelines Version 2.0*. Wakefield, MA: 2011.

Cheng, L., and G. Salembier. "SCUBA-Dive into Reading, Teaching." *Exceptional Children*, 29:6, 68–70 (1997).

Clark, R.E., P.A. Kirschner, and J. Sweller. "Putting Students on the Path to Learning: The Case for Fully Guided Instruction." *American Educator*, 6–11, 2012.

Cohen, P.A., J.A. Kulik, and C.C. Kulik. "Educational Outcomes of Tutoring: A Meta-Analysis of Findings." *American Educational Research Journal*, 19:2, 237–248 (1982).

Conderman, G., V. Bresnahan, and T. Pedersen. *Purposeful Co-Teaching: Real Cases and Effective Strategies*. Thousand Oaks, CA: Corwin Press, 2009.

Corpus, D., and A. Giddings. *Planning & Managing Effective Reading Instruction Across the Content Areas: A Strategic, Time-Saving Guide with Planning Sheets, Model Lessons, and More to Help You Boost Students' Comprehension and Learning*. New York: Scholastic, 2010.

Cramer, S., and J. Stivers. "Don't Give Up! Practical Strategies for Challenging Collaborations." *Teaching Exceptional Children*, 39:6, 6–11 (2007).

Danielson, Charlotte. *Enhancing Professional Practice: A Framework for Teaching*, Alexandria, VA: ASCD, 2007.

Dean, C.B., E.R. Hubbell, H. Pitler, and B. Stone. *Classroom Instruction That Works: Research-Based Strategies for Increasing Student Achievement*. Alexandria, VA: ASCD, 2012.

Dixon, N., A. Davies, and C. Politano. *Learning with Readers' Theatre*. Winnipeg: Peguis, 1996.

Dynak, J., E. Whitten, and D. Dynak. (1996). "Refining the General Education Student Teaching Experience Through the Use of Special Education Collaborative Teaching Models." *Action in Teacher Education*, 19:1, 64–74 (1996).

Eanet, M.G., and A.V. Manzo. "REAP: A Strategy for Improving Reading/Writing/Study Skills." *Journal of Reading*, 19:8, 647–652 (1976).

Eggleston, T. J., and G.E. Smith. "Parting Ways: Ending Your Course." *American Psychological Society Observer*, 15:3 (2002).

Federico, M.A., W.G. Herrold, and J. Venn. "Inclusion Reaches Beyond the Classroom." *Kappa Delta Pi Record*, 36, 178–180 (2000).

Fewster, S., and P.D. MacMillan. "School-Based Evidence for the Validity of Curriculum-Based Measurement of Reading and Writing." *Remedial and Special Education*, 23:3, 149–56 (2002).

Fontana, K.C. "The Effects of Co-Teaching on the Achievement of Eighth-Grade Students with Learning Disabilities." *The Journal of At-Risk Issues*, 11:2, 17–23 (2005).

Fountas, I.C., and G.S. Pinnell. *Leveled Books K–8: Matching Texts to Readers for Effective Teaching*. Portsmouth, NH: Heinemann, 2006.

Friend, M. "The Co-Teaching Partnership." *Educational Leadership,* 64:5, 48–52 (2007).

Friend, M., and L. Cook. *Interactions: Collaborative Skills for School Professionals.* New York: Longman, 2003.

Fuchs, D., and L.S. Fuchs. "Introduction to Response to Intervention: 'What, Why, and How Valid Is It?'" *Reading Research Quarterly,* 41:1, 93–99 (2006).

Fuchs, D., L.S. Fuchs, and P. Burish. "Peer-Assisted Learning Strategies: An Evidence-Based Practice to Promote Reading Achievement." *Learning Disabilities Research & Practice,* 15, 85–91 (2000).

Gately, S.E. "Strengthen Your Co-Teaching Relationship." *Principal Leadership,* 5:9, 36–41 (2005).

Glasser, W. *Every Student Can Succeed.* Chatsworth, CA: Black Forest Press, 2000.

Goodenow, C. "Classroom Belonging Among Early Adolescent Students: Relationships to Motivation and Achievement." *Journal of Early Adolescence,* 13, 21–43 (1993).

Graham, S., and K.R. Harris. "Improving the Writing Performance of Young Struggling Writers: Theoretical and Programmatic Research from the Center on Accelerated Student Learning." *The Journal of Special Education,* 39, 18–33 (2005).

Haager, D., J. Klinger, and S. Vaughn. *Evidence-Based Reading Practices for Response to Intervention.* Baltimore, MD: Brookes Publishing Company, 2007.

Hang, Q., and K. Rabrek. "An Examination of Co-Teaching: Perspectives and Efficacy Indicators." *Remedial and Special Education.* 30:5, 259–268 (2009).

Hosp, M.K., J.L. Hosp, and K.W. Howell. *The ABCs of CBM: A Practical Guide to Curriculum-Based Measurement.* New York: Guildford Press, 2007.

Individuals with Disabilities Education Improvement Act of 2004 (Public Law 108-446).

Institution of Education Sciences. "What Works Clearinghouse Intervention Report: Adolescent Literacy—READ 180." ies.ed.gov/ncee/wwc. October 2009 (accessed June 16, 2014).

Jenkins, J.R., and E. Johnson. "Universal Screening for Reading Problems: Why and How Should We Do This?" *RTI Action Network.* www.rtinetwork.org/essential/assessment/screening/readingproblems. 2008 (accessed June 11, 2014).

Jiban, C.L., and S.L. Deno. "Using Math and Reading Curriculum-Based Measurements to Predict State Mathematics Test Performance: Are Simple One-Minute Measures Technically Adequate?" *Assessment for Effective Intervention,* 32:2 (2007).

Johns, J. *Basic Reading Inventory.* Dubuque, IA: Kendall/Hunt Publishing Company, 2005.

Kauffman, J.M., K.L Wong, J.W. Lloyd, L. Jung, and P.L. Pullen. "What Puts Pupils at Risk? An Analysis of Classroom Teachers' Judgments of Pupils' Behavior." *Remedial and Special Education,* 12, 7–16 (1991).

Kendall, J. *Understanding Common Core State Standards.* Alexandria, VA: ASCD, 2011.

Khan, S. "Let's Use Video to Reinvent Education." *TED.* www.ted.com/talks/salman_khan_let_s_use_video_to_reinvent_education.html. 2011 (accessed June 11, 2014).

Klern, A.M., and J.P. Connell. "Relationships Matter: Linking Teacher Support to Student Engagement and Achievement." *Journal of School Health,* 74, 262–273 (2004).

Klingner, J. K., S. Vaughn, M.T. Hughes, J.S. Schumm, and B. Elbaum. "Outcomes for Students with and without Learning Disabilities in Inclusive Classrooms." *Learning Disabilities Research & Practice,* 13, 153–161 (1998).

Kohler-Evans, P.A. "Co-Teaching: How to Make This Marriage Work in Front of the Kids." *Education,* 127:2, 260–264 (2006).

Kroeger, S.D., and B. Kouche. "Using Peer-Assisted Learning Strategies to Increase Response to Intervention in Inclusive Middle Math Settings." *Teaching Exceptional Children,* 38, 6–12 (2006).

Kroesbergen, E.H., and J.E.H. Van Luit. "Mathematics Interventions for Children with Special Education Needs: A Meta-Analysis." *Remedial and Special Education,* 24, 97–114 (2003).

Larson, W.C., and A.J. Goebel. "Putting Theory into Practice: A Professional Development School/University Co-Teaching Partnership." *Journal of the Scholarship of Teaching and Learning,* 8:2, 52–61 (2008).

Lou, Y., P.C. Abrami, and J. Spence. "Effects of Within-Class Grouping on Student Achievement: An Exploratory Model." *Journal of Educational Research,* 94:2, 101–112 (2000).

Lyman, F. "The Responsive Classroom Discussion: The Inclusion of All Students." In *Mainstreaming Digest,* Audrey Springs Anderson (ed.). College Park, MD: University of Maryland Press, 1981.

Maddux, J. "Self-Efficacy: The Power of Believing You Can." In *Handbook of Positive Psychology,* C.R. Snyder and S.J. Lopez (eds.), pp. 277–287. New York: Oxford University Press, 2002.

Magiera, K., and N. Zigmond. "Co-Teaching in Middle School Classrooms Under Routine Conditions: Does the Instructional Experience Differ for Students with Disabilities in Co-Taught and Solo-Taught Classes?" *Learning Disabilities Research,* 20:2, 79–85 (2005).

Marzano, R.J. *Classroom Assessment and Grading That Work.* Alexandria, VA: ASCD, 2006.

Marzano R.J., J.S. Marzano, and D.J. Pickering. *Classroom Management That Works: Research-Based Strategies for Every Teacher.* Alexandria, VA: ASCD, 2003.

Marzano, R.J., D.J. Pickering, and J.E. Pollock. *Classroom Instruction That Works: Research-Based Strategies for Increasing Student Achievement.* Alexandria, VA: ASCD, 2001.

McNary, S.J., N.A. Glasgow, and C.D. Hicks. *What Successful Teachers Do in Inclusive Classrooms.* Thousand Oaks, CA: Corwin Press, 2005.

Murawski, W.W. *Co-Teaching in the Inclusive Classroom: Working Together to Help All of Your Students Find Success.* Bellevue, WA: Bureau of Education and Research, 2005.

Murawski, W.W., and L.A. Dieker. "50 Ways to Keep Your Co-Teacher: Strategies for Before, During, and After Co-Teaching." *Teaching Exceptional Children,* 40:4, 40–48 (2008).

———. "Tips and Strategies for Co-Teaching at the Secondary Level." *Teaching Exceptional Children,* 36:5, 52–58 (2004).

National Association of School Psychologists. *Communique Handout,* 39:3 (2010).

Nelson, J.R., and S.A. Stage. "Fostering the Development of Vocabulary Knowledge and Reading Comprehension Through Contextually-Based Multiple Meaning Vocabulary Instruction." *Education & Treatment of Children,* 30:1, 1–22 (2007).

Nieto, S. *Language, Culture, and Teaching: Critical Perspectives.* New York: Routledge, 2010.

No Child Left Behind Act of 2001, 20 U.S.C. 70 § 6301 et seq. (2002).

Ogle, D.M. "K-W-L: A Teaching Model That Develops Active Reading of Expository Text." *Reading Teacher,* 39, 564–570 (1986).

Pashler, H. et. al. *Organizing Instruction and Study to Improve Student Learning* (NCER 2007-2004). Washington DC: National Center for Education Research, Institute of Education Sciences, U.S. Department of Education, 2007.

Patriarca, L., and M. Lamb. "Collaboration, Curriculum Development and Reflection as Frameworks for Exploring the Integration of General and Special Education." *B.C. Journal of Special Education,* 18:1, 95–100 (1994).

Pearson, P.D., and M.C. Gallaghe. "The Introduction of Reading Comprehension." *Contemporary Educational Psychology,* 8:3, 317–344 (1983).

Pierangelo, R., and G.A. Giuliani. *Assessment in Special Education: A Practical Approach.* Boston: Pearson, 2013.

Putnam, J.W. *Cooperative Learning and Strategies for Inclusion.* Baltimore, MD: Brookes Publishing Company, 1993.

Reschly, D.J., and S. Wood-Garnett. *Teacher Preparation for Response to Intervention in Middle and High Schools.* Washington, DC: TQ Research & Policy Brief for National Comprehensive Center for Teacher Quality, 2009.

Rosenshine, B. "Principles of Instruction: Research-Based Strategies That All Teachers Should Know." *American Educator,* 12–20 (2012).

Ryan, A.M., and H. Patrick. "The Classroom Social Environment and Changes in Adolescents' Motivation and Engagement During Middle School." *American Educational Research Journal,* 38, 437–460 (2001).

Santa, C.M. "A Vision for Adolescent Literacy: Ours or Theirs?" *Journal of Adolescent & Adult Literacy,* 49:6, 466–476 (2006).

Saphier, J., M.A. Haley-Speca, and R. Gower. *The Skillful Teacher: Building Your Teaching Skills.* Acton, MA: Research for Better Teaching, Inc., 2008.

Scruggs, T.W., and M.A. Mastropieri. "On Babies and Bathwater: Addressing the Problems of Identification of Learning Disabilities." *Learning Disabilities Quarterly,* 25:2, 155–168 (2002).

Scruggs, T.E., M.A. Mastropieri, and K.A. McDuffie. "Co-Teaching in Inclusive Classrooms: A Meta-Synthesis of Qualitative Research." *Exceptional Children,* 73:4, 392–416 (2007).

Slavin, R., and N. Madden. *Students At-Risk of School Failure: The Problem of Its Dimensions.* Johns Hopkins University, Center for Research on Elementary and Middle Schools. Boston: Allyn and Bacon, 2004.

Sousa, D.A. *How the Brain Learns to Read.* Thousand Oaks, CA: Corwin Press, 2005.

Sparks, S.D. "Schools 'Flip' for Lesson Model Promoted by Khan Academy." *Education Week,* 31:5, 1–14 (2011).

Swanson, H.L. "Searching for the Best Model for Instructing Students with Learning Disabilities." *Focus on Exceptional Children,* 34, 1–15 (2001).

Thomas, S.D. "Problematizing Collaboration: A Critical Review of the Empirical Literature on Teaching Teams." *Teacher Education and Special Education,* 27:5, 307–317 (2004).

Thompson, S.J., A.B. Morse, M. Sharpe, and S. Hall. "Accommodations Manual: How to Select, Administer, and Evaluate Use of Accommodations for Instruction and Assessment of Students with Disabilities," *Council of Chief State School Officers.* www.ccsso.org/Documents /2005/Accommodations_Manual_How_2005.pdf. 2005 (accessed June 4, 2014).

Tichenor, M.S., B. Heins, K. Piechura-Couture. "Parent Perceptions of Co-taught Inclusive Classroom." *Education,* 120, 569–574 (2000).

Tomlinson, C.A., and C. Doubet. *Smart in the Middle Grades: Classrooms That Work for Bright Middle Schoolers.* Westerville, OH: National Middle School Association, 2006.

Tomlinson, C.A., and J. McTighe. *Integrating Differentiated Instruction and Understanding by Design.* Alexandria, VA. ASCD, 2006.

Torgesen, J.K., D.D. Houston, and L.M. Rissman. *Improving Literacy Instruction in Middle and High Schools: A Guide for Principals.* Portsmouth, NH: RMC Research Corporation, Center on Instruction, 2007.

U.S. Department of Education, Institute of Education Sciences, National Center for Education Statistics. "Reading 2011: National Assessment of Educational Progress at Grades 4 and 8," *The Nation's Report Card.* nces.ed.gov/nationsreportcard/pdf/main2011/2012457. pdf. November 1, 2011 (accessed June 4, 2014).

Vachon, V., M. Gleason, and A. Archer. *REWARDS for Secondary 6–12 (Intervention).* Frederick, CO: Sopris West, 2007.

Vygotsky, L.S. *Mind in Society: The Development of Higher Psychological Processes* (M. Cole, V. John-Steiner, S. Scribner, and E. Souberman, eds. and trans.) Cambridge, MA: Harvard University Press, 1978 (original work published 1934).

Walther-Thomas, C. "Co-Teaching Experiences: The Benefits and Problems That Teachers and Principals Report Over Time." *Journal of Learning Disabilities,* 30, 395–407 (1997).

Walther-Thomas, C., M. Bryant, and S. Land. "Planning for Effective Co-Teaching: The Key to Successful Inclusion." *Remedial and Special Education,* 17, 255–265 (1996).

Whitten, E. "Intervention Assistance Teams: The Principal's Role Identified!" *CASE in Point,* 23–32 (1996).

Whitten, E., and L. Dieker. "Blurring the Boundaries Through Collaborative Teaching." In *Inclusive Education in the New Millennium,* M. Leng Han Hui and M.G. Moont (eds.). Hong Kong: The Association for Childhood Education International-Hong Kong & Macau and Education Convergence, 2003.

———. "Intervention Assistance Teams: A Broader Vision." *Preventing School Failure,* 40, 41–45 (1995).

Whitten, E., and K.J. Esteves. "Response to Intervention: High Quality Classroom Instruction." *American International College: Online Education Journal* (2010).

Whitten E., K.J. Esteves, and A.B. Woodrow. *RTI Success: Proven Tools and Strategies for Schools and Classrooms.* Minneapolis, MN: Free Spirit Publishing, 2009.

Whitten, E., and A. Hoekstra. *Quality Indices for Co-Teaching Teams.* Unpublished Manuscript (2002).

Whitten, E., and M.W. Sheahan. "Co-Teaching: What Makes It Work." *American International College: Online Education Journal* (2010).

Willingham, D.T. *Why Don't Students Like School? A Cognitive Scientist Answers Questions About How the Mind Works and What It Means for the Classroom.* San Francisco, CA: Jossey-Bass, 2009.

Wilson, G.L. "Be an Active Co-Teacher." *Intervention in School and Clinic,* 43:4, 240–243 (2008).

Wormeli, R. *Fair Isn't Always Equal: Assessing and Grading in the Differentiated Classroom.* Portland, ME: Stenhouse Publishers, 2006.

Yoon, B. "Offering or Limiting Opportunities: Teachers' Roles and Approaches to English-Language Learners' Participation in Literacy Activities." *The Reading Teacher,* 61, 216–225 (2007).

Zimmerman, B.J. "Attaining Self-Regulation: A Social-Cognitive Perspective." In *Handbook on Self-Regulation,* eds. M. Boekaerts, P.R. Pintrich, and M. Zeidner (pp. 13–39). San Diego, CA: Academic Press, 2000.

Zwiers, J., and M. Crawford. *Academic Conversations: Classroom Talk That Fosters Critical Thinking and Content Understandings.* Portland, ME: Stenhouse, 2011.

▲ Print Resources

Deno, S.L., L.S. Fuchs, D. Marston, and J. Shin. "Using Curriculum-Based Measurement to Establish Growth Standards for Students with Learning Disabilities." *School Psychology Review,* 30, 507–527 (2001).

Fuchs, L.S. et al. "Formative Evaluation of Academic Progress: How Much Growth Can We Expect?" *School Psychology Review,* 22, 27–49 (1993).

Hasbrouck, J., and G.A. Tindal. "Oral Reading Fluency Norms: A Valuable Assessment Tool for Reading Teachers." *The Reading Teacher,* 59, 636–644 (2006).

Hosp, M.K., J.L. Hosp, and K.W. Howell. *The ABCs of CBM: A Practical Guide to Curriculum-Based Measurement.* New York: Guildford Press, 2007.

▲ Online Resources

Adolescent Literacy
adlit.org/strategies

aimsweb
aimsweb.com

Alex Catalogue of Electronic Text
infomotions.com/alex

American Library Association's "Great Websites for Kids"
gws.ala.org

Bibliomania
bibliomania.com

CAST: About UDL
cast.org/udl

Center for Digital Storytelling
storycenter.org

Center on Response to Intervention at American Institutes for Research
rti4success.org

Common Core State Standards Initiative
corestandards.org

easyCBM
easycbm.com

Edutopia
edutopia.org

Florida Center for Reading Research
fcrr.org

Fountas & Pinnell Leveled Books
fountasandpinnellleveledbooks.com

Intervention Central: Curriculum-Based Measurement Warehouse
interventioncentral.org/curriculum-based-measurement-reading-math-assesment-tests

Khan Academy
khanacademy.org

National Center for Learning Disabilities
ld.org

National Center on Universal Design for Learning
udlcenter.org

National School Reform Faculty
nsrfharmony.org

Reading A–Z
readinga-z.com

Research Institute on Progress Monitoring
progressmonitoring.org

RTI Action Network
rtinetwork.org

What Works Clearinghouse
ies.ed.gov/ncee/wwc

▲ Resources for Academic Assessments

Accelerated Math Intervention
renaissance.com/products/accelerated-math-intervention

Grades K–12. This system from Renaissance Learning allows educators to create math assignments and assessments tailored to each student's current level of intervention. Allows for individual progress monitoring. Administration time varies.

Developmental Reading Assessment*
(2nd Edition PLUS) (DRA2+)
pearsonschool.com/dra2

Grades K–8. From Pearson, this set of individually administered, criterion-referenced reading assessments is modeled after an informal reading inventory. Administration time: 15–45 minutes.

Edcheckup
edcheckup.com

Grades K–8. This progress monitoring system is a series of CBM tests that measure student growth in the basic skills of literacy and mathematics. The program features electronic scoring that allows instant access to progress reports. Administration time varies depending on subject area.

Gates-MacGinitie Reading Tests

riversidepublishing.com/products/gmrt

Grades K–12 (and adult). This group-administered reading survey from Riverside Publishing is designed to test students' achievement in reading. It can be used as a diagnostic or progress-monitoring tool and is developmentally appropriate for all learners. Administration time: 55–75 minutes.

KeyMath-3: A Diagnostic Inventory of Essential Mathematics (KM-III)

pearsonclinical.com/education.html

Grades K–12. Individually administered tests from Pearson are designed to determine a student's level of math achievement. Administration time: 30–90 minutes. (Search for "KeyMath-3" at the listed website to locate the specific product.)

Slosson-Diagnostic Math Screener (S-DMS)

slossonnews.com/S-DMS.html

Grades 1–8. These tests from Slosson Educational Publications can be administered individually or in a group. They assess students' conceptual development, problem solving, and computation skills in math. Available in five grade ranges. Administration time: 30–50 minutes.

STAR Math and STAR Reading

renaissance.com/products/star-assessments

Grades 1–12. These Web-based assessments from Renaissance Learning evaluate students' skills in math and reading and are well suited to RTI screening. Progress-monitoring tools are available. Administration time for each test: 15 minutes.

Wechsler Fundamentals: Academic Skills

pearsonclinical.com/education.html

Grades K–12. These individually administered tests from Pearson assess reading abilities, spelling abilities, and math calculation skills. These tests can be useful in determining whether intervention is needed. Administration time: 45 minutes. (Search for "Wechsler Fundamentals: Academic Skills" at the listed website to locate the specific product.)

Woodcock-Johnson IV

riversidepublishing.com/products/wj-iv

Ages 2–90+. This system brings together tests of cognitive abilities and achievement, along with an oral language battery. When used in conjunction, these tests can be used as a diagnostic means to identify specific skill strengths and deficiencies. Administration time varies.

Index

Note: Page numbers in *italic type* and **bold face type** indicate figures and reproducible forms respectively.

A

Ability grouping, 39
Academic assessment
  as core component of RTI, 3, 6
  determining eligibility for special
    education, 88–90
  determining level of support, 85–86
  diagnostic evaluation, 76–79, *83*
  example, 88
  finding time for, 84–85
  indentifying characteristics of
    students at risk, 74
  movement across tiers, determin-
    ing, 86–87
  outcome assessment, 82, *84*
  progress monitoring, 79–82, *83*
  resources, 207–208
  screening process, 73–76, *83*
  using multiple measures, 74–75
Academic Conversation: Classroom
  Talk That Fosters Critical
  Thinking and Content
  Understanding (Zwiers and
  Crawford), 41
Academic conversations, 41, 54–58
Academic motivation
  common difficulties, 78
  inventive ways of revisiting con-
    tent, 134
  research-based strategies and
    programs, 149, 150–151, 153,
    167, 185–186
  student goal setting, 132
Academic readiness grouping, 39, 41
Academic screening, 11
Active learning, *23*
Administrative support, 108
Adult advocates, *25*
Advance organizers, 133
Alternative teaching model, *118,*
  118–119, *121, 123*
Analytic thinkers, 44
Annotating Text, 144, 150
Anticipation Guide, 149, 150–151
Assess, Set Goals, Instruct, and
  Monitor (ASIM)
  as component of RTI, 3, 6
  example, 88
  goal setting, 132
  growth mindset implementation,
    22
  implementation of, 7, 27–29
  student and family involvement, 88
Assessment
  baseline assessment of school
    readiness, 27
  as core component of RTI, 2
  determining instructional needs, 18

  purpose of, 15
  of student interest, background,
    skills, preferences, 32
  by support teams, 21
  Tier I, *11*
  Tier II, *13*
  Tier III, *14*
  using a variety, *24*
  See also Academic assessment;
    Behavioral screening
Association for Middle Level
  Education (AMLE), 23–25,
  84–85
Audio-Assisted Reading, 142, 151–152
Audiobooks, 143, 152
Auditory learners, 44
AVID, 148, 153

B

Behavioral screening, 11
Beyond SMART, 148, 153
Bloom's Taxonomy, 134, *135*
Brainstorming, 145, 154
Buck Institute for Education, 138
Business involvement, *25*

C

CALL UP Note-Taking, 149, 154
Challenging curriculum, *24*
Chat, 50
Classroom aides, 117
Clock Grouping, 12, 51–52, *52,* **70**
Coat of Arms, 47–48, **68**
Collaboration
  among leaders, *24*
  among students, 34, 35, 138
  as core component of RTI, 2, 3, 6, 9
  meeting Common Core State
    Standards, 19
  Tier I, 12
  Tier II, 13
Collaborative learning, 136
Collaborative problem solving, 41–42,
  54–58
Collaborative teaching. *See*
  Co-teaching; Team approach
Common Core State Standards, 19,
  132, 138
Common planning time, 106, 107
Communication skills, 41
Community building, 2, 3, 16, 24, 47–51
Community involvement, *25*
Complementary teaching model,
  111–112, *112–114,* 114, *121, 122*
Composition. *See* Writing to
  communicate
Conflicting Texts and Quotes, 147, 156
Content-area literacy skills, 19, 20

Conversation norms development,
  57–58
Co-teaching
  alternative teaching model, *118,*
    118–119, *121, 123*
  benefits and objectives, 105–106
  choreographing the dance, 111
  complementary teaching, 111–112,
    111–114, 114, *121, 122*
  as core component of RTI, 2, 3
  parallel teaching, *117,* 117–118, *121,*
    123
  quality indicators of success,
    106–111
  shared teaching, 119–120, *120, 121,*
    123
  station teaching, 114–116, *116, 121,*
    122
  Two Plus One Reflection Log, 114,
    115, **129**
  using multiple models, 124
  working with classroom aides, 117
CRA, 148, 156–157
Critical thinking
  common difficulties, 78
  encouragement for, 134–135
  research-based strategies and pro-
    grams, 140, 147–148, 156–157,
    161–163, 176–177, 193
Cueing, 133
Curiosity inciting, 133
Curriculum-based measurement
  (CBM), 79–81, 82

D

Data-based decision making, 7
Determining level of support, 85–88
Diagnostic evaluation, 76–78, *83,*
  91–103, 145–149
Differentiated instruction
  as complement to universal design
    for learning, 131
  as core component of RTI, 2, 5
  co-teaching effectiveness, 109
  first-year focus model, 18
  Tier I, 11
  See also Research-based teaching;
    Small-group instruction; Team
    approach; Tier III instruction;
    Tier II instruction; individual
    instruction
Digital content, 4, 21, 43, 141
Digital storytelling, 48–49, 81
Discrepancy formula, 6
Discussion, 133
Diversity in the classroom, 2
Documentation, 77
Drop-out risk factors, 74

E

Educational philosophies, understanding, 110
Evaluation Team, 22–23, 81
Evidence-based strategies
    Clock Grouping, 12, 51–52, *52*, **70**
    as core component of RTI, 2, 7, 8
    first-year focus model, 18
    Interactive Word Wall, 12, 144, 145, 163–164
    Jigsaw, 12, 54
    Think Pair Share, 12, 56, 144, 183
    Tier III, 14
Explicit, teacher-directed instruction, 136

F

Family involvement, 13, 21, *25*, 76–77, 88, 89
Feedback, 132
Fidelity of implementation, 13, 14
First-year focus model of RTI, 18
Fixed mindset, 22
Flipped classroom, 139
Focus lessons, 136
Forced Freewriting, 145, 157–158
Formal reading inventory, 74
Fountas & Pinnell Leveled Literacy Intervention System, 142, 158
Frayer Model, 144, 158

G

General education teacher, *8*
Global thinkers, 44
Goal setting
    common difficulties, 78
    as core component of RTI, 1
    first-year focus model, 18
    growth mindset, 22
    for intervention, 88
    for schools and classrooms, 28
    strategies for improving, 148, 153, 159–160, 167
    strategy instruction across subjects model, 20
    student involvement, 15, 132
    traditional model of RTI, 17
Goal-Setting Protocol, 148, 159–160
Gradual Release of Responsibility Framework, 136–137
Grouping. *See* Purposeful grouping
Growth mindset, 22
Guidance services, *25*
Guided instruction, 136

H

Health wellness, *25*
Heterogeneous grouping, 36–37, *37*, 38
Higher-level thinking promotion, 134–135, *135*
High-Preference Strategy, 148, 160
Homework, 134
Homogeneous grouping, 36, *37*
How Do You Know?, 147, 148, 161

I

Identity development, 6–7
Illusion of knowing, 132
Incoming students, 11, 14, 75
Independent learning tasks, 136
Independent study, 2
Individual instruction, *37*, 41
Individuals with Disabilities Education Act (IDEA), 6, 88
Informal reading inventories (IRIs), 74, 81, 88
Initiation of a task, 148, 156–160, 170–171, 185–186
Inquiry and research skills
    common difficulties, 78
    research-based strategies and programs, 140, 146–147, 164–165, 188–190, 198–199, 200
Instructional Teams, 21, 74, 85
Interactive Read-Aloud, 147, 148, 162–163
Interactive Word Wall, 12, 144, 145, 163–164
Interest grouping, 39
Interventionist, *8*
Intervention Plan, 76, 86, 88, **98**
Interview Grids, 146, 147, 164–165

J/K

Jigsaw, 12, 54
Job application, 42, **59**
Joke books, 143, 165
Khan, Sal, 82
Khan Academy (website), 82, 139
Kinesthetic learners, 44
Kinesthetic Writing, of Sorts, 146, 165–166
KWL-Plus, 148, 167

L

Language and vocabulary development
    common difficulties, 78
    research-based strategies and programs, 144–145, 158–159, 163–164, 168–170, 186–187, 199–200
Leadership qualities, 24
Learning approaches, use of variety, *24*
Learning disabilities, 1, 23, 88–90
Learning preference grouping, 38
Learning preferences, 33, 44–45, 109, 134
Learning Profile, 3, 21, 76, 85, 88, **91–103**
Learning strategies. *See* Self-management and learning strategies
LINCS + VOC, 144, 168
Literacy instruction. *See* Reading comprehension; Reading fluency; Reading instruction
Literacy skills, 1, 19, 20, 74
Literature Circles, 144, 168–170
Literature Circles: Voice and Choice in Book Clubs and Reading Groups (Daniels), 170

M

Making Choices, 148, 170–171
Mastery grouping, 38
Metacognition, 132
Middle school students
    academic and behavioral histories, 73
    challenges for, 1–2, 5
    characteristics of students at risk, 74
    involvement in diagnostic evaluation, 76–77
    involvement in goal setting, 88, 132
    knowing themselves, 33
    qualities of, 32, 34, 41
    social, emotional, and academic development, 6–7
MIT + K12 (website), 139
Mnemonic Devices, 149, 171–172
Monitoring. *See* Progress monitoring
Motivation. *See* Academic motivation
Multiple learning approaches, *24*
Multisensory instruction, 134

N

National Association of State Directors of Special Education (NASDSE), 15
Navigation team, 20–21
No Child Left Behind (NCLB), 6
Note-taking
    common difficulties, 78
    research-based strategies and programs, 149, 154, 189

O

Observations, documentation of, 77
One-on-one instruction, 14
Online collaboration tools, 107
Online instruction and monitoring, 82, 139
Opportunity grouping, 39
Organizational structures, *25*
Outcome assessment, 82, *84*

P/Q

Paraeducator, *8*
Parallel teaching model, *117,* 117–118, *121, 123*
Parent Contact Log, 77, **103**
Pashler, Harold, 132
Pattern Sorts, 142, 172
Peer collaboration, 138
Peer leadership, 14
Peer-paired note review, 116
Peer pairing, 38
Peer relationships, 1, 6, 31, 34, 41–42
Peer tutoring, 53–54
Personalized instruction, 2, 5–7, 42–50
Personalized learner assessment, 7, 85
PIRATES, 148, 173–174
Positive learning environment
    as core component of RTI, 3
    personalized instruction, 31–34

philosophy, 31
purposeful grouping, 34–41
requirements, 31
strategies for building, 42–46
Possible Sentences, 143, 174
Prior knowledge activation, 133
Probes, 79
Problem-solving process
   collaboration, 41–42, 54–58
   for co-teachers, 110, **127–128**
   silent conversation, 56–57
   Tier II, 13
Process Approach, 145, 175–176
Professional development, 11, 12, *24,*
      141
Progress monitoring
   as core component of RTI, 6
   curriculum-based management,
      79–81
   example, 88
   of group progress, 40, 41
   informal reading inventories
      (IRIs), 81
   Khan Academy, 82
   overview, *83*
   purpose and method, 79
   questions for assessment of
      methods, 81
   for schools and classrooms, 29
   student involvement, 15
   Tier II, 13
   Tier III, 14
Project-based learning, 134, 137–138
PROVE-ing What You Know, 147, 148,
      176–177
Purposeful grouping
   ability grouping *vs.* academic readi-
      ness grouping, 39
   aims of, 35
   Clock Grouping, 12, 51–52, **70**
   as core component of RTI, 2, 3, 5, 8
   guidelines, 35–36
   guiding questions, 36, 40
   individual instruction, 37
   Jigsaw, 12
   peer tutoring, 53–54
   random grouping, 39
   within RTI tiers, 40–41
   Shuffling the Deck grouping, 53, **71**
   Think Pair Share, 12
   Tier I, *11,* 40
   Tier II, 12, *13,* 40–41
   Tier III, *14,* 41
   whole-class instruction, 36, *37,* 40,
      119–120, *120, 121*
   See also Small-group instruction
QAR, 143, 144, 177

R

RAFT, 145, 178–179
Random grouping, 39
READ 180, 144, 181–183
Read-Aloud, 142, 143, 179
Readers Theatre, 143, 180

Reading comprehension
   assessment, 74
   common areas of difficulty, 78
   progress monitoring, 81
   research-based strategies and
      programs, 56, 143–144, 150, 174,
      177, 181–183, 190–192, 193–195,
      196–197
Reading fluency
   common areas of difficulty, 78
   research-based strategies and
      programs, 142–143, 151–152,
      158, 165, 179, 180–181, 184–185
Reading instruction
   integration of, 8
   meeting Common Core State
      Standards, 19
   progress monitoring, 81
   research-based teaching, 140–141
   strategy instruction across subjects
      model, 19, 20
Read Naturally, 142, 143, 180–181
REAP, 143, 182–183
Reciprocal teaching, 55
Reflecting time, 107, 114
Research. *See* Inquiry and research
      skills
Research-based teaching
   characteristics of, *23–25*
   as core component of RTI, 3
   evidence-based instructional
      methods, 131–138
   flipped classroom, 139
   knowing theories behind, 110
   strategies and programs, 150–200
      (*See also* specific program,
      strategy, or subject area)
   strategies *vs.* programs, 140
   strategy instruction across subjects
      model, 19–20
   Tier I, 11
   Tier II, 13
   training for, 117
   What to Try When charts, 142–149
   See also Academic assessment;
      Assessment; Behavioral screen-
      ing; Co-teaching; Purposeful
      grouping
Response to Intervention (RTI)
   assessment of, 9
   characteristics and beliefs, 23–25
   Common Core State Standards and
      literacy and, 19
   as complement to universal design
      for learning, 131
   core beliefs and principles, 15–16,
      131
   core components of, 1–3, 5–9
   determining level of support, 85–88
   digital content, 4, 21, 43, 141
   family involvement, 13, 21, *25,*
      76–77, 88, 89
   first-year focus model, 18
   as general education initiative, 5,
      16, 18, 85
   growth mindset, 22

implementation of, 9–16, 27–29,
      200
   key concepts, 2–3, 7–9, 131
   meeting Common Core State
      Standards, 19
   strategy instruction across subjects
      model, 18–20
   team models, 20–25
   terminology, *8*
   traditional model, 17–18
   value of, 1–2
   See also Academic assessment;
      Assessment; Collaboration;
      Co-teaching; Positive learn-
      ing environment; Progress
      monitoring; Research-based
      teaching; Team approach; Tier
      III instruction; Tier II instruc-
      tion; Tier I instruction
*Response to Intervention: Policy
   Considerations and
   Implementation* (NASDSE), 15
Reverse Outlining, 145, 183
REWARDS, 142, 184

S

School environment, *25*
School-wide academic student
      baseline, 18
School-wide screening, 75–76
Screening process, 73–76, *83, 85*
Screening Team, 88
SCUBA-Dive into Reading, 142,
      184–185
Self-efficacy, 32
Self-management and learning
      strategies
   common difficulties, 78
   research-based strategies and pro-
      grams, 140, 148–149, 150–151,
      153, 154–155, 159–161, 167,
      170–174, 185–186, 189
   strategy instruction across subjects
      model, 18–20
Self-Regulated Strategy Development
      Model, 132–133
Self-regulation, 32
Self-Talk, 148, 149, 185–186
Sentence Building, Elaborating, and
      Pruning, 144, 146, 186–187
Shared teaching model, 119–120, *120,
      121, 123*
Shared vision, *24*
Shuffling the deck grouping, 53
Silent conversation, 56–57
6 + 1 Trait Writing, 145, 146, 187–188
Skill area grouping, 38
Small-group instruction
   benefits, *37,* 138
   Clock Grouping, 51–52, **70**
   community building, 34
   determining composition, 36–37
   dialogue within, 134
   heterogeneous grouping, 36–37, 38
   homogeneous grouping, 36, 37
   instructors, 21

Shuffling the Deck grouping, 53, **71**
Tier I, 11
Tier II, 12, 13
Tier III, 14
traditional model of RTI, 17
types of groups, 38–39
Social awareness, 15
Special education, 6, 88–90, 105
Special education teacher, 8
Specialized personnel, *8*
Specific learning disability, 89–90
SQ3R, 146, 147, 188–189
Station teaching model, *114,* 114–116,
    116, 121, 122
Strategy-based instruction, 132–133
Strategy instruction across subjects
    model of RTI, 18–20
Structured Note-Taking, 149, 189
Student choice grouping, 39
Student-generated questioning, 133
Student-initiated learning, 136
Student Interest Inventory, 33, 43,
    60–62
Students. *See* Middle school students
Students as Problem Solvers, 146,
    189–190
Study skills
    common difficulties, 78
    research-based strategies and pro-
        grams, 149, 150–151, 171–172,
        185–186
Subtext Strategy, 143, 190–191
Summarizing by Drawing, 143, 191–192
Supplemental classes, 12
Support Team, 21–22, 75, 85

T

TAG (Writer's Workshop), 145, 146,
    192
Take a Side, 147, 193
Teacher-student relationships, 31,
    32–33
Teaching approach
    balancing theory and practice,
        understanding educational
        philosophies, 110
    differentiated instruction, 109
    flexibility and spontaneity, 108–109
    See also Co-teaching; Purposeful
        grouping; Small-group instruc-
        tion; Team approach; Tier II
        instruction; Tier I instruction
Team approach
    academic assessment, 85
    as core component of RTI, 3, 6, 9, 16
    meeting Common Core State
        Standards, 19
    types of teams, 20–22
Technology, 82, 134, 139
TED-ED (website), 139
Terminology, *8*
Test-taking
    common difficulties, 78
    research-based strategies and pro-
        grams, 149, 170–171, 173–174,
        185–186

Text Rendering, 144, 193–194
The Read Aloud Handbook (Trelease),
    179
THIEVES, 143, 194–195
Thinking and Self-Questioning, 145,
    195–196
Thinking styles, 33, 44–45
Thinking Styles and Learning
    Preferences Inventory, 45,
    63–65
Think Pair Share, 12, 56, 144, 183
*This We Believe: Keys to Educating
    Young Adolescents* (AMLE),
    23–25, 84–85
Three-Tier Model of Instruction,
    9–16, *10*
    See also Tier III instruction; Tier II
        instruction; Tier I instruction
Tier III instruction
    alternative teaching method, *118,*
        118–119
    approach, 7
    characteristics of, *10*
    components of, *14*
    examples of co-teaching models,
        121
    first-year focus model, 18
    grouping, 41
    identifying students needing, 21, 22
    movement from, 41, 87
    movement to, 13, 14, 86–87
    overview, 9, 14
    screening of students receiving,
        75–76
    strategy instruction across subjects
        model, 18–20
Tier II instruction
    alternative teaching method, *118,*
        118–119
    approach, 7
    characteristics of, *10*
    components of, *13*
    examples of co-teaching models,
        121
    first-year focus model, 18
    flipped classroom, 139
    grouping, 40–41
    identifying students needing, 21, 22
    lesson plan, *126*
    movement to, 41, 85, 87
    movement to Tier III, 86–87
    overview, 9, 12–13
    screening of students receiving,
        75–76
    strategy instruction across subjects
        model, 18–20
Tier I instruction
    academic assessment, 85
    approach, 7
    characteristics of, *10*
    complementary teaching method,
        111–112, *112–114,* 114, *121, 122*
    components of, *11*
    example, 12
    grouping, 40
    lesson plan, *125, 126*
    movement to, 13, 41, 87

    movement to Tier II, 85
    overview, 9, 10–11
    peer tutoring, 53
    screening process, 85
    strategy instruction across subjects
        model, 18
Time management
    common difficulties, 78
    research-based strategies and pro-
        grams, 148, 153, 160, 170–171,
        173–174
Traditional model of RTI, 17–18
TWA + Plans, 143, 144, 146, 196–197
Two Plus One Reflection Log, 114,
    115, **129**

U/V

Universal design for learning (UDL),
    10, 131
Value young adolescents, *23*
Visual learners, 44
Visuals, 133
Vocabulary development. *See*
    Language and vocabulary
    development

W/Y

Web-Based Bookmarks, 147, 198
WebQuests, 146, 147, 198–199
What Makes a Great Teacher? form,
    46, **66**
What's in My Bag activity, 48
What to Try When charts
    critical thinking, 147–148
    inquiry and research, 146–147
    language and vocabulary develop-
        ment, 144–145
    reading comprehension, 143–144
    reading fluency, 142–143
    self-management and learning
        strategies, 148–149
    use of, 3, 74, 76, 132, 141
    word recognition, 142
    writing to communicate, 145–146
What Would You Do? form, 46–47, **67**
Where I Come From activity, 49–50
Whole-class instruction, 36, *37,* 40,
    119–120, *120, 121*
Wonderopolis (website), 139
Word recognition
    common areas of difficulty, 78
    research-based strategies and pro-
        grams, 151–152, 158, 172, 184
Word Sorts, 145, 199–200
Working Backward, 146, 200
Work plan
    strategies for improving student
        response to, 148, 159–160,
        170–171, 185–186
    student development of, 137, 138
Writing to communicate
    common difficulties, 78
    research-based strategies and pro-
        grams, 145–146, 154, 157–158,
        165–166, 175–176, 178–179, 183,
        186–188, 192, 195–197
Yellow Pages activity, 51, **69**

About the Authors

Kelli J. Esteves, Ed.D., is an associate professor of education at Butler University. Kelli holds a B.A. in learning disabilities, an M.A. in teaching children with visual impairments, and an Ed.D. in special education. She is also the coauthor of *RTI Success: Proven Tools and Strategies for Schools and Classrooms.* Kelli speaks locally and nationally on response to intervention, children's literature, and various topics related to special education. She has consulted with schools across the Midwest and is a frequent presenter for professional organizations such as the International Reading Association and the Association for Supervision and Curriculum Development. Prior to her time at Butler, she was the director of the Learning Disabilities program at Aquinas College in Grand Rapids, Michigan. She was also a special education teacher and literacy specialist in the K–12 public school system. Kelli and her husband Dean have two lively, creative, and fun-loving children, Ava and Alex. To arrange a consultation or workshop, contact Kelli at kesteves@butler.edu.

Elizabeth Whitten, Ph.D., has public school experience as an elementary and special education teacher and administrator. She is a professor of special education and administration at Western Michigan University holding a Ph.D. in special education, an M.A. in special education, and a B.A. in elementary and special education. As a teacher and an administrator, she has worked in Illinois and Michigan, as well as at Department of Defense Schools in Germany. Elizabeth has provided professional development and consultation across the United States and throughout Germany on topics related to response to intervention, collaborative teaching and teaming, differentiated instruction, data-based decision making, and other topics related to inclusion and special education. She is a frequent presenter of her research at professional organizations such as Council for Exceptional Children, Association for Teacher Educators, and Teacher Education Division of CEC. She is the coauthor of *RTI Success: Proven Tools and Strategies for Schools and Classrooms.* Contact Elizabeth at whitten@wmich.edu.

Download the free PLC/Book Study Guide at freespirit.com/RT-MS-PLC

More Great Books from Free Spirit

RTI Success
Proven Tools and Strategies for Schools and Classrooms
by Elizabeth Whitten, Ph.D., Kelli J. Esteves, Ed.D., and Alice Woodrow, Ed.D.
256 pp., PB, 8½" x 11". For teachers and administrators, grades K–12. Includes digital content.

The PBIS Team Handbook
Setting Expectations and Building Positive Behavior
by Beth Baker, M.S.Ed., with Char Ryan, Ph.D.
208 pp., PB, 8½" x 11". For K–12 PBIS coaches and team members, including special educators, teachers, paraprofessionals, school psychologists, social workers, counselors, administrators, parents, and other school staff members. Includes digital content.

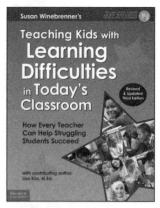

Teaching Kids with Learning Difficulties in Today's Classroom
How Every Teacher Can Help Struggling Students Succeed (Revised & Updated Third Edition)
by Susan Winebrenner, M.S., with Lisa M. Kiss, M.Ed.
288 pp., PB, 8½" x 11". For K–12 teachers, administrators, and higher education faculty. Includes digital content.

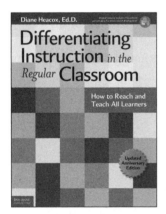

Differentiating Instruction in the Regular Classroom
How to Reach and Teach All Learners (Updated Anniversary Edition)
by Diane Heacox, Ed.D.
176 pp., PB, 8½" x 11". For teachers, grades K–12. Includes digital content.

Making Differentiation a Habit
How to Ensure Success in Academically Diverse Classrooms
by Diane Heacox, Ed.D.
192 pp., PB, 8½" x 11". For teachers and administrators, grades K–12. Includes digital content.

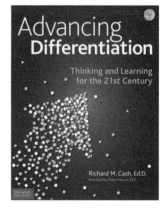

Advancing Differentiation
Thinking and Learning for the 21st Century
by Richard M. Cash, Ed.D.
208 pp., PB, 8½" x 11". For teachers and administrators, grades K–12. Includes digital content.

Interested in purchasing multiple quantities and receiving volume discounts?
Contact edsales@freespirit.com or call 1.800.735.7323 and ask for Education Sales.

Many Free Spirit authors are available for speaking engagements, workshops, and keynotes.
Contact speakers@freespirit.com or call 1.800.735.7323.

For pricing information, to place an order, or to request a free catalog, contact:

217 Fifth Avenue North • Suite 200 • Minneapolis, MN 55401-1299
toll-free 800.735.7323 • local 612.338.2068 • fax 612.337.5050
help4kids@freespirit.com • www.freespirit.com